The Light of the Moon

Life, Death and the Birth of ATLS

By Randy Styner

Edited by Tony Farley, Sue Fisher, and Steve Quinn

Published by Lulu Press, Inc., Raleigh, North Carolina.

Copyright © 2007 by Randy Styner.

All rights reserved. No part of this book may be reproduced or used in any manner whatsoever without written permission except in the case of brief citations in critical reviews or articles.

Published in the United States by Lulu Press, Inc. Lulu is a registered trademark of Lulu Press, Inc.

The Cataloging-in-Publication Data is on file at the Library of Congress.

ISBN 978-1-300-88996-0

Book and cover design by Randy Styner.

www.lulu.com

Printed in the United States of America

For Mom

Charlene Ann Styner

1944-1976

If you would not be forgotten
As soon as you are dead and rotten
Either write things worth the reading
Or do things worth the writing.

-Benjamin Franklin

Introduction

February 18, 1976, just after 2 a.m.:

The light of the moon broke free of the clouds that had reached menacingly across the sky in all directions until only a couple of hours before. It bathed the wreckage of a small airplane that lay in a vacant field. It bathed the path of debris strewn behind it toward the gap it had ripped through the trees. It bathed frozen sap that had oozed from ragged stumps and it reflected off the ice of a frozen pond. It bathed a man's swollen eyelids as he squinted to consider it through the broken Plexiglas of the cockpit windshield. It bathed him as he climbed out of the twisted mass and stumbled away. It bathed him until he was out of the sight of his son, left sitting there amongst the remnants of his family - now all alone.

Several miles away Ricky and David walked across a cold factory parking lot toward David's car. They were both beat from another long shift and were anxious to get home. The fat orb of the moon had emerged above Hebron, Nebraska, and the town slept quietly below, in suspended animation, encapsulated by the crystal clear frozen air of the winter that was draped over them.

When Ricky and David had come to the small factory late yesterday afternoon the sky had been plastered with a low layer of gray clouds which had been over the region for a few gloomy days, but these had now all but evaporated. The clouds' passing revealed the moon and a deep, dark sky beyond dotted with a brilliant and endless field of bright stars. Around the town the land rolled away and the moon illuminated the barren and empty fields and the skeletal woodlots that surrounded the town and ran off in all directions, melding seamlessly beyond with the vast, frozen Nebraska prairie.

A cold breeze would have wafted around them. I imagine a thermometer nailed to the wall of the factory just outside the door saying 26 degrees and they probably believed it. Puddles of water would have turned to ice and the clumps of snow that managed to stick to the ground from the last storm were now ugly frozen blocks of white speckled with black dots of soot. They would have experienced nights like this enough over their lives out there to know what freezing cold felt like. They could tell by the sharp chill of the air in their sinuses with each breath they took, and how it penetrated into their cheeks and nipped at their ears and the tips of their noses as they walked quickly toward the car hunched into their heavy winter coats.

I picture Ricky walking to the passenger side and grabbing the frozen handle of the door which he jerks open with a creaky groan.

He slid into the big front seat as David got in on the other side and started the frozen engine. The ignition would have strained over several times before the engine coughed to life with a rough rumble. I picture him waiting a little while to let it warm up some more, then popping on his headlights which illuminated the cloud of white exhaust that poured out of the tailpipe into the freezing air and washed over the car with the breeze. Then he dropped the shifter and guided the old car slowly forward out of the parking space and over the patches of ice and snow as he maneuvered toward the entrance of the lot, pausing when he got there, then pointing the car toward the outskirts of town and home.

There would be no one out here this time of night, and I bet they were happy about that. They would have been tired and the last thing they needed was to get stuck behind a slow moving semi-truck or someone lost from I-80, some sixty miles to the north of them. I imagine the solitude of the highway was one of the benefits of the night shift. But now, they were probably looking forward to the warmth of home, a cold beer, some T.V., and bed.

Upon reaching the darkened Highway 81, Ricky turned the car north and accelerated into the night. As they glided across its frozen asphalt, the bright headlights would have played off thin, wispy fingers of mist gathered in low spots and crossing the road in irregular intervals, breaking up like specters as the car rushed through them.

A few minutes later, they saw Dad.

He was on the side of the road, waving his arms above his head.

Dad saw the car rapidly slow and pull off onto the shoulder, the headlights washing over him as he stumbled slowly through the dust that enveloped them. At first both Ricky and David thought his grotesquely disfigured face was some kind of mask, and they stared in disbelief. His clothing was tattered and covered in dark stains as well, but they hadn't seen any sign of why this man was here or where he had come from. Dad could see on their faces a mixture of horror and shock.

For a moment they all wondered what was about to happen.

It was almost thirty years later and I never even saw the car that almost killed me.

A few minutes before, I had finished topping off the teardrop-shaped tank of my beloved black and chrome Harley Davidson, glinting in the afternoon sun. I loved my hog. Dad, when I told him of my new toy, wasn't too happy about it, of course. He had spent a significant portion of our childhood slamming on the idea of motorcycles. He always had said that the only good thing about them was they kept the world supplied with healthy and young organs for transplants. Even now, I must say that I don't agree with this. I know many responsible riders who have spent years on the back of their bikes with nary a scrape. When I began to ride, I was determined to be one of them. I was careful, and as long as I was in control, I'd be fine.

I never thought about the moments that were out of my control as I replaced the gas nozzle into the fuel pump then threw my leg over the leather saddle, pulling the bike upright and turning the key in the ignition. I watched the indicator lights blink on and popped the shifter into neutral, then depressed the chrome starter button on the handlebar with my gloved thumb. The engine kicked over and sprang to life with a sharp roar, and for a moment I enjoyed its throaty growl as it pulsated powerfully under me. The vibration resonated through my body as I settled into the saddle.

The feeling was amplified as I gunned the engine a couple of times, just to feel it.

It felt good.

I popped the clutch into first gear with a clunk, rolled the throttle a touch, and eased forward pulling out of the gas station and making a right turn toward the intersection just to the north. I entered the left turn lane and stopped at the red light short of the crosswalk.

I waited at the light, enjoying the feel of the fine-tuned engine rumbling smoothly beneath me like an old friend, strong and true and never failing. Its loud growl announced to all that I was coming and made me feel bigger than I was.

In a flash, the green arrow popped up and I and eased the bike into the intersection to begin my turn.

The imaginary Director in my head suddenly yelled: "Cut!" and everything disappeared.

Witnesses said that I sprang up off the bike in an apparent attempt to get clear, but was impeded by the windshield of the on-rushing SUV which had blown the light from my blind spot. It impacted hard, knocking my bike out from under me and bouncing me off its windshield and over a smooth arc through the air before I landed back on the rough asphalt in a crumpled heap. My helmet smashed forward into the ground, thrusting my face into the visor which opened a large gash on my forehead and erupted my nose in a crimson gush. My limbs spun out from under me in all directions, and I flopped across the street on my belly like an unnaturally posed rag-doll.

I lay immobilized as bystanders ran to the scene and swarmed around, blood spilling out of me from my nose, my mouth, my head…I stared sideways at the scene in front of me through the red smeared visor, now cracked and askew, eye-level with the asphalt. I found much to my distress that I was unable to move or talk or even breathe. I don't remember any pain but I knew I was hurt.

That hardly mattered now. Darkness began to envelop me and very gradually, against the fight I put up in my spinning brain, I faded out - as did the sounds of the commotion around me, leaving me with the feeling that I was slowly sinking backwards, falling in slow motion deeper and deeper.

It was like entering a dream, then suddenly, to my surprise, I felt warm and good. A rushing sound surged through my head like water through a semi-kinked hose and was pleasant and somewhat comforting. It blocked out the panic I had felt closing in on me a scant second before, as well as the pain I was sure was coming once my brain sorted it out. The dream wrapped itself warmly around me, and I found myself suspended in a sort of bubble. Outside of it, I was only vaguely aware of bright, painful light and chaos as people rushed about around me. But in here it was safe and calm.

For a moment, it was kind of nice.

In fact, I think I was all ready to stay put right there, but then I became distinctly aware of a familiar, foreboding, and bad feeling.

From some corner of my battered mind the ethereal image of Staff Sergeant Phillips, my most feared and loathed Drill Instructor, materialized and burst into the fabric of my dream - just like he had entered our squad bay so many times back at the Marine Recruit Depot during boot camp all those years ago. He came, as he always did, from out of nowhere and was now standing over me as I cowered, that familiar menacing grimace on his face; a combination of rage, loathing and disgust. The image of him towering there over me made me suddenly very afraid.

"WHAT ARE YOU DOING DOWN THERE, YOU WORTHLESS MAGGOT?!" He bellowed at me from the periphery of my scrambled brain in his thick Trinidad accent.

The words echoed as if spoken in a large cave and tore through the haze that separated me from the reality of my pathetic and disfigured form, still sprawled on the asphalt of the road. My bubble began to quiver.

"WHAT KIND OF MARINE LIES DOWN ON THE FRIGGIN GROUND LIKE A GOL-DARN RAGGEDY ANN DOLLY??!" he bellowed.

"IS THAT WHAT YOU ARE?? A GOL-DARN RAGGEDY ANN DOLLY?! YOU BETTER GET UP! OPEN YOUR EYES, MAGGOT!!" he screamed mercilessly and unconcerned about whether or not I thought I was going to die. He hadn't told me I could die, after all.

"OPEN YOUR EYES!!!!"

With a soundless pop the bubble disappeared, and I was thrust back into the world.

The director in my head: "Fade in – AMBULANCE…"

I opened my fluttering eyelids very slowly and the painful light pierced throbbing into my foggy brain.

"…what happened?" I sputtered through puffy and swollen lips, but as the world resolved itself before me I already knew. Out of my field of vision the attendants tried to calm me, sounding slightly surprised. I could not move. I was strapped down and immobilized on the stretcher and my neck was in a plastic collar. I could taste the iron of my blood. It oozed down the back of my raw throat. It was disgusting.

"You got hit, man," one of the attendants said. He sounded like a kid. "You got hit on your motorcycle."

I could not grasp it. Hit on my motorcycle? Not possible. I just didn't get it. I was totally confused. I was wanting so desperately to cast off the hazy weight that held me fast to the thin foam of the stretcher mattress and emerge into a different reality, but was unable to muster the strength. So I just lay there, baffled.

After an eternity of listening to the undulating whirl of the siren, the ambulance slowed and we pulled into a hospital emergency entrance. They jerked me out of the vehicle gurney and I was rushed into a brightly lit emergency room, which turned out was at the University of California Irvine Medical Center. I was under the care of one of the best hospitals in the world, and, ironically, the entity where my own father had learned medicine long before any of this. Of course, at the time I couldn't have cared less.

My best friend in the world was now a husky and friendly young man with a neatly trimmed goatee and purple scrub suit named Danny. He struck me as the kind of guy whose friends probably describe him as a big old teddy bear. I trusted him completely. He must have felt bad for me, for he never left my side. He told me calmly and with an appropriate level of sympathy that it appeared that my hip and shoulder on my right side had been dislocated, and were probably also fractured, that my neck might have been broken, and that I most likely had suffered some level of head injury.

He did something to my IV and a rush of cold liquid flowed into my arm. They had removed my helmet at the scene and cut off my beloved leather jacket. Now the detached tickle of scissors made their way up my legs and side as the rest of my clothes were cut away, exposing me completely and leaving me feeling utterly helpless.

Danny determined immediately that there was no need for me to be intubated with a breathing tube as my trachea was uninjured and seemed to work, but they did fit me with a catheter, which was not comfortable. When I threatened to throw up, they jammed a suction tube up my nose and into my throat, so I wouldn't aspirate anything. On my bare chest, they placed small pads that were hooked up to an EKG machine. My bodily functions became summarized by small red and green blips leading various solid lines across a screen.

They rapidly assessed my immediate injuries in the emergency room, but a CAT scan would still be necessary, so off I went. I spent what seemed like a very long time in the cramped tube, listening to the bored and monotone sounding voice of the technician on his microphone in the control room telling me not to breath or that I could breathe again while the machine beeped and whirred around me.

We stopped in another room where they took some x-rays of me then I ended up back in the emergency room. Terri had finally made it to the hospital and was being briefed as I rolled in. She came to my side and grabbed my hand. I was glad to see my wife. She stood beside me, looking down at me on the gurney with a brave but worried look. I tried to look tough for her benefit, but at that point pulling it off would have been quite a trick. I don't think she would have bought the act anyway.

Danny appeared again and patted her hand, then enthusiastically announced that he was going to reduce my shoulder and hip - meaning he was about to pop them back into place. I still wore the uncomfortable neck brace which held my throbbing head perfectly still, and the only thing I could see was the water stained white acoustical ceiling tiles occupying my immediate field of view.

"This might hurt a little at first," Danny said, as he poked his head into my field of vision to look at me and began to work his hands around my shoulder. "So tell me if you feel too much pain and I'll give you something."

He must have felt the tension in my muscles as a bolt of fire sprang toward my fingertips, because he relaxed and looked at my eyes to see if I was about to scream.

I was.

I gurgled, trying my best negotiation voice. Anyway, I knew from long experience what phases like 'this might hurt a little' meant.

"Tell you what," I rasped. "Give me something now, and you can torque those joints around as much as you want."

"My man!" he said with a smile. I imagine that my attitude made his life a little easier. He left then returned a few moments later.

"This will do it," he said out of my view.

A few seconds later I felt a warm feeling rush into my arm through the IV tube protruding out of it. A peaceful, floating sensation embraced my body and I suddenly felt incredibly happy and pleasantly stoned.

"Whoa…" I exclaimed, as my head begin to spin and I began to feel more and more giddy. "That's…the good…stuff…"

"Sure is!" Danny said with an edge of humor in his voice. "Now relax and let me do my thing."

I drifted slowly away, probably humming the Partridge Family theme, on a soft white fluffy cloud while squeezing my wife's hand as the valium worked its way quickly into my system. On the other side, Danny worked my twisted limbs back into place. I came to a few seconds later to his smiling face. He looked quite proud. I found out later from Terri that only a few seconds earlier he had been raising his voice at me, reminding me to continue to breathe before I re-emerged once again and took that responsibility back for myself. She has never talked about that moment again.

"All done!" Danny said cheerily. I cracked a lame smile and thanked him for the good work.

But then I felt sorry for myself. I was pretty sure that if I were going to die now, he'd be a little more serious. Still I knew life as I had known it was probably over. Danny saw this in my face. He gently patted my newly replaced shoulder.

"You're going to be okay," he said. Then he turned away to tend to another task somewhere in the noisy, pulsating emergency room. Someone somewhere was hollering in anguish. Nearby, a small child was crying. It was a normal day for the staff.

Numbness held me limp and I looked at my wife through glassy and bloodshot eyes and tried to smile weakly. I could see she wasn't having a good time with this either. I was now thoroughly exhausted and drifted off into sleep.

At some point, Dad came to see me. I was fully expecting some version of I Told You So, but he didn't bother. Still, I knew what he was thinking and I was embarrassed.

"I'm sorry, Pop," was all I could think to say. He smiled softly and looked at me with a sympathy I don't think I had ever seen from him before.

"That's okay, Son," he said. I could still see the scar etched in his own forehead. "I crashed an airplane once…"

And I finally got to experience ATLS.

I have known about Advanced Trauma Life Support practically my whole life. At least I knew vaguely what it was about and what it was for, and it went something like this…

Many years ago, some doctors determined that there was a disease that wasn't really being recognized for what it was. This was a special disease, because unlike other diseases, this one didn't inflict itself primarily on the weak and old. In fact, the victims of this disease were more often the young and the strong--people in the prime of their life. And it was killing them by the thousands and thousands.

They called the disease trauma. It was unique because in its individual pieces it appeared as auto accidents and gunshot wounds. Kitchen knife lacerations and falls from roofs. Individual accidents and emergencies. They were not diseases in the traditional sense of the word. But nobody was looking at these single cases from a larger perspective. When they did, however, they quickly realized there were common threads that ran through all of them. And when that thread was pulled, an epidemic was revealed.

Doctors decided that if it was a disease, then there could be a common way to treat trauma in all its forms. They began to study the disease, figure it out, then found a way to fight it. Simple facts that had not been considered about the disease before—and considering a new way of looking at trauma treatment in general--began to emerge. And ATLS was born soon after.

Before this time, there was no standard of care for the trauma patient in the United States, or anywhere else for that matter. The primary accepted method for any emergency room patient including a trauma victim was the same for all cases, and generally consisted of a diagnosis of the patient, starting at the head and working down to the toes. The findings from the lengthy exam was then the basis for the treatment on that complete diagnosis of the whole patient.

Hopefully while all of this was done your patient didn't die. ATLS changed that. As they found how trauma worked, a new treatment philosophy was developed. It was based largely on the fact that what looks bad on a patient at first glance may not be the worst of their worries, and the real problem may not be apparent at all. A system of treatment was needed to recognize the priorities of what would kill them the fastest.

For example, upon my arrival to UCI a series of diagnostic events occurred in a specific order and in the same way they are done in every emergency room throughout the United States and in many other countries throughout the world: The ABC's of trauma (or more correctly, the A, B, C, D and E):

In a nutshell, the first thing they did was to protect my cervical spine (with that goddamn collar!) and then immediately checked if I could mechanically breathe – assessment of my airway, which is A. Then they checked to make sure I was really breathing (which is B), and to ensure that the undamaged airway was actually functional. Then, when they saw I was breathing, they quickly searched me for serious bleeding (C for Circulation). Then they diagnosed my spine, head, and neck for injury (D for Disability). Then they made sure I had external resources to quickly receive fluids (or suck them out), medication, and oxygen, as well as to monitor my vitals (that's E, for Environment).

Everything happened in a set and specific order, and each problem was found and fixed before the next was diagnosed. Fortunately for me I got to the hospital within the 'golden hour' of the injuries, after which serious problems tend to become exponentially worse and more dangerous with each passing moment.

These are the basic tenets of Advance Trauma Life Support, or ATLS. It is now the standardized method of treating trauma throughout much of the world. It is based on a very simple principle: Know what will kill a patient fastest, and treat that first - before moving to the next thing.

If, for example, my trachea was crushed there would not have been much sense in treating anything else because lack of oxygen due to severe trauma will kill a human being quicker and more surely than almost anything else. Quicker than blood loss, quicker than a non-immediately fatal head injury, quicker than anything. So it makes sense to treat that and only that first. Focus your resources; attack one target at a time, then move to the next one.

Doctors found that trauma deaths generally occur in one of three stages. The first stage happens when the victim is killed very quickly of grave injuries before intervention can arrive. The second stage is within a few hours of the initial trauma as the initial injury begins to cause peripheral system failure. The third stage is in the days and weeks following the injury due to infections and sepsis. From this, doctors determined that although there was not a lot they could do during the first stage, they could work to improve the response process and equip the EMTs and paramedics in the field to better care for the patient at the scene. This would automatically increase the chances of victims avoiding a stage two death. Consequently, if they could improve the treatment of the patient entering the emergency room from the scene, the victim would have a better chance of avoiding a stage three death.

So doctors tried it-and it worked, better than they could have ever imagined. Lives began to be saved by the thousands.

For those who study trauma now, it seems like a basic concept. But in reality it was one that was pretty much unknown in the medical community until one fateful night in 1976. Until the events of that night, nobody had really ever thought about it, at least to the extent of doing anything about it.

ATLS is not unique, insomuch as it exists. There have been many significant advances in medicine over the years in neurology, cardiology, oncology, and stem cell research, for example. But it is the genesis of the inspiration of ATLS that is different and significant.

The story behind ATLS does not come from laboratories and research or funding grants and committees. Instead it is a story that starts with that moonlit and twisted airplane smashed in that dead and frozen field, smeared with the blood of a family.

Every practitioner trained in ATLS has read about the event. It is discussed in the History section of the ATLS Student Manual by Irvine Hughes, which strikes the reader hard, pulling them down to the moment, down to that field. Doctors who read it say that those words carry an impact that made them understand the gritty nature of trauma medicine. It made them understand what force it was that drew them to this vocation and which was more powerful than the stress or the long hours or the horrors at the center of it all that they would surely witness. In a brilliantly simple way, Hughes' words capture it:

"**<u>The Nebraska Concept and Inception:</u>**

The Delivery of trauma care by doctors in the U.S. was at best inconsistent before 1980. A tragedy occurred in February 1976 that changed trauma care in the 'first hour' for the injured patient in the U.S. and in much of the rest of the world. An orthopedic surgeon, piloting his plane, crashed in a rural Nebraska cornfield. The surgeon sustained serious injuries and 3 of his children sustained critical injuries, and 1 child sustained minor injuries. His wife was killed instantly. The care his family received was inadequate by the day's standards. The surgeon, recognizing how inadequate his treatment was, stated: 'When I can provide better care in the field with limited resources than what my children and I received at the primary care facility, there is something wrong with the system and the system has to be changed'"

The system had to be changed. That led to one of the most revolutionary advances in trauma care ever, and one which is still being practiced relatively unchanged today. It has saved countless lives all over the world.

But to me, the words of that passage smell of dark and cold and mud. To me, they mean everything. I was there, a child critically injured in that field. I was freezing against that cold. That mud packed itself into the ripped tissue of my body. That was my mom, my dad, and my siblings.

And I have carried the scars of the birth of ATLS with me through my entire life. I look at them every day.

I was born in 1968 in Denver General Hospital, where Dad was a resident physician. We left Denver when I was two and I grew up with my family in Lincoln, Nebraska. It was a pretty pleasant place to grow up, and, to this day, I consider myself a native Nebraskan.

It was then, and I imagine still is, a town where kids play outside by themselves, and you can walk alone downtown at any time of the day or night without fear. By Lincoln's standards my childhood was nothing short of normal until that night in the field, just three months past my seventh birthday.

We had a nice big house in the Lincoln countryside sitting proudly on a hill in the middle of ten acres of land at the end of a rocky road off what then was Rural Route 1. I spent countless hours with my brothers and neighbor kids exploring the countryside on foot or on the back of one of the horses which lived in a large barn on the back five acres of our land. We only had three T.V. channels on our old wood-box Zenith with the big picture tube jutting out of the back, so the outside world was our only real source of entertainment.

Mom took care of all of our needs, and made sure we were clothed and fed and loved and kept in line. Dad worked hard as an orthopedic surgeon at various Lincoln hospitals and his private practice to provide us with a comfortable life, but consequently I never saw him too much. Mom was our total support system, and somehow she kept her three crazy boys from killing themselves or each other. Don't ask me how.

She was like a saint, though. She had incredible patience and no matter how hard she was working to keep our home clean and comfortable, she was there. Whenever I had a question or problem or fear, she would always stop everything and dedicate all of her attention to me. It was the same for my siblings. She was never too busy for her children, and no question was meaningless; no time for explanation was too long.

Trouble began shortly after she was killed. Dad, emotionally wrecked from it all, immersed himself in his work and this new concept of ATLS. He was the Chief of Surgery at Lincoln General, which in and of itself was a huge commitment of his time. Add in his ATLS work and all of his time was now taken.

I knew all along that whatever he was doing, it was important, both for us and him. I believe in my father. I always have. He is a good man.

But the result of all this was that my brothers and sister and I had to move forward through life largely by ourselves, without much of a guide. We were lucky, though. We had a home at least and were in a secure environment, relatively. Through it, an interesting mix of people began to move in and out in the form of Dad's girlfriends or care givers, sitters, etc., each offering some hope for the stability we all craved, but most disappearing too soon.

But Dad tried his best through it all to do right by us kids. He was lonely and wanted us to have a Mom again, so he remarried to a young twenty-one year-old nurse from the hospital not quite a year after the crash. She was as much a distraction for him as she was an attempt to provide some kind of maternal figure for us. Dad meant well and we all loved her immediately. She was young and beautiful and full of energy and seemed to love us back. But it was just an illusion – for all of us, including her.

The salt-of-the-land mentality of the Midwest has always been such that when life kicks you down, you get up. You don't complain; you just keep moving. I believe in this and I still do, but as a child I never saw a psychologist or counselor to talk about what happened to Mom, or the fear and anger I felt every day. I should have, but had no idea about any of that kind of stuff. I was just a kid.

So I internalized it. I got good at internalizing.

To her credit, our step mother tried to deal with and raise four very messed up and confused children, still trying to make themselves understand that Mom was in fact never coming back. She grew up in the farm country where spare the rod, spoil the child was the rule of raising kids, and she reverted to that philosophy quickly. The beatings started soon after she moved in.

It hurt. Largely because that brand of discipline was new to us in a horrible and shocking way. Mom had never laid a finger in anger on any of us. She would have defended us from the likes of that with her life. But she wasn't there. Dad seemed oblivious to it all, and we never talked about our "discipline".

We endured it all in silence for the next three years. We moved away from our Mom's beloved country home and into the city to live in a soulless, flashy house in a rich neighborhood where we tried to get some consistency.

But nothing ever seemed good enough for her and she finally left Dad. We were all too much for her in spite of her iron fist. I was glad when she was gone, but we had no mom - again. I hated her for years for that until one day I realized she was just a kid, too.

Dad was crushed. He had protected himself from the emotional fallout from Mom's death with his new wife, so now the absence of that bunker almost buried him. But he soon picked himself up and found himself once again in his work. It's just how he is. I admire him for having the strength to do it.

But for me, I realized that I was truly on my own one day a few months later, as a 7th grade student at Pound Junior High School. Some of the many bullies there, who had always been drawn to my small size and meekness to target with their taunts, viciously dumped my books from under my arm between classes one day. I struggled to hold on to them, but with little success. My papers disappeared into the churning frenzy of feet of the uncaring students in the crowded hallway, jumping on them like sharks to blood.

The bullies then taunted and humiliated me mercilessly as I cowered and I ended up being pushed down in the middle of the hallway, where I sat stunned for a few seconds before I broke into sobbing tears, much to the delight of the other students. I can still hear their tinny, miserable laughter.

When I looked up, I saw two teachers standing in their doorways, looking pathetically down on me and shaking their head with a complete lack of sympathy. I don't know how much they saw, but they did nothing to intervene or to help me. Then the bell rang and they all vanished like good little citizens into their rooms, leaving me alone in the hallway, in total desolation.

After a few minutes, the halls cleared of students and I was left alone in my misery. I calmed down a bit and tried to regain some dignity, then rose to my feet to slink off, not bothering to gather my notebooks or assignments now scattered all up and down the hallway. Most of the assignments were unfinished anyway. I guess no one bothered to tell Dad about the episode. I didn't. I figured that was just how life was.

But inside me, as I lurched about for the rest of that day, a door clanged shut. I didn't cry for the next twenty years.

I used to sneak out at night. I never looked for trouble, I just needed to get out and walk around. Often, I would walk across the cornfield behind our house to the cemetery where mom is buried. I would just sit by her grave. Sometimes I would fall asleep there and be gone all night. It would greatly upset Dad, who assumed I was up to no good being out all night, especially since I was always vague as to where I was. We had begun to drift apart, and I didn't want to bring Mom into it.

I turned to what one could say was "my duty to distract Dad from his own misery" the best I could, which I did by not staying out of trouble for very long. This culminated with me crashing my brother's car into a ditch beside a country road sixty miles from home one night (I was fourteen and obviously unlicensed)-- and this finally got me sent to military school in Wisconsin, starting as junior in high school.

Dad placed me under the care of my aunt Mary Lou, my dad's sister, who lived in Chicago. During breaks and over the summers in high school, I stayed with them. Mary Lou and my Uncle Pat understood my need for structure and did their best for me, but I was a pretty hard package.

I did all right in military school, for a while anyway, and once the school year began. The old stone of Northwestern Academy in Lake Geneva became my home away from home…away from home. I got good grades for the first time since I was a little kid, succeeding in getting on the honor roll my second semester. I was active on the Northwestern Rifle Drill Team and a varsity soccer player. I was promoted quickly and became the editor of our school paper by the end of my junior year. I was picked to be a Cadet Staff Officer for my senior year, and, for the first time that I could remember, people began to treat me with respect.

Then I got busted for getting in a fight with a senior ranking cadet. It was stupid. I somehow caught a break, though. They stripped me of my rank and position but let me stay and graduate, for which I was thankful. But the faculty, my aunt and uncle, my family…they were all very disappointed in me, but especially my dad who thought I had moved beyond that brand of bullshit. He never told me so, but I knew.

The Academy was torn down years later, and I was sorry to see it go. It had meant something important to me. I tried college for a semester after graduation, but I drifted aimlessly around the huge University of

Wisconsin- Madison campus without any semblance of a compass. Despite military school, it turned out I possessed a total lack of discipline. On my own I wasn't ready for it, choosing the trappings of the social scene over anything as mundane as classes. It wasn't long before I was out of the University's good graces and slammed on probation.

When I was at the Academy I had a friend and roommate named Jim. Jim was a Marine at heart. He was in the Young Marines and often talked about the day he would join up. His father and grandfather were both Marines, too. His dad was a helicopter pilot in Viet Nam, and his grandpa was a World War II veteran who had stormed beaches in the South Pacific. I met both of them at the Academy and thought that they could have been brothers since they both looked much younger than their ages. They appeared powerful and ruggedly handsome with chiseled features. To me they were the epitome of manliness.

Seeing that first hand made me consider enlisting as a Marine, but then I quickly discarded that thought. Mostly, I couldn't get my head around a four year commitment and, at 17 years old, that was like an eternity. Besides…me? A Marine? I bet those kids at Pound Junior High would be laughing their asses off about that.

Yet, one day over Christmas break from college and still on probation, I found myself before a tall Marine named Sergeant Sinclair. He was wearing a sharp dress blue uniform and standing casually in the doorway of his office at the recruiting center in Palatine, Illinois, looking like something out of those old movies. I had just finished my first semester in college with straight Fs, and it had been suggested by some both at the University and other places that I seek a new path.

With a single glance, Sergeant Sinclair immediately recognized the look of me. He put his arm firmly around my shoulder and guided me into his office, sweeping me up in his spiel of the glory of his beloved Corps. It was what I needed to hear and I bought all of it -- hook, line, and sinker. That was not to say that he was pulling my leg or anything. I can honestly say that everything that the Corps ever told me during my entire enlistment was true. Nobody ever lied to me about anything. The truth may have been difficult to hear sometimes, but it was still true.

I had never had any serious thoughts that I could ever be a Marine. I thought Marines were all over six feet tall, made of steel, and feared nothing. I, on the other hand, was five-foot-six, made of weak flesh, and feared everything. But Sergeant Sinclair assured me that I could be one, too - and that I would be.

He took me under his wing as my mentor and gave me direction and a focused purpose for the first time in my life. He made me get in shape and quit screwing around. I went to boot camp the following February with Recruit Training Platoon 2021 at the Marine Corps Recruit Training Depot in San Diego and, to my own surprise, I excelled. I quickly became a Squad Leader and, by the end of boot camp, I was one of the fastest and fittest recruits in my training battalion. I shot at an expert level with the M-16 rifle (which I could strip clean in seconds and reassemble correctly just as fast blindfolded), and quickly learned everything the Corps would teach me about the Marines.

In the Corps, I had once again found a home and a family. Eventually I accepted that the Corps loved me. It was a tough and sometimes a brutal love, but it was love and care for me and my future and well-being nonetheless. Granted, I was akin to a piece of equipment in many aspects, but there was never any secret about that. In return, I got to be a Marine--One of the Few—which was no small thing. It is something all Marines feel and it's why we stay Marines, even long after we get out.

I was stationed at the Marine Corps Air Ground Combat Center in Twentynine Palms, California, as an Armor Crewman, otherwise known as a 'Tanker.' I was assigned to the "Jokers" of Bravo Company, Third Tank Battalion, 3rd Platoon, where I would stay throughout the rest of my enlistment. I mastered every job from loader to Tank Commander and ended up as a driver on a big M-60 A-3 Main Battle Tank that we named the Night Stalker.

I loved tanks. In my mind, that was the only way to travel. My friend and fellow tanker, Hank, gave us our motto: "When I move the earth rumbles. When I speak people die." That suited me. Tanks have lots of guns, and I found that I liked shooting guns. The bigger, the better. Over my tour I learned to fire many and the Corps made sure I was deadly accurate with all of them. But it wasn't the violence or fantasy of killing my enemy that attracted me to my job. I never wanted to kill anyone. It was the craftsmanship of these war tools and the skill needed to use them that fascinated me. And if these tools were to be my business card, I figured I'd better know how to flash them.

It was about that time when, as a 20 year-old Lance Corporal, I met Terri. We met at Disneyland one weekend when a mutual friend of ours said he wanted to introduce us. Who was I to refuse?

Immediately, when I saw her, I was stunned. She was amazingly beautiful, like no one I had ever seen. I was struck by her open smile, piercing dark brown eyes, and long black hair. She was smart and well-spoken. I quickly recognized her incredible intelligence. She is still one of the smartest people I have ever known.

Yet we immediately could not stand one another. I figured that she was a spoiled California brat and she assessed me as a stupid wannabe-bad Marine. We spent the whole day defending our opposing points of view until finally I got sick of arguing and walked away with my friend to get into whatever trouble we could find on our own.

Whether by fate, chemistry or dumb luck, we both found ourselves at the same party the following weekend. This time, however, we immediately connected and ended the night kissing each other with great passion. The next day, after gathering my courage, I called to see how she was doing and if she wanted to see me again. Even though I should not have not been surprised, to my delight she said yes.

We started dating over the long distance between Twentynine Palms and her home in Orange County. After a month or two of that, she decided to come out to the desert to be with me full time. We moved in together into a little shoebox of an apartment in town just off of Adobe road and Highway 62, much to the chagrin of my beloved Corps, which looked at all non-marine women as trouble for their poor, innocent young troops.

But I didn't care. In the swirling heat of the desert nights, I found comfort in her arms. We would stay awake in silence and listen to the coyotes howl at a nearby oasis, or talk softly about the things to come. When I finally told her about Mom and my many strange adventures she was surprised, but I imagine it explained a thing or two about me.

I tried to convince her and myself that it was behind me; that my love for her would make it all right. And I did find that I loved her with all my heart. She made me feel alive, and I hadn't felt that as long as I could remember.

But even with her beside me, I still thought about Mom and the airplane almost every day. I could not escape it. I never understood the why of it all and figured I never would. It just had become part of my life.

Every time I watched another family, whole and complete, spending their time together, I thought about Mom. Secretly, I was jealous of their unity and resentful that they didn't have to know what life would be like without each other.

I thought about her when the first snow began to fall back in the Midwest, and the ground would start to freeze.

And I thought about her when I lay staring at the dark ceiling night after night trying to recapture and retain the fading memory of the sound of her voice, the feel of her touch, the smell of her hair… She never really left me.

Terri and I married in September and by the following August I would move out of the Corps and into my new life and the promises of the civilian world. In the meantime my unit was getting ready to go overseas for two weeks in Thailand, and we were all looking forward to that. Tank units don't get to go overseas much, and many of us had never been. We would finally cross the equator and would earn our tattoos. The following February my enlistment would end and I would get out of the active duty Marine Corps and Terri and I could truly get our life started.

Then, on the 2nd of August, 1991, Iraq, a country I was only vaguely familiar with and had always thought was our friend, invaded a country I had never heard of called Kuwait, and in the blink of an eye all of our plans were put on hold. Third Tanks was immediately deployed to Saudi Arabia, and we were there for almost nine months, the entirety of Operation Desert Shield and Desert Storm. I ended up getting my tour extended to stay in Saudi Arabia and fight the war in Kuwait with my unit.

Third Tanks had been assigned to the First Marine Division during Desert Shield, and then was further assigned into Task Force Ripper. On February 23, 1991 we blasted our way into the meat grinder of Desert Storm. Four days and four hours later, our smoking weapons ceased fire. Behind us lay a mangled and bloody path of human destruction, the likes of which, just a few days before, I could have never imagined.

I got back home to a hero's welcome and got out of the Corps a month later, my tour of duty finally and honorably completed. Even though I was still too stunned by the war and my subsequent thrust into the civilian world to know it, I was as proud of my service as a Marine as anything I would later know in my life.

I learned many lessons as a Marine that I have used ever since, often completely unaware that I was using them. During my tour, I met true heroes and living mountains of men like Gunny Russ Williams, Staff Sergeant Frank Cordero, Staff Sergeant Jeff Daniels, Lieutenant Colonel Buster Diggs, Warrant Officer Tim Cook, and my Drill Instructors--Staff Sergeant Shafer, Staff Sergeant Dixon, Staff Sergeant Phillips, and Staff Sergeant Binkley. They were all the type of men I had never met in the civilian world, which seemed far too small and meek for them.

My tour as a Marine was the first major thing in my life that I had ever started and then finished without screwing it up. The Corps gave me pride and a new direction when I needed it. I could say it saved my life. But, like so many things, it came with a cost.

Terri and I moved to the Midwest to work on a campground that my Aunt Mary Lou and Uncle Pat owned. We both attended Western Illinois University in Macomb, Illinois, where I immersed myself in college and tried to adapt to civilian life as best I could. I missed the Corps, though, and compensated somewhat for it by joining the Illinois National Guard.

I was assigned to the Second Battalion, 123rd Field Artillery, Battery B, a crack artillery unit stationed at the Macomb armory. I had a lot of fun there and quickly won the respect of my fellow soldiers. I served my four year inactive reserve service requirement with them and wore that uniform with the same pride with which I wore the uniform of a Marine.

But the memory of Desert Storm had become an unwelcome and constant companion to me. A few months after I returned, I started to get "walk guard," which was this inexplicable need to wake at 2 a.m., with a wrenching tension knotting through the core of my body, then dry heaving until I passed out. At this same time, I also began to dream about that tank and the blood-soaked and mangled vehicles and bodies. Suddenly the dreams of Mom were replaced by the horrors of what I had seen and done in that desert in southern Kuwait. People started calling these types of ailments "Gulf War Syndrome." The reality is that this was simply a catch-all phrase to distract people from a still unexplained range of ailments and diseases, which were as varied as the individuals who served there.

Several years later, when I finally sought help from the Veterans Administration, I was diagnosed with PTSD, which I realize now, explained a lot.

And, the death of Mom hadn't really gone anywhere. She was still there, floating on the fringes of my subconscious – and another thing I had yet to deal with. But I did the best that I could and, with Marine tenacity, I managed to get a life together for Terri and me.

Then I crashed my bike and it all came back.

I awoke with a familiar jerking start one night, reliving the phantom impact, just like I relived the war. But it was becoming exhausting. Sitting there in the dark that night, I just thought I can't do this anymore. If it was PTSD, it was consuming me. So, I should really get...help?

I hated the way the word felt in my brain, like I had a disease. It made me feel weak and pathetic. But I was sick of being at the mercy of the traumatized part of my psyche and I had to try to do something about it.

The next day I drew a random name from the list of psychological services my insurance company gave me and made an appointment the following week.

When I walked into Carol's office, I sat down on the comfortable armchair, which, annoyingly, disappeared at some point and was replaced by an ottoman. Carol greeted me with a warm and trustworthy smile. I took comfort that she was a social worker, not a psychologist or psychotherapist, because to me, seeing her instead of some shrink meant that I wasn't that far gone.

I gave her a brief synopsis of my life. She furrowed her brow and tapped her pen as I reeled it out. I must have sounded like a real piece of work, but she accepted the challenge. She, for the first time in my life, was able to get me to honestly talk to myself, listen to myself and finally start to confront my fears. It seems funny to me now, but in reality it was the beginning step of a long journey that I have made since, and am still making.

A couple years later, I had what they refer to in psychological circles as a turning point. Following a family trip to Kauai, Terri told me she was pregnant, and our son James was born the following October. When I looked into his eyes for the first time, it was as if I were reborn myself. With him, I began to truly believe the fracture of my own childhood life could begin to heal through his life.

But sometimes, even now, when I look at my son, I am aware, despite my shame, that I am jealous of him as I watch him with his mother. I am jealous that he has a chance to know her, to talk to her, and to tuck himself into the safety of her arms. I realize in those moments how much I miss Mom. I have spent my life wondering about all of the things I don't have, and will never have, because she wasn't there.

She was thirty-two years old when her life ended in that field. Thirty-two…that seems so young to me now. I remember thinking on my thirty-third birthday that I was now older than she was. It is an odd thing to become older than one's parents, particularly when you are not that old. I felt at that age like I was still just starting my life, yet hers had ended.

But I am no victim of life. Writing this story has saved me from that. I want neither pity nor condolence from anyone for anything. I can't change the road that led me here so I continue on ahead. Something the Corps taught me was that while you need to know what is behind you, the battle is before you. "Watch your six, but continue to march."

So I march. And as I do, I find that every day above ground is a good day.

On these pages is the story of something that happened one cold night, in a remote farmer's field, and how, as I sought that story, of how it ended up changing the world, and me along with it.

This isn't just a story about an airplane crash. And even though I was there, this story was never about me, either. It was about people I didn't even know, would not meet for many years, or, sadly, never met at all. It was about people who put their lives aside to find us, to rescue us, to care for us, and to make something good from something so bad. These were people who didn't even know what the others did, or the roles they played that night when the world changed for me…and for you.

It's about my mother and one small tragedy in a world of tragedies. It's about my father, an unwitting hero who did what he had to do.

It's about a concept called ATLS, and how it came to be. How through it, at the end of my mother's life, maybe she made it possible for others, so many others - maybe even you and maybe even me - to live.

I have written about it, and how it all came together, and to give credit to those people who came, and to say out loud that the entire world is maybe a better place because of them.

And I also realized that writing this story is one of the most important things I have ever done or ever will do.

Now you know me a little, and I think that's important. Here is the story of that night, and the consequences of it – both for me and the rest of the world. It was a blip in time, which I cannot distinguish as the worst night of my life, or the best. When life ended and began at the same time. It was a moment that blurs the difference, making each concept irrelevant in the presence of the other.

Good, bad…it all depends on how you land, I guess.

You know.

Chapter 1

February 17, 2006.

Dr. James Styner stood in front of a small wooden lectern and nervously sized up his audience, trying to grasp the gravity of the moment. Before him sat two hundred or so of the most respected trauma surgeons in all of Europe, if not the rest of the planet for that matter. Each of them distinguished members of the Royal College – the group he came across the Atlantic to address.

The room he found himself in was a two hundred and seventy year old amphitheater. It could have jumped from one of the old movies where the young doctors sat in rows, looking down on the professor performing an autopsy on the body of a peasant, or some other procedure. Many, many great men and women had stood in that exact spot, and that alone was unnerving. The great and ancient hall was silent except for the beating of Dad's thudding heart.

They had asked him to come to this place in Dublin, Ireland, to speak about that night. He was the only speaker for this, the annual 81st lecture of the College. He would find out later that the 81st lecture, named for Abraham Colles - a noted surgeon and anatomist who died in 1843, was significant because it was reserved for those whom the College deemed the most important and distinguished speakers.

He didn't consider himself all that important just then, nervously standing there before that crowd, a picture of a wrecked airplane projected on the screen behind him. He felt weird that they had given him a check for five hundred dollars as a speaking fee, which was customary. He tried to politely turn it down, but they insisted.

He never wanted money for it. From his point of view, he helped on an idea, wrote it down, presented it to some people, and then went on with his life. He had left his home in Lincoln for good in the mid-80's, and had become quite content with his new practice in California. It was quite a pleasant change, being away from the thousand-mile-an-hour life of a trauma surgeon. He had faded into anonymity, and ATLS had gone on into perpetuity without him. And that was fine with him.

But now others -- fellow doctors, surgeons and researchers -- wanted to hear him talk about it.

A couple of months earlier and seemingly out of the blue, he was asked to speak about ATLS at an American College of Surgeons convention in San Francisco. That was the first time he had ever told the story in public. His presentation ended with a standing ovation. Doctors from all over the world enthusiastically shook his hand and thanked him for what he had done. And that speech led him here.

He felt privileged and humbled. It was indeed a great honor, to stand there before this crowd. They all knew of him. Perhaps they had discussed him and his story, although never by name--until now. For almost thirty years, he had been to them a mythical sort of figure, sculpted in the form of darkness and shadow from the words of the ATLS textbook. Dr. James Styner was always someone they wondered about, but never thought they'd actually meet. Some probably wondered cynically if he even existed at all.

Now he stood before them, flesh and blood, not at all at home in the long black academic robe that they gave him to wear, draped neatly over his shoulders and making him look like an old-time professor. The look wasn't really his style, but he went along with it.

He lowered his head to consider the words on the pages stacked neatly on the lectern before him. He thought about the date. The significance of it, February 17, 2006 – exactly thirty years after the crash -- did not escape him, of course. It wasn't planned this way, of course, but he, of all people, knew that some things just have a funny way of happening.

He spoke, softly at first. He thanked the President of the College who had introduced him, and then turned his attention to the audience. He took a slow, deep breath and paused to shift his mind back to the field, the cold, the blood. Drinking from the memory he began to speak:

"It has been my observation that countries are closer together if they possess something in common," he said. "I was fortunate, if that's the right word, to participate in such a development. I am here tonight to share with you my experience."

He glanced back to the pages, more aware of the thudding of his heart in his ears, then back at the audience.

"As in so many cases," he continued "It starts with a tragedy and then the recognition of a need." The memory held him fast now. His hands trembled slightly as he turned to the first page.

"Thirty years ago…to this very day," he said, glancing at the large clock in the back of the room, "at about this very time…there was an airplane crash."

He paused and saw the audience was held rapt at his words, making him slightly uneasy. But there was no turning back now, so he pressed on, giving himself to the emotion surging up from deep within him.

"Out of the mass of metal, the injured, and the dead, ATLS was born…"

February 17, 1976.

Mom awoke early that morning, got dressed, and crept softly downstairs to Grandma's kitchen to make coffee and prepare for breakfast. She wanted to have plenty of time to get us all ready to go home.

We had all traveled to California from Lincoln a week prior, and now our vacation had come to an end and had been a success. My cousin Mike, a recording engineer who mixed huge rock and roll bands like America and the Eagles, had married a beautiful Hollywood wardrobe mistress named Jennifer three days earlier (on Valentine's Day, of course), and they had sped off to their honeymoon in Tahiti among a flourish of laughter and good will.

Mom was happy how everything had come to pass. The wedding festivities were over, and she had gotten to see all of the family on Dad's side and spend a few days with her mom and her sister. Now she was ready to head home, and get back to regular life.

We were planning to leave for the airport in Fullerton fairly early, once everybody got their things together. One of the benefits of having your own plane was that you could come and go as you pleased and not be tied down by an airline itinerary. That lack of stress alone made it worth it.

One by one that morning we all awoke and made our way downstairs for breakfast. Mom already had gathered my 3 year-old sister and she sat in a highchair and sucked on her bottle. Then came my brothers Chris, who was 10 years old, and Rick, who was 8, then me. I was 7.

We gathered with our mother at the breakfast table near the big glass door that overlooked Grandma's lush garden out back. Bright morning sunshine filled the room. My brothers and I did our regular breakfast routine as Mom chatted with Grandma and sipped coffee, alternating between that and us kids to sort our cereal, milk, and orange juice issues. Four kids had made her a pro by that time, and she carried it all off without missing a beat, as always.

After a while, Dad came down and joined us too. He had been up since before Mom and had gone for a run, showered, and changed before coming down. He greeted Grandma with the usual pleasantries and she reciprocated.

Grandma never really got along with my dad too well. She loved him, insomuch as he was the husband of her daughter and the father of her grandchildren, but she never really seemed overly fond of him. He would tell me the story years later, about how he began to see Mom, a beautiful nursing student at Rio Hondo Hospital, where he worked as a lab tech while he attended medical school at UC Irvine. Grandma hadn't approved of him. He was a little too rough around the edges for her.

Dad was born in Los Angeles in 1934 to a true American working class family. His father, Kenneth (I always called him Pappy), worked various jobs before jumping up after the attack on Pearl Harbor with the rest of America. He immediately enlisted in the Navy and went on to serve as a Chief Petty Officer aboard the USS Pennsylvania, or the Pennsy, as most people called her. Much like it had been for me, the service was what he needed to get his life together.

He had boarded his vessel at Treasure Island in San Francisco after it had been refitted at the only usable dry dock at Pearl Harbor, having been only lightly damaged in the attack. The USS Arizona, the Pennsylvania's sister ship, had sunk and was still smoking in the harbor while they feverishly worked on the Pennsy. She was one of only three battleships left in the Pacific Fleet still floating in Pearl Harbor after the attack. She would spend the next four years leading the way as America sought revenge for the treachery of Imperial Japan.

Pappy served under a young and funny officer from Nebraska named Johnny Carson in the communication section of the huge ship. Yes, that Johnny Carson. Carson was stationed in the radio room with Pappy during battle stations, which was probably often enough. Years later, while we all watched Johnny on T.V, Pappy would tell the story about playing an occasional game of chess with him during the down time inherent in all naval combat.

By the time it was over, the Pennsy had fired more ammunition than any other ship in the war, and perhaps in all of history. She took two torpedoes to her stern one day near Okinawa, but still stayed afloat. Pappy told the story about how they had to stuff the holes in her with seat cushions and mattresses to keep the water out. The image always cracked me up as Pappy spun the story, painting the image of this huge battle ship cruising along with mattresses sticking out of her.

But Pappy always tempered the humor with a far-off look as he told me of the men and friends they lost that day…the ones who died outright when the torpedoes hit, and the ones who drowned shortly after when they were trapped in the rapidly flooding compartments after their comrades were forced to seal off that section of the ship by closing watertight doors. It had to be done to save the ship. He said they could hear the clanking of wrenches on the bulkheads for what seemed like a long time as the doomed sailors pleaded for their lives before eventually all was silent. I don't think he ever forgot that sound, and it probably haunted his dreams, too.

After the war, once she had outlived her usefulness, the Pennsy was nuked (not once, but twice) at Bikini Atoll during the atomic tests in 1946. Yet she would not sink. Two years later, they towed her to an area near some small island in the South Pacific, opened her seacocks, and sent her down quietly and peacefully to her final resting place somewhere deep under the blue waves, her mission finally complete.

During the war, my dad's mom, Hazel, worked as the proverbial 'Rosie the Riveter' at the Douglass aircraft factory in El Segundo, California. She helped build the Dauntless and Devastator dive bombers for the Navy and Marines until the war was over. She, my dad, Uncle Jerry, and Aunt Mary Lou were a typical war family of the time, supporting the war and their sailor until he would return home.

My grandfather was a rough man. He was a hard drinker and tough talker, and could back it all up, too. He smoked three packs of unfiltered Lucky Strikes or Camels every day for thirty years. He was his own man and was smart, but was also a firm believer in personal salvation through physical labor. He believed that the greatest thing you could do in life was build, create and fiddle with things.

My grandparents moved in to take care of us after Mom died, and thank God for them. Pappy taught me my multiplication tables, and, being a self-proclaimed "rock hound," he taught me everything about rocks and gems, too. He showed me how to make pancakes and how to garden. He was everything I thought a real man should be. I stood in awe of him.

Years later, Pappy survived a stroke that hit him on a fishing trip near Guadalupe Island, 250 miles from San Diego along the Baja coast. Thankfully, my Dad and his medical partner Bruce were there and kept him alive and stable until they got back to San Diego twelve hours later. A Lear jet met them at the San Diego Airport and flew them all back to Lincoln, Nebraska, for his care. It was the kind of thing that would have killed most people, but not Pappy.

Despite his invincibility to me, he finally died of stomach cancer, ten years after ovarian cancer took his wife, my Grandma Hazel. I was training with the Marines at Fort Irwin in the Mojave at the time, so I attended his funeral in my uniform and got to salute his remains as a Marine. I knew he was proud of me, and that made a difference. Dad sent his flag to the U.S.S. Pennsylvania Reunion Association in Washington.

After his graduation from high school, Dad followed his father's footsteps and also joined the Navy. As if a foreshadowing of his eventual career, he enlisted to become a Corpsman, which is a field medical specialist, often assigned to Marine field units. He had enlisted with the intent of fighting with the Marines in Korea. However, the Corpsman were a favorite target of the enemy. Dad recalled that the instructor told them as much on the first day, and that those not wanting to continue as a Corpsman would receive a different assignment. But, after a few seconds, nobody moved, so the instructor went on with the training.

Fortunately for Dad, and ultimately for me and my siblings, the Korean War ended in July of that same year, just before Dad finished Corps school. He avoided combat, but saw in detail its horrible results. He served out his tour at the Veterans Hospital in Bremerton, Washington, as a Corpsman, helping the bloodied Korean vets try to be put back together. It was long hours of frustrating bureaucracy and thanklessness, but the experience taught him the value of education and also provided him with the means to seek it through the GI Bill. It also gave him a new interest: Medicine.

After the service, Dad went to college at Humboldt State University in California's far north, and then came back to Los Angeles to attend medical school. He also needed a job, so he managed to get work as a lab tech at Rio Hondo. He was briefly married to a woman named Sandy, but that's all he ever said about that. Then he met Mom. She was so beautiful, he told me later, and immediately caught his attention. She was sweet and nice to him, which was a welcome change to the grind of working and medical school.

He had brains but seemed to lack some serious refinement. My mother's mom, Grandma Carter, thought that he came across as a bit of a playboy, with his crew cut, cocky attitude, and sharp wit. He certainly didn't fit the mold of an academic type. He had divorced Sandy only shortly before he had met Mom, and Grandma didn't approve of that at all.

Grandma had hoped that her daughter would go for one of those nice boys from church. She had been sort of seeing a clean cut Christian boy, but now she was drawn to this man. Grandma was not happy with this situation.

Mom's father, Ray Carter, thought Dad seemed all right, and his approval for Dad to see his little girl was what was truly important. He thought that at least Dad would be able to get a job as a doctor and give his daughter a secure future.

Grandma and Grandpa Carter were from the old school. They had traveled to Southern California during the dust bowl from South Dakota. Their small dairy farm had fallen victim to the shifting sand, so they made their way west with the rest of the stricken Midwest farmers. They settled in a small Dutch community called Cerritos, and started their lives again.

Mom was born in Los Angeles in 1944 and was ten years Dad's junior. She was barely a woman when she and Dad met in the fall of 1963. She enjoyed the fun things that the youth of the era did back then, like rock and roll and fast cars. Her teenage record collection included Paul Anka, Frankie Vallie, and a new kid named Elvis, and she loved to dance. She was on the flag drill team at her High School, and was in a car club that liked to gather at the local car hop and cruise the streets of the 1950's L.A. suburbs. In Dad, she found all of those things she liked – which was exactly what worried Grandma.

It was impressive that Dad had somehow found the courage to tell Grandpa Ray when Mom got pregnant with my oldest brother Chris before they were married. When he heard, Ray slapped his forehead in disbelief, looked back and forth at both of them for a second or two hoping for a punch line. When none came, he closed his eyes.

"Not the doc..!" he said.

Ray Carter, was a big man. At five-foot-nine, he wasn't tall, but he was stocky, tough and a heavy smoker. He helped to build the skyscrapers in Los Angeles, and, according to family stories, was a force to be reckoned with. Apparently, my grandfathers got along great, being cut from the same cloth. They were a breed that all but disappeared sometime between the early seventies and late eighties. They were men who always wore hats and ties, changed their own oil and tires, and insisted on opening doors for ladies. Like Pappy, Grandpa Ray was also at Pearl Harbor during the war. He was a civilian welder, and worked there for almost two years to help clear the debris and rebuild the base.

It took guts for Dad to be honest, but that was Dad. Grandpa Ray had grown to like and respect him, and Dad for his part promised to make an honest woman out of Mom, and quickly, which he did. The shotgun was not necessary at the wedding, but I'd be willing to bet it wasn't too far away.

I wish I had gotten to know Grandpa Ray, but he died of a heart attack while on vacation in Orlando with Grandma when I was still a baby, only a few years before that morning in the kitchen. I share his name, though (my middle name), and take great pride in that. I take comfort in knowing that he had held me and proudly looked at his grandson.

Grandma did not see in Dad what Grandpa Ray did. She was cordial, but never got too close. Mom was always honest with her mother, so Grandma certainly knew all about Dad, the good and the not-so-good. I'm sure she thought Mom could've chosen more carefully.

People are often slow to come around, but in the end she did. After so many years of blaming my Dad for what happened to Mom, he was the one she wanted by her side as she lay dying of kidney failure years later. In the end, she had forgiven him.

My dad was dedicated to his family and his work from the start. He didn't want the hard life his dad had lived, and knew that medicine was his out. Beside he was damn good at it, and loved it. He loved his family, too and would do well by them.

In spite of Dad and Grandma's early relationship, Grandma loved my two brothers, my sister, and me. She was always quick to spoil us when we came out to visit her in California. We always had a good time on those trips. And now here we were and this trip had been fun too. Grandma smiled at me sitting next to Mom as I ate my cereal.

I had a nice time with Mom just the night before. She had been taking some rare relaxation time in the tub upstairs. I peeked in to ask her something and she motioned for me to come sit down and talk. That was how she was. She was fascinated by her children and always wanted to know how we were doing and what was new with us.

I am not sure what specifically we talked about, but I remember I sat on the edge of the tub for a long time. It was just her and me. I remember feeling so privileged that I could have her all to myself for a while. I remember her like an angel and I loved her with all of my being. I hope that I told her that.

The next morning in the kitchen, we finished our breakfast and began to get our things together. My mom's sister, Aunt Betty Lou, had come over to help Mom wrangle us and get us ready to fly home. She lived in Fullerton, near the airport where our plane was parked. Coincidentally, it was the same airport where I would learn to fly little Cessna 172s many years later.

We spent a lot of time at Aunt Betty's house in the hills above Euclid Avenue with Uncle Ken whenever we made one of our west coasts visits, swimming in their pool with my cousins Jeff and Daren. But not today. Today we were heading straight to the airport. My parents and Betty Lou packed our bags into her and Grandma's cars, then Dad went back inside and called his partner Bruce to tell him we were getting ready to go.

Bruce and my Dad owned our plane together, and Dad always kept in contact with him whenever he flew, as best as he could in the days before such things as cell phones. They did it with land-line calls before every take off and after every landing. It was a standard practice with pilots.

While he did that, the rest of us piled into the cars--me, Rick, and Mom into Betty Lou's Audi, and Dad, Kim and Chris in Grandma's big blue Cadillac. Rick and I messed around in the back seat while Mom and Betty chatted as sisters do up front for the twenty minutes or so until we made it to the airport. Had I been given a glimpse into only a few hours into the future, I'd have paid more attention to what Mom said, no matter what it was.

The orange and white with brown stripes 1969 Beechcraft Baron B-55 N3600H sat gleaming in the hazy morning sun, tied down on the tarmac of the transitive parking area of the Fullerton Municipal Airport. It was a beautiful plane, by all accounts. It held six people and their luggage comfortably. Its two big Continental engines mounted into the front of each wing cranked out 300 horse power each, the dual constant-speed propellers driving the sleek craft to a cruising speed of around 230 mph. It could go over 1,800 nautical miles on a tank of gas and could climb 1,700 feet per minute. It handled as good as any plane of its kind and the B-55 Baron is still generally respected in the aviation community as a top notch airplane.

Mom loved to fly with Dad and she loved the Baron. It was a wonderful airplane. She had taken many trips with him in it. So enamored by flying was she that she had recently taken a copilot class and was in the process of becoming a student pilot to learn to fly herself. She wanted to be a solo pilot someday so she could split the load of flying back and forth on these long trips.

Or whatever. She just loved to be up in the air with Dad. She watched and followed along as he methodically walked around the plane checking the wings and tail and flaps as he went through his pre-flight checklist.

The plane was fueled up and ready to go. Grandma and Betty Lou kept us together off to the side while Mom and Dad loaded our luggage into the nose of the plane, then Mom opened the little cargo door that accessed the two back seats and more cargo space in the tail. In there she loaded a few more bags.

She joined Betty and Grandma while Dad went into the small terminal to get a standard weather report and file his flight plan. They said that it was nice and clear all the way to Farmington where we would land to take a break and have lunch. It was a perfect day for flying.

And it was time to go.

I remember how my Grandma kissed me and hugged me tight before we went. Betty Lou hugged me goodbye, too. There were hugs all around and my Grandma even hugged Dad.

"Remember this is precious cargo," she told him. "You must be very careful."

Rick crawled through the little cargo door at the rear of the plane through which Mom loaded the suitcases a few moments before, and on into the back seats. Once he had maneuvered himself into the seat farthest from the hatch, I crawled in behind him, got into my seat on the right side, and arranged the seatbelt around my waist buckling it and pulling it tight.

Mom patted me on the leg and blew us both a kiss, then closed the hatch with a muted thump, insuring it was tightly secured and locked. Meanwhile, Chris had climbed up onto the right wing to go through the main door and worked his way into the seat behind the left pilot position. When he was all situated, Mom handed Kim to him so he could buckle her into the other seat, which he did. Then she stepped back off of the wing so Dad could climb up and enter the cockpit.

Dad positioned himself in the pilot seat where he continued his preflight checks. Finally, Mom climbed in and fastened herself into the copilot seat, closing the door behind her and insuring it was locked. It was snug in the plane with all of us crammed in there, but not uncomfortable, for such a small space.

The interior of the plane muffled the sounds both outside and in. Dad had placed his David Clarke aviation headset on his head as did Mom, and he was going through his checklist with her. I knew the drill well and waited in anticipation while Dad methodically flipped switches and checked gauges as Mom read each item. Then suddenly, he yelled out:

"Left prop! Clear!"

The left engine coughed out rapid high pitched staccato bursts then blasted into full action with a roar. He let it warm up and continued to work through the checklist. Then he yelled again:

"Right prop! Clear!" The right engine followed suit. Once everything checked out, Dad gently pushed the engine throttle forward and the plane slowly glided out of its space and into the taxi lane, stopping between the rows of planes.

He flipped the radio to the automated weather briefing. Mom listened and jotted down the bits of information that came forth. Dad then requested clearance to move to the run-up area near the end of runway two-four, and then with an increase in throttle guided the plane over to it. Once there, he did a series of run up checks and adjusted the pressure setting on the altimeter based on what he heard during the weather briefing. When complete, he moved the plane to the end of the taxiway, stopping short of the runway threshold, and called the tower to get permission to take off for a right downwind departure.

Permission was granted and the engines increased their pitch as we moved forward and turned to take our position on the runway. Once Dad got the plane properly oriented roughly west and more or less into the light breeze, he opened the throttle to full and the plane smoothly thrust forward, quickly gaining speed and pushing the blood to the back of my head and my body into the seat. A funny dropping feeling in my stomach made me know that the plane was lifting gracefully from the earth, into the cloudless sky above Orange County.

Dad reached climbing speed then raised the landing gear. It whirred and clunked into place under us. He guided the plane to the pattern altitude, and with a gentle and wide bank to the right, he turned to point the compass east. He continued to climb into the sky, setting a course that would take us far above the deserts and mountains of Southern California and Arizona, and on toward Farmington.

Our home lay a million miles beyond.

I found all kinds of ways to pass the time on these trips, but mostly I just stared out of my little window at the changing landscape below. We flew over snow-capped mountains, green forests, and deep canyons, then out over the sandy brown California desert. We flew a route roughly parallel to U.S. Intestate 40, skirting the southern fringes of the Rocky Mountains, which majestically extended northward like towering sentinels.

From up here the world looked like one of those big model train set ups; everything in detail, but miniature. People were way too small to see, but I could see trains on their rails and small specks of cars on the highways.

I had spent a lot of my childhood back in that seat. Sometimes the trips got boring, but I could forget the boredom as I was absorbed into the tiny world moving slowly below me. I always wondered what was down there. I wanted to be there, at the top of that mountain or deep in those woods. It was a game I played.

I still do when I fly. I always anticipated the day I'd be big enough to be allowed to go into the plane through the front, walking onto the wing and through the main door like Chris did, but for now I was happy back there in my snug little compartment next to Rick, while I watched the world moving slowly below.

Next to me, Rick had fallen fast asleep and eventually I too was lulled into drowsiness by the incessant purr of the engines and the rocking of the little plane, rolling gently side to side like a cradle. Slowly, my head flopped to rest on Rick's shoulder and I dozed off too, the big world spinning almost two miles beneath me.

Presently, we began to descend toward the New Mexico high country. Farmington came into view and Dad lined up with the runway and glided the plane into to a smooth landing. Rick and I awoke with a slight start to the thump and chirp of the wheels under us as they touched down. Dad slowed the rushing plane, pulled off the runway, and stopped. He contacted the Farmington ground control and got permission to move onto the taxiway and over to the transitive parking area, and then found a spot to park.

The engines shut down one at a time and once they were silent we piled ourselves out of the plane, stretching our cramped bodies and rejoicing in being firmly back on the ground.

Dad went into the terminal building to check the weather again and call Bruce while the rest of us made our way to the little café adjacent to the runway where we could get some lunch and watch as other little planes came and went.

Rick and I loaded wads of paper into our drinking straws, secretly shooting them at each other and the unsuspecting diners around us. From time to time, the people gave stern looks right at us, but we pretended that we were innocent and probably believed they really didn't know where the shots had come from – what with us being the only kids in the place. I guess they all took pity on my Mom with her three rambunctious boys, for no one said a thing. Rick and I congratulated ourselves for being clever.

Our food arrived and I munched on my hot dog. Dad came in to join us and get some food as well, and we sat and ate a quiet lunch as a family one more time, together in that little airport café. Nothing particularly special was going on. It was the same scene as it is with anyone played out a million times across the globe every day, I suppose. It's difficult to realize how big of a deal such a mundane moment can be.

For the rest of my life, if I could've ever been granted a wish for one instant in time to capture in a photograph, it would have been that one, right then. We couldn't have known the innocence we left sitting there amongst our wadded up napkins placed haphazardly on ketchup stained plates as we got up, gathered our things, turned our backs, and walked away.

Back at the plane, we conducted the same drill as before. We got ourselves situated in our same places and were shortly climbing back into the sky. It wasn't far now. Not far at all.

After what seemed a long time, I looked around the clean white interior of the plane, bathed golden by the slowly setting sun sliding gracefully into the sea beyond the horizon far behind us. Mom had taken my sister into the front to sit on her lap where she had fallen asleep. I could see her closed eyes over the seat back, propped up on Mom's shoulder as Mom stroked her hair. I could see the back of Mom and Dad's heads over their seats, the green headphones cupped over their ears. I could see Chris' hair poking up over his seat back in front of Rick. Beside me, Rick was asleep again.

Slowly, with the darkening of the clear sky, listening to the droning of the engines propelling us perpetually forward, I gently laid my head back on my big brother's shoulder and drifted into sleep once again, closing my eyes as a child for the last time.

Chapter 2

Shelley crossed the terminal of the Ontario, California airport towards where I sat, carrying a cup of coffee in each hand. It was around 6:30 in the morning and she, our other colleague Ross, and I were taking the first flight out to Atlanta to attend nuclear emergency response training at a FEMA facility in Alabama. We were all excited to be there and had been looking forward to the weeklong break in our normal work routines.

I looked over the edge of the copy of the backpacking magazine I was reading and smiled pleasantly at Shelley as she approached, pulling myself from the story of a kid who had gotten his arm stuck under a boulder in some Moab canyon while hiking alone. He ended up having to cut his mangled forearm off with a dull knife, negotiate the rest of the canyon, set up and rappel one-armed down a sixty foot cliff, and then hike out some twenty miles before he ran into a couple of other hikers who helped him get to safety.

What must that have been like?

I placed the magazine on the worn vinyl of the seat between me and the armrest. Shelley returned the smile and handed me the extra cup, then sat next to me, sipping her coffee.

I liked Shelley. She was one of those people who carry an unthreatening and honest demeanor, and she had an easy and direct way about her. With her, what you saw was truly what you got – an admirable trait for anyone.

Before that trip, I had never really had many serious conversations with Shelley other than the standard work fare, but nonetheless we got along well. I had learned a lot about her and she was always kind to me. She's a good friend. Since I had to take this trip with people from work, I was glad one of them was her.

I trusted her - and that was a rare thing for me.

We passed the time in the terminal chatting about inane things as we counted the minutes until boarding. Ross snoozed in the seat on the other side of me, and presently the soft voice of the gate attendant came over the speakers above us to announce our flight. We made our way up to the jetway and boarded, shuffling through the aisle until we found our row. We buckled ourselves to the outer two seats in the center column somewhere in the middle of the big Delta L-1011 jet. Ross had a seat in another part of the plane, but Shelley was sitting next to me. I was glad she was. It was good to have someone to talk to.

I use to work on the road doing freelance audio-visual production jobs for various companies. I flew many times doing this, but always hated to fly alone. Generally, I never talked to anyone because I always found those situations awkward, sitting trapped next to a stranger, not knowing what to say. I read a lot on those trips.

I hadn't told the whole story about "it" outside a structured setting in quite some time. Maybe that was why it seemed different this time. Ever since the motorcycle crash, and in my subsequent conversations with my therapist, Carol, it had been heavy on my mind. I guess that's why it wasn't surprising that while Shelley and I chatted about the ins and outs of air travel the way people do while the plane prepares for the upcoming act of lurching itself into the air, fighting against gravity and the weight of a full load of passengers, luggage, and fuel, the subject of air disasters came up.

For me, I have found, this is a natural thing. Perhaps it is a basic part of the human psyche. It comes from the belief that specific air disasters are never predicted and occur as a sort of surprise. The logic following this dictates that if you talk about the possibility, it somehow spoils the surprise - and then it won't happen.

So, to thwart the possibility of disaster of some shape or form in advance, you analyze the things that can go wrong on takeoff, like that one in Chicago when the engine fell off, or landing, like that one in Dallas that was slammed to the earth by a sudden and cataclysmic wind shear during their final approach. Or somewhere in between, like that one in Iowa that had its rear engine ripped apart in midair, and ended up rolling in a fiery ball down a Sioux City runway.

It was a slightly morbid line of conversation, I was aware, but it didn't bother me. To my gratitude, Shelley didn't seem to mind either, perhaps sharing my illogical logic. In truth, probably neither of us bought it, but if nothing else, it was an interesting topic with which to pass the time.

As if on cue, the plane jerked slightly as it moved back from the gate, breaking the flow of our conversation. I chuckled nervously, and fiddled with the emergency card in the seat back. There was an uncomfortable pause while I thought of something to say. Maybe the topic really had made me uncomfortable. Maybe it was the silence I hated. Either way, I began to speak, unable to stop the words:

"In case you were wondering," I said, matter-of-factly, "you are statistically much safer while I am on this plane."

It came so casually--almost as an afterthought--like I was talking about walking a dog or reading a good book.

"Really," Shelley said, turning her head slightly to glance at me curiously. "And why would that be?"

I regretted it immediately. Telling the story always brought an element of weirdness. The whole thing has always made me feel a little like a freak. I didn't want her to know that I was a freak. Besides, I hadn't told the story in so long that I was a little unsure how to start. I squirmed in my seat now.

"Well..." I blurted out, trying to figure the best way to put it. "I was...kind of in a plane crash...once."

She blinked and sized me up. I now had her full attention. I crawled in my skin under the weight of her stare. Why couldn't I ever just keep my big mouth closed?

"Shut...up!" she said wide-eyed with pointed disbelief.

I understood her reaction fully. I guess it's a strange thing to hear from someone seated next to you, particularly when you are strapped into an airplane getting ready to taxi. I guess most people don't give such statistics much thought.

Except me.

In a lot of ways, the idea of statistical safety is what allowed me to ever get back on an airplane, funny as it may be.

"Yeah...," I continued, awkwardly, "So statistically, you are safer ...because I am on this plane."

She blinked again. I felt like an idiot.

"I mean what are the odds?" I babbled on. "Of it happening twice, I mean..." I glanced at her and shrugged.

Shelley's stare weighed on me as she sized me up, probably at least to some extent unsure whether or not I was just pulling her leg. I had seen her expression so many times on the faces of others, so at least I was ready for it. Nobody really knows how to respond when I tell them about that. It must be a bit surreal. I always feel like they are waiting for me to give them the punch line or something.

But I could see that she did believe me, just by the look in her eyes. Not everybody does. Some people have told me I was flat out lying. I guess I have always kind of understood this too, looking at it from their point of view. It is a hard thing to fathom, that this person here was in a plane crash.

It is especially odd to hear when you're sitting right there next to them, with all their limbs and parts seemingly intact…with them alive. People just don't know a whole lot of airplane crash survivors, because if nothing else, they are pretty sure that not many people survive airplane crashes.

As for us who do, it is something you shouldn't bring up at all unless you are prepared to take some questions. It is simple human nature to inquire about such things. Maybe someday I'll figure that fact out and shut up. But not that day.

I have spent my life seeing the reaction just like the one I got from Shelley, but honestly I had forgotten about it and how it made me feel until right then. I turned my attention to the plastic tray table folded securely into the seat back in front of me, and wanted to smack my head into it.

"Wow…" Shelley said after a pause, seemingly with a lack of words, which I knew from knowing Shelley was probably rare. She didn't strike me as the type of person who was often at a lack for words. The jet had begun taxiing by that point as we made our way to take off.

The funny thing about the story is that it only comes up on one of two occasions--when I am on an airplane with someone I don't know too well, or when someone I do know suddenly notices the cross-shaped scar that dominates the right side of my forehead. I've known people for years who never notice it then one day out of the blue, they stop in their tracks.

"Whoa…" they say. "Where'd you get THAT?"

I've heard it more times than I can count. And, over the years I have tried to think up a witty response, such as bull fighting accident, raging clown, alien abduction…

But usually the answer comes out as a mumbling about a bad accident I was in once. If I am lucky it stops there, but it rarely does. Like I said before, accidents are a source of interest for people. That's just the way it is. So eventually I told the story to everyone I was close to.

The folds of my forehead have begun to hide the scar, at least mask it somewhat, so people don't seem to notice it too much anymore. In fact, it was such a common occurrence that the whole thing had become just like any story to me. It lost its significance somewhat. It seemed that through telling it all of those times, I managed to bury the feelings associated with it somewhere down deep, and left them there.

But now that I had started it, I was unable to keep my mouth from moving for a long time, as almost by force I was drawn to toss it all out, even though it was painful. Shelley, to her credit, seemed interested to listen and was an attentive audience. It was certainly not something she had ever heard before. Besides, she was trapped beside me so where was she going to go?

So I told it again. But as the words came out this time, I realized that as I relived each of the moments, even the ones I didn't think I could possibly know, I could feel my insides churn and squirm with anxiety. For the first time, maybe because of the amazed way that Shelley looked at me, I think I actually realized it was me I was talking about. For whatever reason, telling it that time really affected me, and I couldn't stop until it was all out.

When I finished, we sat in silence for a while as the big jet lofted us on our way to Atlanta. I stared at the seat back again, mentally exhausted, trying to play it off as no big deal, but feeling like a clown. Shelley took it all in, but I knew what a heavy thing I had just laid on her, talking so intently about something so personal. I was a little embarrassed by it all now.

"Have you ever tried to write that down?" she asked after awhile. I looked at her.

"Yeah, I have," I said. Actually, it was more that I had simply thought about writing it. Terri had been telling me for years that I should. So did Carol. Lots of people had.

The problem was, beyond my desire to write something, I knew so little about the real story. As I tried to get the words down in a coherent and systematic form, it would become just that; a story, a tall tale. I mean, I was there, but I was just a little kid and unconscious most of the time. I only knew what I'd been told over the years, meted out in small, intermittent strands.

And because I didn't know what really occurred for those large stretches of time, I would end up creating a story filled with guesses or might-have-beens.

One thing I did know for sure was that I didn't want to tell a fictional story about it. If I was going to write about it, I wanted to tell the entire truth. Except that I didn't know the truth. No one person did. It was horribly discouraging, and I would always lay my proverbial pen down and walk away after a few pages, or paragraphs, or even sentences. It always left me with an empty and depressed feeling.

I explained as much to Shelley.

"Why don't you find some of those people, then?" she suggested with barely a pause. "Ask them about it?"

As she said it, her words swirled in my mind, finally attaching themselves to some kind of meaning. I was a little dumbfounded. It made perfect sense. Any thought I had about doing something like this before had seemed futile or even impossible, so I never gave it too much consideration. Yet, here was Shelley, just a friendly coworker sitting next to me on a plane, asking me what I really should have asked myself all along.

Why didn't I ever find those people?

"Nah," I said, retreating once again to the comfort of denial. "I don't even know where to look…and even if I did, who'd remember anything?"

Shelley turned to face me again. "Do you really think someone would really ever forget *that*?" She said bluntly.

I glanced at her and in seeing the intensity of her look, faced away and stared at my lap, like I had been caught in something. I thought about those words very carefully.

"No," I said finally. "No, I don't suppose they would."

"There has got to be someone around," she concluded, and settled back in her seat with the confidence of someone who knows they are right. More importantly like someone who knows YOU know they are right. "You just have to look."

I cannot describe the sensation that hearing her say those words had on me, but it was akin to being struck by psychological lightning. I tried to stoically play it off, but the thought made me squirm inside.

Could it be possible? Why had I never given it more serious consideration? Why did I want to believe what Shelley had said was NOT true, even though I knew in my heart that it was??

I was cornered. I couldn't deny the truth in her words. They rang in my head the rest of the flight.

We got to Atlanta and we didn't crash, kind of proving my point about statistical safety. We picked up our rental car then drove to our hotel to rest for a while. An hour later we all went out for a nice dinner, followed by a visit to a bar in Buckhead to celebrate our safe arrival.

I got really drunk.

Sometime after midnight, Ross drove us back down Peachtree Street in the direction of the massive Turner Center and back to our hotel. I swayed in the elevator till the doors opened and then staggered out. I turned and mumbled an incoherent 'night' to my friends, then walked down the corridor and found my door, opened it, and poured myself into the room.

I clumsily pulled off my clothes then flopped onto the stiff bed, draping my arms across it and reaching for my cell phone. I called Terri, who wondered why I got so drunk and we argued about it for a while, then I fell spinning into fumy sleep.

I dreamed a fitful yet familiar nightmare about fog and frozen, dirty ground. I wandered lost and afraid, not sure where I was or where I could go for help. I slipped further and further into the mist until I tripped and plunged into an endless void, twirling and tumbling downward…

"Ungh!" I shot up with a start, thrashing my arms to free myself from the sweat soaked sheets that entangled me like a net. The darkness that held me down filled my senses with still, dead air. I wasn't quite sure where I was for a second, but came around as objects began to resolve from the blackness that held me.

I was in a hotel room. I was in Atlanta. It was early in the morning.

My head swam in a haze of old beer and adrenaline. My heart raced. The room was hot and muggy. Suddenly I felt sick.

Stumbling into the bathroom, I slumped to my knees in front of the toilet and considered it for a moment while waves of nausea rolled across me. Suddenly the waves crashed and I thrust my face into the toilet to let loose with a violent spasm twisting deep in my gut, feeling like a piston was ramming through my innards. I heaved up a small remnant of the night's repast, and a bit of beer, then dry-retched for several agonizing minutes.

Eventually the waves subsided and I lay down, curled up on my side in a fetal position, gratefully embracing the gentle sensation of feeling better as it slowly washed over me. Of course, I knew the sick could return, but it didn't. I lay there for a long time, my skin drenched with clammy sweat sticking to the cold tile floor, the scene all too familiar from my years after the war.

When it all finally passed, I collected my wits, pushed myself to my knees, and slowly stood. I shuffled the short distance to the sink to turn on the cold water and splashed it over my face as it flowed from the tap. There was an acrid and bitter taste in my mouth, so I fumbled for my toothbrush and quickly brushed my teeth. Then I rubbed my hands over my face and stared into the mirror at the dark bags under my eyes. They drooped heavily, making me look tired and numb, defying the indecipherable stream of ringing thought still flowing through my head.

With a huff, I turned and left the little bathroom, flicking out the light with a flip of my hand as I went. I stumbled across the room and found the darkened air conditioner under the front window. I fiddled blindly at the switches until it began to blow slightly more cool air into the stuffy room, then I grunted and fell back on the bed, spinning again into restless sleep, whirling like a vortex behind my thudding eyes. I wasn't sure where these familiar feelings were coming from, but I knew I had opened a long-sealed tomb somewhere in the depths of my head.

Great.

I tried to shake off the rough night and intrusive thoughts the next morning with a lot of coffee, and eventually managed to get my head focused on the reason I was in Atlanta, which was to learn emergency response procedures to radiological incidents. Like so many times before, I suppressed the intruding thoughts as they entered my mind. They were the same images I had seen thousands of times throughout the years. They never changed.

A week later, we returned to California and Ross was greeted at the airport by his wife and little boy, who ran up to him, grabbing his leg and hugging it with a locked grip. I smiled as he said goodbye to Shelley and me, and Ross walked off with this troop, his loving family.

Seeing this made me miss James and Terri. It was good to be home.

Shelley and I rode the airport bus to the remote parking lot and found my silver Xterra. We loaded up our bags in the back and got in. I started it and turned up Blood on the Tracks a little in my CD player, then pulled out of the lot and headed for the entrance of the freeway, and on toward Riverside to drop Shelley off. Then I could finally travel home to Terri and James. We drove in silence for a while, while Lilly, Rosemary and the Jack of Hearts filled the void.

"Are you going to write about that crash?" Shelly asked a few minutes after we got on the freeway. I thought about it for a few seconds.

"Yeah…" I said finally. "Yeah, I think I will."

"I think it'll do you good," she said. I knew she was right.

Eventually, we pulled up in front of her house and I helped her get her suitcase out of my car. We said goodbye, and I watched as she trundled her way to her door, pausing to wave back at me. I waited till she went inside, then the door closed and the porch light went out, leaving me alone with my thoughts. I turned to go and inhaled a deep breath of the cool California desert air, taking in the dim glow of reflecting lights on the horizon below a dark, clear, star-filled sky, finally alone.

Suddenly I felt good. I felt inspired. I felt motivated. I had said I would do it, and now I had to do it. I climbed into my truck and made my way home.

When I walked in, I was greeted by the loving arms of my wife and son. It was good to be back, but Terri immediately saw in my eyes that something was up. After fifteen years, you just know these things about your partner. I told her about my revelation and of my plan to find the facts and tell the story, and she was genuinely happy, if not relived. "And I'll do anything I can to help you, Terri said.

Now I really wanted to do it.

I just needed to figure out how.

After so many years and cycles of starting and stopping, I had finally convinced myself that the story would never be told, and that my Mom would be forgotten. It had made me desperate and depressed, and I had to force my way through that now. I began to think really hard about it for the first time in my life, and set my determination to get it done.

Chapter 3

Days later, I sat in front of my computer monitor for the umpteenth hour, lost in the thoughts that raged disjointedly through my head. I had never researched the crash or even thought about how I would. By then I had regressed back to my old mindset that was sure that there wasn't much information out there, especially after thirty years. Nobody probably cared anyway.

I had a definite image of that day in my head, but, without much more information, creating a draft or even an outline was impossible and wrought with frustration. I realized that this quest would require that I do some real research.

Damn.

The good news is that I am pretty good at research – in fact it is a large part of my day job. But, unfortunately, it is a royal pain in the butt to get started when you don't even know what you're looking for. Generally, the research I do day to day has some basis in knowledge that I already possess, so I know where to start.

But here, with this? How do you find such an insignificant event in such a huge world? Where would I go to begin? Who could I talk to? It was the proverbial needle in an impossibly huge haystack. It was so long ago, that there couldn't be much if anything. And even if I did find it out, I didn't know the first thing about writing a book. I mean me, a writer? Who the hell was I kidding?

I was clueless, and it was utterly defeating in its weight. After a while I pushed back my seat and stomped away from the computer to sit outside on my back patio. I stared out across the lawn, watching the phoebes dive and twist in aerial acrobatics as they snatched insects from mid-air over the grass. The cool spring breeze wafted over me.

I closed my eyes and retreated to memories of college. This was really the same as doing research papers I used to do on something like Cell Biology, or recumbent DNA, or Drosophila Melanogaster. As a perennial under-achieving student, I always began by staring into the massive whirling, sucking void of blackness known as the Academic Body of Knowledge, all of which represented the universe of stuff you don't know.

If you let it overwhelm you, which is easy to do, you end up cowering alone in the darkened corner of some smoky bar a little later, trying to escape it with cheap college beer and cigarettes bummed from kind strangers. And, of course, you really piss off the professor when you hand in something akin to a smiley face drawn in crayon on construction paper entitled, "My Sell Biologoogly Stuff." And, for the record, I only did that once...

But, if you are committed and motivated, you look in the right places, and keep at it, eventually the answers seem to magically resolve before you. Put them together and you've done...Research!

My eyes snapped open - I remembered! I did learn something in college, after all!

Still, I had to push away the growing desire to find something else to do instead of wasting my time with this. I considered giving into the cynicism for a moment, but then I remembered how I used to get through those mountains of paper in the stacks of the library at Western Illinois.

As I walked through those stacks, I realized that everything that has ever been learned in the academic world can, in fact, be found somewhere. And for the most part written down. All I had to do was pull that information together and give it to my professor in a neat and organized format--properly referenced, of course.

That is what all research is all about. I got a lot of A's this way, and remembering it now emboldened me. I determined that I would seek out what I could. No harm in trying, I figured. If I could do twenty pages of dribble on the human lymphatic system, I could do this, for crying out loud.

I went back and sat at my desk and stared at the Google home page on my computer screen for a long time. The cursor defiantly blinked at me, daring me to figure out what exactly the hell I was trying to do. Where do I start? I wondered...I couldn't say if there were too many places to go or too few, but nothing came to mind. I racked my brain.

I remembered that many years ago I had seen a report of the crash. I didn't remember then what it said exactly, but I figured it must have been from an official agency. Who would do that...the FAA? The NTSB? The NHSA? Who?

After a moment of trying to figure it out for sure, I concluded, what the hell? and typed in "FAA" to see what would happen. I clicked on the first link that Google provided and was brought to the Federal Aviation Administration's webpage. At the top, I saw a link that said *Accident and Incident Data.*' Encouraged, I clicked it. When the next page popped up I immediately spotted another link that said *Aviation Accident Reports and Statistics – National Transportation Safety Board (NTSB).* With building enthusiasm, I clicked on this link. In a flash, the National Transportation Safety Board's website link popped up. Although I was doubtful, I thought that maybe there would be some sort of database of crashes there.

Then the very first thing my eyes rested on was a link that said: *Accident Database & Synopses - Descriptions of more than 140,000 aviation accidents - search capability available.*'

I blinked and a moment later delayed disbelief splashed over me. There was no way it could be that easy! Skeptical, I clicked the link. The page that popped up said:

'*The NTSB aviation accident database contains information from 1962 and later about civil aviation accidents and selected incidents within the United States, its territories and possessions, and in international waters. Generally, a* **preliminary** *report is available online within a few days of an accident.* **Factual** *information is added when available, and when the investigation is completed, the preliminary report is replaced with a* **final** *description of the accident and its probable cause. Full narrative descriptions may not be available for dates before 1993, cases under revision, or where NTSB did not have primary investigative responsibility.*'

Holy bejeezus! I thought. The mother lode! Just like that!

I scanned over the data input boxes and with excited and trembling fingers, typed in the information for my query.

Date range: February 17, 1976.

City: Hebron

State: Nebraska

Aircraft Category: Airplane

Make/Model: Beech Baron

Investigation type: accident

Injuries…I considered this. The only choices were fatal and Non-Fatal. I clicked fatal. That felt weird.

That was all I knew. I clicked 'Submit.' The computer thought for a few seconds and then a mostly blank page popped up.

'Not found.' It reported, matter-of-factly.

Erghf! I hated computers! I tapped my finger on the pad beside the mouse, but then I saw near the top of the page there was a small link advertising 'Index of Months.' I clicked it.

Just like magic, the screen filled with a list of headings of years from 1968 to the present. Each year was followed beneath it by links to each individual month of that year.

Ah-ha! This looked promising. I was excited again. I scrolled down until I located the row for 1976 and clicked 'February.' Columns of information popped up. It was a list of incidents that occurred by each day of that month! It listed the location, the type of aircraft, the registration number, the severity (fatal/non-fatal), and the status of the report with a link to it labeled 'probable cause.'

Still not totally believing what I was seeing, I scrolled down to the heading of Tuesday, February 17, 1976, and began to read the list of locations:

Michigan City Indiana, Two Buttes Colorado, Artesia Wells Texas, Austin Texas, Bowie Texas, all nonfatal...Flagstaff Arizona, Fatal(1)...Yuma Arizona, Brawley California, Chipley Florida, Atlanta Georgia, all nonfatal...Cuba Missouri, Fatal(2)...Hebron...

Hebron. I knew the name well. It was held in my subconscious as a blurry and foreboding presence, only defined by the menacing feeling with which the name hit me.

Hebron. That was the place. I read on. It said:

Beech B55, Number N3600H, Fatal (1).

My god, I thought. I recognized the tail number…it was us! My heart thumped. I stared at it for a second. I was overcome that I was able to find any information at all, but there it was. Still, I hesitated to click on the link that would show me the report. I was aware of my heart throbbing in my head. Suddenly, I was afraid.

I think that there are basically two types of fear. One is a fear that motivates a person to take action, be it fight or flight, but the other is a fear that causes paralysis and keeps them from doing anything. The kind that makes you just stare at the oncoming light streaking through the tunnel growing bigger and bigger while you stay on the tracks, unable to move.

For any scary situation, I think either type of fear can occur, depending on a person's state of mind. At that moment I realized that I had been paralyzed by my fear of finding the truth for my entire life. It wasn't the fear itself that held me back; there was nothing wrong with being afraid. It was simply my perspective of that fear.

I took a deep breath and forced myself to position the mouse arrow over the link. Then with a single click, I smashed through the paralysis and into action, and in doing so set into motion a momentum that would lead to one of the most important journeys I had ever taken.

On the screen it flashed:

NTSB Identification: **MKC76AK043**
14 CFR Part 91 General Aviation
Event occurred Tuesday, February 17, 1976 in HEBRON, NE
Aircraft: BEECH B55, registration: N3600H

FILE	DATE	LOCATION	AIRCRAFT DATA	INJURIES F S M/N	FLIGHT PURPOSE	PILOT DATA

3-0365 76/2/17 HEBRON,NE BEECH B55   CR- 0 1 0   NONCOMMERCIAL PRIVATE, AGE 41
TIME -
1830   N3600H   PX- 1 4 0   PLEASURE/PERSONAL TRANSP TOTAL HOURS, 103
DAMAGE-
DESTROYED   OT- 0 0 0   NOT INSTRUMENT RATED. DEPARTURE POINT   INTENDED
DESTINATION
  FARMINGTON,NM   LINCOLN,NE
  TYPE OF ACCIDENT   PHASE OF OPERATION
   COLLIDED WITH: TREES   IN FLIGHT: OTHER
  PROBABLE CAUSE(S)
     PILOT IN COMMAND - IMPROPER IN-FLIGHT DECISIONS OR PLANNING
     PILOT IN COMMAND - CONTINUED VFR FLIGHT INTO ADVERSE WEATHER CONDITIONS
     PILOT-VISUAL FLT AT ALT INSUF TO CLR OBST TRRN
     MISCELLANEOUS ACTS,CONDITIONS - SEAT BELT NOT FASTENED
FACTOR(S)
    WEATHER - LOW CEILING
    WEATHER – FOG

WEATHER BRIEFING - BRIEFED BY FLIGHT SERVICE PERSONNEL, BY RADIO
WEATHER FORECAST - FORECAST SUBSTANTIALLY CORRECT
   SKY CONDITION   CEILING AT ACCIDENT SITE
    PARTIAL OBSCURATION   600
   VISIBILITY AT ACCIDENT SITE   PRECIPITATION AT ACCIDENT SITE
    1 MILE OR LESS   NONE
   OBSTRUCTIONS TO VISION AT ACCIDENT SITE   WIND DIRECTION-DEGREES
                          FOG   360
   WIND VELOCITY-KNOTS   TYPE OF WEATHER CONDITIONS
    18   IFR
   TYPE OF FLIGHT PLAN
      VFR
REMARKS- ATMTD FLT BLO FOG BANK,DARK NIGHT.R PAX BELT.

I was utterly and completely stunned and transfixed, like someone had just pulled the rug out from under me. Before me were these incredible details about our crash. I was numb with disbelief.

It all looked so…cold. So statistical. I don't know what I expected, but this defied any expectation I did have. I took a moment to peruse the document, having to figure out the abbreviations.

CR meant crew, PX meant passengers. I guess OT stood for others. F was for fatal, S for serious, and M/N for minor or none. Mom had been reduced to PX F 1. I was one of the PX S 4. Dad was now CR S 1.

I already knew some of this information, from the story as told by my brother and Dad, but it was strange and interesting to see it in a formal format, so devoid of emotion and so simply factual. I looked over the document for a very long time, taking in all of what it meant.

I considered again the numbers used to classify my family and my mom for statistical purposes. I felt strangely offended by them, in a way. It was like they robbed my mom of what she was as a person. I was aware that by taking offense at this, I felt a little childish. After all it wasn't the numbers fault, or even the person who put them there in the first place. We are all statistics at some point, I guess. I would come to recognize a lot of this kind of angst as I continued my research.

But for now, I shook off the angst of the numbers, and thought about the report from a more clinical point of view. It was a good start, and provided a good deal of information. Moreover, it gave me hope to find more. I clicked the browser's back button once, and then paused. I suddenly got a strange feeling that made me go back to the accident list.

I looked over the other reports of fatalities that occurred on that day and began to study them, too. I felt suddenly like I owed those people that. I wondered if anyone else would ever look for them here.

The first one happened in Flagstaff. The pilot, who was the only one on board, flew his Cessna 105G into thunderstorm-related turbulence and ended up crashing. It was a commercial flight, but he was alone. I pictured his chiseled face and set jaw as he struggled with the controls, trying to retain control of the aircraft even as it was wrenched from his grasp by the turbulent and undulating air. He was screaming a mayday into his headset as the earth rose to meet him. The report said the aircraft was totally destroyed. It made me shiver.

The other fatal accident that day happened in Missouri and appeared to be a flight instructor and student in their Grumman AA-1B, doing touch and go landings at the airport when they lost control and went nose down in front of the runway. The report noted that the instructor was drunk. Not hard to picture that one. I shook my head. I thought about that flight again a year or so later while landing a Cessna 172 with my own instructor.

We were in the process of a simulated power failure and were making a turn back to the runway at Fullerton. Just before we got there, I moved the flaps to full. The nose of the plane raised but my mind was elsewhere for the critical moment and I didn't notice the airspeed drop from the indicator like a rock. Suddenly I could hear the stall warning horn begin, and my instructor pointedly telling me to get my nose down-NOW! I pushed the controls forward and brought the runway back into view, increasing my speed again, and a few seconds later thumped into a bumpy, but passable landing.

If my instructor had been drunk like that guy, we would have stalled, and during the uncoordinated turn we were in, we most certainly would have spiraled into the ground a couple hundred feet below, just like they did. The end of two great stories, as my instructor put it – his and mine. I take their example with me into the air every time I fly now.

With a curious and morbid fascination, I began to click on the vast list of other reports from the NTSB database, each with its own story that played out in my mind toward their violent and fiery conclusions. I became immersed in this task, only pausing when I realized I had spent two hours doing it. It was fascinating, but wasn't very productive to my immediate cause.

Overall, I concluded that it wasn't an atypical day as far as airplane accidents go - only directly significant to me and the few others who were flung variously to the earth that day and lived. I did note though, that in all of the reports I glanced through, ours was the only one where survivors and totally destroyed aircraft were synonymous. The thought gave me pause. What do I know of luck?

I was tired from my day of discovery, and worn out from what I had found. I had to sort out the questions that intruded into my mind. This was going to take some time. It was time to call it a day. I pushed back from the computer and shuffled into the living room to spend the rest of the evening with Terri and James.

A couple of days later I was rejuvenated and decided to resume my search. I had spent the intervening time thinking about the specific groups of people that may have had something to do with the incident. I figured if I could identify them, I could contact them and see if anyone specifically knew about the crash, or even had heard about it.

The County Sheriff where we crashed had come to mind, and I decided that I would start there. I figured that would be an excellent source of records, and there may have even been someone there who remembered the whole thing. My rudimentary knowledge of Nebraska geography was insufficient to remember what county I was talking about. But I was armed with modern search engine technology so I typed: "Hebron Nebraska."

I was immediately rewarded with a list of topics to choose from. The first one I clicked was a link to the official site of Hebron. This proclaimed the place 'A nice place on the Trail,' as well as the proud keeper of the world's largest porch swing. I didn't immediately get the trail reference—ashamedly, since I was raised in Nebraska and should have known this as the Oregon Trail--but the porch swing comment made me chuckle. I guess you learn something every day.

A quick look at the site revealed that the town was in Thayer County. I went back to Google and typed in 'Thayer County Sherriff,' and waited. A webpage immediately popped up. To my annoyance, it contained only a phone number. No website or email address. But, eager to start somewhere, I picked up the telephone on my desk and dialed the number. A very Midwestern sounding lady answered at the other end. After several moments of trying to explain what I was doing, she told me to hold on. She would ask around and I was clicked on hold.

She came back a few moments later and informed me that no one there knew of it, which she wasn't very surprised about as most of the department was in their thirty's and wouldn't have been involved in the search anyway, as they were all kids at the time. She also said all records that old would have been destroyed years ago, so no luck.

Dejected, I thanked her and she wished me good luck and clicked off. Where to go now?

I thought about it some more, and another thought hit me. How about the hospital? But there was no way that they'd remember. I was sure nobody at the hospital that night would still be there today. I mean it had been thirty years! Besides, if the County Sheriff didn't even have a web address, what could I expect from some tiny hospital? But maybe they had a record - at least somewhere to start. I figured it was worth a shot.

I searched the Hebron City home page for a reference to the Hebron hospital, but was instead drawn to the link to Thayer County Health Services. I clicked it. In front of me popped up a very nice website, the kind you'd find from a real hospital, with a picture of a large and modern looking facility.

I blinked at it. I am not sure what I expected the hospital to be – maybe something like a crumbling one room brick building with a rickety old metal exam table and dirty glass jars full of cotton balls and thermometers soaking in alcohol. It was a totally unfair image.

And they had an email contact link. I clicked it and a blank email screen popped up. I typed:

"Hello..." then stopped. I realized that I didn't really know what to say. I hadn't exactly thought about it. How could I briefly tell about what I was doing and not sound like some kind of weirdo? Moreover, what if someone did remember, but were still mad at my Dad for some things he said in the wake of our trip there?

It occurred to me that I probably couldn't even get the information for the rest of my family, what with privacy laws and the like. They probably didn't even keep records for that long. I felt again like I was wasting my time.

The motivation I had felt moments earlier quickly drained from me.

I pointed the mouse to the X at the upper right-hand corner of the window and clicked it. The email page disappeared unceremoniously back into cyberspace. I stared at the bottom of the Thayer County Health

Services homepage again. The email option sat quietly before me, waiting for me to continue, but I hesitated.

I was scared and paralyzed again. My stomach had twisted up and my jaw was locked and rigid, grinding my molars into each other. Why? Why would I be afraid of this? It was just a request for information. Information was what I needed. It can't hurt you, I thought. It can't! Besides, you weren't going to find anything anyway...

"Bah!" I muttered, trying to fling off the feeling. I clicked on the link again renewing my energy and typed in:

"Hello. I am writing because I was a survivor of a small airplane that crashed in a field near Hebron on February 17, 1976. I believe that the Thayer County Health Services was where we made it to after being rescued from the scene and was where we received our initial care prior to transport to Lincoln General Hospital. I am looking for anyone who remembers that night, and would like to talk to them about the incident. Please let me know if anyone is around from that night, or if you know of anyone locally who might remember the incident. Anyone with any information at all can contact me."

I hovered the mouse arrow over the send icon and, physically forcing myself to overcome the fear that tried to stop me, depressed the button under my index finger with a slight click. The email disappeared.

A moment of regret stabbed me in the side, but was over quickly. I considered the sensation left by the whole thing, and then concluded that it had not been so bad. It'll probably take weeks to get a response anyway, if anyone responds at all.

I suddenly now felt like I had actually accomplished something. This was becoming a project again! I felt reinvigorated and I went back to the Google homepage, and studied the bright white screen, waiting for inspiration to guide me where to go next.

Who else..?

Twelve hundred miles away and a few micro bleeps later, a small box declaring that new mail had arrived popped up on the screen of Hospital Administrator Joyce Beck's desktop computer at the Thayer County Medical Center in Hebron, Nebraska, which by then had become one of the best and most important hospitals in the region. She was out when it came, but found it there when she returned later that day.

She mouse-clicked her way into her email in-box and saw the heading from a name she had never heard of before. The words in the heading caught her attention first as she began to scan my note.

What was that about a plane crash?

She hesitated then began at the top and read the entire email. Her better judgment was telling her to refer it to the legal department or something…it sounded like the beginning of a lawsuit. But instead she stared at the words for a long time. She found that she was touched by them. They carried a silent sort of desperation. She thought that whoever had sent this was looking for something very badly.

She looked away from the computer screen and thought about what to do. Perhaps, she thought, there would be no harm in asking around. There were a few staff members still here that were around in the seventies, after all.

Besides, she was curious. She was a pilot herself, and seeing the words of a survivor of a crash was very intriguing. As it is with all pilots, there were lessons that could be gleaned from those who have ridden a plane into the ground. It was the strange wisdom of survivors. There were indeed things to be learned; things only they could know.

With a new determination, she decided to help. If she was wrong, she was wrong. But she didn't think she was. She hit the reply icon and rattled off a quick response:

"Randy, I am the CEO of the hospital. I have not had the time yet to investigate this but I am sure I can help you. Give me some time and I will get the information for you. I look forward to meeting you. I will be in touch."

Then Joyce pushed her chair back from the desk, got up and strode into the hallway, looking for Helen.

Chapter 4

Dad peered through the window of the Beechcraft Baron and on into the gathering gloom. We were somewhere over Kansas. It would be night soon.

Small rumbles of turbulence rocked the plane. Several miles ahead and far, far below, Dad studied a low lying wind storm that swept over the flat dusty ground, roiling a cloud of soot and ice particles a few hundred feet into the swirling air. From this altitude it looked like a brown layer of fluffy cotton spread over the surface of the earth. The weather report he'd gotten in Farmington had predicted the possibility of the storm, and it would probably get a little rough as we flew over it, but it wasn't supposed to be too bad all the way up here.

Darkness crept up on the little plane from the eastern sky. As the plane began to be lightly buffeted from the updrafts created by the storm below, Dad squinted from behind his Ray-Bans toward his new concern. A thin grey line of clouds had crept into view from over the horizon. It expanded across the horizon from north to south directly across the path of our airplane flying through the rapidly darkening sky. This front, too, had been mentioned in the forecast, so it wasn't unexpected, but it appeared much lower than he'd thought it would have been.

"Better check that weather," he said to Mom. She saw the clouds too and nodded. She flipped through the pages till she found the correct radio frequency for the nearest flight service station in Minneapolis and turned the knobs on the radio until it was correctly displayed.

The storm below had closed most of the airports in the region to visual, or VFR flight, which was Dad's highest FAA certification. If he knowingly entered a situation where he had low or no visibility, like a cloud bank or snow storm, he would be in big trouble with the FAA. You have to be instrument, or IFR certified, to fly in those conditions. Dad had flown IFR with Bruce many times, so he knew how. He had the hours, but had never taken the IFR certification test. Without that certification, he could only legally fly so long as he had visibility.

There was a low pressure front stationary over the area in front of him, explaining the cloud bank extending from left to right like a grey wall before them. It had been reported as a high system, starting at 5,000 to 6,000 feet, which he could easily get under and still fly VFR. But, as the pressure in the area unexpectedly dropped, so did the clouds.

Dad considered his options. The top of the clouds weren't that high, but he was very hesitant to increase his altitude and go over them. If he did that, and lost view of the ground, he would also lose critical landmarks. Of course he could do the calculations and time the flight, and that should put us close, but the odds were that he'd still have to go through the clouds to get down once we got to Lincoln, which was likely with overcast like this.

Another option was to just put down and wait. He didn't really want to fly through this system; however, the wind storm in Kansas wasn't any good and would have created dangerous wind conditions on the ground for miles around, so diverting that way wasn't really a good option either. He considered cutting southeast toward Missouri to avoid the system, and landing in Kansas City or somewhere close, but even if it was clear there, that would cut his fuel short, and he didn't want to push his luck there. Most aviation accidents were a result of fuel exhaustion, he knew, and he didn't want to be one of them.

So there was left the option to go under the system, and try to stay above the deck. Beside, these clouds didn't contain any bad weather, just overcast conditions.

He asked Mom to get out the sectional chart for the area. She flipped on a small directional light above her and pulled it out, folding it into a manageable size and put it on her lap. He glanced at it, noting the altitude of Lincoln at about 1,000 feet above sea level. He wasn't sure of his exact position on the map, but the change of altitude wouldn't be that great from Lincoln.

He was presently cruising at 6,500 feet above sea level, so a gentle decent to an altitude that would get him under the clouds, but above, say, 1,500 feet would suffice. If things got too bad, like if the cloud layer got too low to safely fly under, he could always find a farm or small town runway to land at. With his wife and kids, it was the last thing he wanted to do, but if he had to, it was an option.

He would be able to see the lights on the ground. And if he could see lights, he could tell if he was getting low.

As the airplane approached the leading edge of the system near the Kansas-Nebraska border, he gently reduced the power and the plane began to sink through the rushing air into an easy descent, aimed for the bottom of the dark bank of clouds. The sky behind had grown from orange and blue to steel grey as the sun submerged itself somewhere back over the horizon. Under the clouds the air was black. The altimeter slowly ticked off the cushion of air under us, gravity pulling us gently down. Thin wafts of clouds hanging from the bank reached down to grab at the plane as it was pulled towards earth. They momentarily enveloped the plane for a few seconds at a time.

The night sky below the clouds wrapped us completely, but below it the air was clear and the dotted lights of the civilization of rural America appeared on the ground, sporadically dotting the wash of black over the ground, trailing off to the horizon in all directions. Dad continued his decent to stay about 500 feet below the ceiling and restored the power to the engines and leveled the flight.

Nothing to it. He turned and smiled at Mom. She saw and smiled back at him, then flipped the light off. The cabin went dark, save for the lights of the instruments. It wouldn't be long now. The sing-song droning of the engines eased Dad back into the seat and he thought of what he'd have to do once they landed. This and that. Call Bruce...all the little things.

Occasionally, he glanced down at the panel. The flight remained nice and smooth. It was clear sailing from here, so to speak. He was significantly lower than usual when he flew this route, but never gave it another thought. As long as he was higher than Lincoln, there was nothing to worry about. He had a little wiggle room if he needed it.

A poignant thought, as the clouds began to settle around the plane again and the ceiling dropped a little more. Dad cursed this. The pressure was still dropping and the clouds had lowered themselves. The red-flashing anti-collision beacon and wing tip lights reflected off of them forming a multicolored halo around the plane alternating between green and red hues, and white flashes from the strobes, punctuated by intervals of blackness.

Dad reduced power again and eased the plane down through the clouds until he could see the lights on the ground again. He looked at the altimeter. He had room. Lincoln was still way down there.

Sometime later, the same thing. The clouds kept coming down, as if to push us lower, and he kept getting lower and lower to get under them. In the pilot world, this was called 'scud-running.' Everyone knew it was a good way to get into trouble. But unfortunately in situations like this, without IFR training it was all you could do without getting in trouble with the FAA. He had done it before. The trick was to just not get too low, and, according to the weather report, the clouds were not supposed to get that low that night.

He knew that weather reports didn't guarantee anything, though. Clouds can do anything, so he wasn't afraid to go IFR if the clouds forced him to an unsafe altitude. It just wasn't necessary yet. And there are reasons why there is an IFR certification in the first place. It is easy to get off course or otherwise askew when you can't see in an airplane, especially in clouds where everything looks the same. A pilot can easily get completely inverted and not even know it, and if not well trained, have a very hard time re-orienting themselves when they realize their error, often at a cost of their lives and that of their passengers.

He hadn't trained to that extent, but still felt comfortable to simply go through the cloud layer to the clear air above without getting turned over, and then report to the nearest flight service station, acknowledge his error, and request a vector to Lincoln. They'd want a word with him when he got there, but it was better than the alternative. There wasn't turbulence or wind, so it would be a simple steady course, until the clouds were below him.

But until then, he just had to watch the altimeter. Keep high enough, above Lincoln's elevation, and he'd be okay. He hadn't wandered off course. The compass had not changed overly dramatically during the trip down, and they hadn't been buffeted too badly. There was a slight crosswind from due north, but nothing that he couldn't compensate for.

Besides, he could still see light far beneath him. As long as he could see the lights on the ground, he'd know roughly how high up he was.

He was keeping his eye on one particular bright light in the far distance to use as a reference. From where he sat it was a long way down still, letting him know that there was still plenty of altitude between the plane and the ground.

But still, he had a tingle telling him to watch his butt. He was getting lower than he liked, that was for sure. He preferred to be high. He'd be happy when Lincoln appeared.

What he didn't know as he brought the plane ever lower was that the ground was actually slowly rising towards him. A small ridge extended from north to south directly in his flight path. He had made the assumption that the elevation of the ground was consistent, and at ten-thousand feet it would have been a good assumption. But this low, it made all the difference. He was about to find that out.

The altimeter needle slowly approached 1,650 feet. 1,500 feet, 500 feet above Lincoln, was as low as he was willing to go. If the clouds moved in any more he'd have to just fly IFR and deal with it. He turned to Mom.

She held Kim in her lap and stared out the windshield into the darkness beyond, looking uneasy. Her face was silhouetted against the intermittent flash of the wing tip strobe beyond her window. She glanced at him, and smiled nervously. They were thinking the same thing. Dad spoke into his microphone.

"Were going in pretty low," he said. "Why don't you give Kim to Chris, and help me keep an eye out. We should try to get our bearings in case the clouds move in again. I might have to go through them."

Mom smiled again. She flipped on the cabin light and unbuckled her seatbelt and turned to get Chris' attention. He was sitting awake in his seat and smiled at her immediately as she caught his eye. He leaned forward to hear her. She covered her microphone and loudly spoke over the drone of the engines.

"I need you to hold Kim for a little while, okay?" she said.

He smiled and held out his hands. Mom gently lifted the sleeping little girl toward Chris over the front seat. Chris unbuckled his belt and softly took her to him and positioned her on his lap so she faced forward. Her head lulled back onto his shoulder as he pulled some slack out of the seat belt to make room for her, and then clicked it securely around them both. Kim settled back into the security of her brother's embrace and fell quickly back asleep. Mom looked at her oldest boy and was proud of him.

"I love you," she mouthed to him, and smiled.

Chris smiled back and wrapped his arms around his baby sister. Mom blew him a kiss and turned back around, then settled back into her seat. She focused on the task at hand, rummaged in the map case, and pulled out the appropriate chart, spreading it over the console in front of her. She turned on and positioned the light above so she could see and began to look the maps over.

"Where do you suppose we are?" she asked.

"Not too far…southwest of Lincoln," Dad replied. "Maybe…eighty or so miles?"

She looked back out the window. With the light on, she couldn't see much of anything but her reflection.

The altimeter swept down to 1,600. Dad increased the engine power a touch to slow the descent slightly. The small light he had been focused on still appeared to be fixed on the horizon, but was quickly lost in clouds.

Mom was nervous. She didn't like the feeling she was getting, either.

"Jim?" she said.

From the kitchen of his neat farmhouse, 1,558 feet above sea level, Charles Braun lifted his head and stared suddenly into the quiet space of the house, listening intently. He could suddenly and distinctly hear a low pitched drone approaching from a distance off, somewhere outside the house to the west.

"Cara!" he called to his wife in the kitchen. "Do you hear anything?"

"Sounds like a swarm of locust!" she replied. He pushed himself up and walked from the kitchen back into his living room and paused, concentrating on the sound. He walked over to the T.V. and switched it off, focusing his hearing farther.

It was there again. The drone was still distant, but definitely coming closer. It sounded like an airplane, but no one would be flying that close to his house. The airport was on the other side of Hebron. They must be lost and looking for it. He went to the front door and opened it.

The low clouds extended thickly into the distance all around the farm, becoming fog at some points as they caressed the ground. That was a strange phenomenon for that time of year. The noise came from the clouds toward the southwest, and continued growing and growing.

He stepped fully outside looking into the misty air toward the source of the sound. It quickly had grown louder and louder still. Then his eyes locked onto blinking lights, dim at first, but brighter with each passing moment as they pierced through the fog, racing toward him. He raised his reading glasses to his eyes. The lights looked like they were practically on the ground, and moving quickly toward him.

Suddenly with a crescendo roar, a small airplane resolved from the darkness and raced past, just in front of the house and practically right above him. It streaked by, maybe thirty feet high! Alarmed by the spectacle he crouched down slightly, keeping his startled eyes locked to the plane.

It shot right toward the windmill near his barn but somehow missed it by what had to have been inches and roared on.

"What the hell are they doing?!" He exclaimed and watched the plane speed into the night growing exponentially quieter as it flew away. He was flabbergasted. He listened to the drone for a few moments as the blinking lights were reclaimed by the fog. He stood stunned, shaking his head in disbelief.

Cara appeared behind him at the door, and asked what was going on.

"I have no idea!" he said, somewhat shaken. They must have gone higher. He listened for a few moments more, and shrugged.

They must have been trying to find the airport, he thought, but people should be more careful in those things! They went back in, closed the door, and turned the T.V. back on.

Dad had suddenly become disoriented and was growing very concerned. He had been concentrating on the clouds and when he looked where he thought the light that he had been watching should have been, he could no longer see it or any other lights out there for that matter. The world outside had gone completely black. The cloud ceiling was still just overhead. He looked at the altimeter, which hadn't moved. He was okay, though, he still had at least 500 feet. But it was time to start thinking of biting the bullet and going into the clouds.

He tried to relax and loosened his grip on the controls a little, preparing to slowly add power and enter the clouds. Mom watched Dad intently. She felt tense but unafraid. Dad knew what he was doing, even if they were low. Once they got through this bank of clouds, she and Dad would be able to get oriented and would be okay. We were very close to the ground, but also very close to Lincoln. We would get there, she was sure.

She fixed her stare out the window, then reached up and switched off the light, eliminating the glare, and tried to lock on to some kind of point to focus on, looking for some indication of a house or farm or something on the ground.

The clouds parted before her and for a split second she caught a glimpse of something. It appeared to be rushing toward them. She immediately knew it wasn't right. She knew it was no cloud.

Her eyes opened wide as the first tree scraped the bottom of the fuselage and a wall of larger trees bore down on the plane. Her heart felt like it was thrust into her throat in horror at what she saw. She screamed:

"JIM!!!"

Her final word, her husband's name, was frozen in the space between her and Dad. The world was held perfectly still for a moment as the realization of the unfolding event came upon him, even as he could not right then accept it as fact.

The fact that time was up.

Chris' eyes shot toward Mom's seat as she screamed, and he locked his arms instinctively around his sister sitting in his lap. Within the same moment, the world exploded as the airplane smashed into the wall of trees at 168 miles per hour.

His whole body and the world around him surrealistically lurched as it was rocked by a tremendous wallop, like it had been placed in the path of an approaching freight train. His senses were assaulted by a simultaneous and insanely loud chorus of shrieking, ripping, and snapping.

The plane jarringly dipped hard to the right flinging him around in his seat. The glow of the panel lights went out plunging him into total darkness. In the same instant, a blasting crescendo of noise accompanied by a violence he had no way of comprehending ripped through the plane. The fuselage next to Mom explosively disintegrated in a hail of metal, wood, and leaves, disappearing into the darkness.

Chris was instantly assailed by a massive blast of cold air smashing into him as the airplane was violently jerked sideways to the left. His stomach floated into his throat as it dropped, crashing from the sky. With an enormous smashing thud, the plane impacted into the earth.

He was flung forward hard into Kim, and they both pummeled into the oxygen tank strapped to the back of Dad's seat. He could feel her little body go limp like a rag doll, but gripped her as tight as he could. The plane spun to the left, the force of which flung him and Kim in the opposite direction, toward the gaping hole in the fuselage, straining the belt that held them to the seat and inside the plane. Clumps of debris hurled around the cabin showering over him as the plane slid across the ground with a sickening, screeching groan.

Chris never screamed. He was never afraid. He didn't have time to be scared. The whole thing couldn't have lasted more than a few seconds.

With a sudden and rocking jolt, the plane stopped and was still. Chris' heart pounded like a drum in his head and his body resonated like a freshly struck tuning fork. Eerie and total silence settled slowly over him like a heavy, cold blanket.

He trembled as he tightly closed his eyes and squeezed the limp body of his little sister to his chest. He bit on his lower lip and waited. He thought Kim must be dead and he would be soon too. Death wasn't so bad, he figured, now that it was so close, but he never thought it would be like this. He was probably dead already and just didn't know it. From behind the blackness of his eyelids he listened to the sound of the breeze and waited calmly for death's dark embrace.

From the depths of the still and twisted fuselage of our destroyed little airplane, wrapped in darkness and wisps fog, not a sound or motion came.

Chapter 5

The wheels of a Frontier Airlines twin turboprop commuter plane struck the runway with a bouncing chirp, and I was amazed to find myself in Omaha again.

We taxied around the airport until we arrived at our place on the tarmac, and I unbuckled my seat belt and moved to the door, gingerly working my way down the steps extending from the plane. I walked briskly through sunshine and the smell of airline exhaust across the tarmac and into the terminal.

All airports have a unique smell, and Omaha was no different. I remembered its signature aroma immediately. I walked over the polished and smooth floor, strolling my small carry-on bag behind me toward the rental car desk to claim my ride for the next week.

Eventually I slid into the driver's seat of a white Pontiac Grand Am. After several adjustments to the mirrors and seat from those made by the incredibly tall person who had sat there before me, I started it up and guided it out of the parking structure into the brightness of the Midwestern day.

I hadn't been here in so long I could scarcely recognize the landscape that rolled gently away from me as I wheeled down the road. The radio played music from the local rock station coming softly through the speakers. Omaha is not a small city, but it retains its Nebraska roots everywhere you look in the forms of stockyards, grain silos, and railway yards full of the miles of freight cars which send the American prairie's bounty to the rest of the world.

I rolled my window down letting the wind blow across my hair. The smell of the cool, clean air brought me back to surprisingly good memories, and soothed the anxiousness I thought I would discover while I was here-- back in Nebraska, hunting for the truth.

I had never actually expected to be back here like this, but the information I found during my research back home had emboldened me to search further. What I had found released a virtual landslide of new and surprising revelations. At every step, it seemed, I had lent no faith to any of it bearing any kind of fruit, and yet at every step, I was proven wrong.

My success with the NTSB gave me more ideas about where to look, and as I did, I found more and more people who were there. Every one of them spoke to me as if they knew me, and they all wanted very much to meet me and tell their stories. I had been given a reason to come. Hell, I was compelled to come. I had to meet these people, and learn their stories if I had any chance of telling mine. Shelley was right. Without coming here, I could have never known how much I had to learn.

I had asked my sister Kim to come along, or rather she had volunteered to meet me here. I had told her about my plans for the trip a couple of weeks prior, and much to my surprise, she said she wanted to come with me. She arranged to go out a few days ahead of me to hang out with our family friend Jill, and I would meet her at Jill's house once I got into town.

It would be good to see Jill. She had been Dad's girlfriend once for ten years and came to my family's rescue in the dark days following the horrors of mom and my step mother. She always seemed so cool and hip. She was totally connected with the world and life, and her confidence and grace gave me hope for myself.

She gave us all hope. She took Kim under her wing and helped her through her adolescence, into becoming a smart and beautiful woman. I am not sure how things would have been for Kim, or any of us for that matter, were it not for Jill. She got Dad through too. I never told her, but she has always been my hero. We all owe her more than we can ever repay.

Dad and Jill almost got married, but she was much younger than him, and there were many pressures that kept them from taking that step. Eventually they broke up, but she fell in love and married Jim. Jill and Jim raised their family in the quiet and comfortable neighborhood in Omaha, where I now found myself, shifting the car into park and getting out before their beautiful stone covered house.

I was struck by her unchanged beauty as I walked toward her and was suddenly transported back in time. She had not aged in all of these years, and I suddenly felt like I still knew her so well. I realized at that moment that in all of the time I lived in Nebraska after the crash, she was the closest thing to my mother that I had known.

I hugged her tightly, and, for a moment, I held my face to her shoulder as I tried to try to hold in the sobs that suddenly and unexpectedly sloshed around me. I was overcome by the maternal way she held me, the way her hair felt in my face, by the complete sincerity of her embrace, by the way she was so glad to see me after so long. For a moment, I just wanted to just hold her and cry to her like the child I suddenly felt, but I was embarrassed and afraid of causing a scene, so I choked it back. After a few seconds, I collected myself and pulled away with a sheepish smile.

"It's good to see you," was all I could manage.

She had two wonderful little boys, Adam and Alec, and each of them treated me like I was some kind of rock star or something from the moment I arrived. Jill had told them I was coming and they had been waiting excitedly for me all morning. They swarmed around me as soon as I pulled up, which made me feel really, really good.

After a while we loaded into Jill's car and went to a circus-themed burger restaurant in a new subdivision nearby. The boys argued with each other as to who would sit next to me in the car on the way. I guess it pays to be a celebrity!

Jill bought me and Kim dinner. I patted Adam's head who colored intently next to me, while Alec was lost in his own thing at the other end of the table. He reminded me of my son, and it made me miss my family terribly, even though I had just left them that morning.

"What made you decide to start writing about it?" Jill asked, after a while of chatting.

"Weeeell..." I trailed off and really thought about it. I wasn't at that moment really sure why I had decided to drop everything, take a week of my vacation time, leave my family, and come out here to learn about something that was not much more, or so it seemed, than a distant memory.

"I guess the time just seemed right." I said after some thought. I found I was having a difficult time at that moment formulating a sensible response to such an easy question.

The time was right, that was for sure. Everything had just fallen into place with an ease that I could never have imagined. I had never been much on the phenomenon of planetary alignment and such, but I was quickly becoming a believer. People I had never even known about really existed, and they wanted to talk to me.

I began to realize that the truth, all of it, could really be out there. I just had to go and gather it up. I began to believe that things really happen exactly when they are supposed to, and not a minute sooner or later. This was one of the few times in my life I just rode with it, and it was taking me exactly where I had to go, for better or for worse.

We spent the night at our childhood friend Cindy's house in Omaha. Kim and I drove toward Lincoln the next morning, bright and early. We had things to do today. We were going to see Clarke later that morning.

Clarke Mundhenke had been our pastor at the little church we attended as kids. He was a true family friend, although it had been a while since I had seen him. He knew a lot about that night and had played a big role for us. Bigger than I ever knew at that time. My brother had mentioned his name as a good source of information, so, using expert investigative technique, I called Lincoln 411 information and got his number.

Clarke's wife Sharon had answered the phone. The last time I saw her was just after I got back from Desert Storm. I had just gotten out of the Marines and was heading out to Illinois to set things up for Terri and me to start college. I had stopped over in Lincoln to see some old friends and found myself at Clarke and Sharon's house, near the big house where I grew up. Sharon had taught me to play the piano as a kid after the crash, which was one of my few outlets for the pain I was in. It was like my therapy. Music still is.

Seemed like a long time ago. I guess it was.

When Clarke came to the phone, he was excited to hear from me and when I told him what I was trying to do, he immediately offered his home for us to stay in while we were in town. I happily accepted. I thought of how good it would be to see him, and it made me smile.

The sixty miles from Omaha to Lincoln down I-80 brought back many memories. I used to make the trip from Lincoln to Omaha and back on occasion for trips to the Henry Doorly Zoo, or the Spaghetti Plant, or for a weekend with my family at the Granada Royale Hotel, with its neat swimming pool and waterfall. Dad would go to the historic Ak-Sar-Ben Race Track to see horse races sometimes, and later as a teenager, I would sneak up here with my friends for a concert at the Civic Auditorium, or college parties. They were good times I had all but forgotten.

Just like from the memories of my childhood, the air was cool and clean and filled with the soft drone of cicadas, although not as thick as their sound would be come July and August when they would drown out practically all other noise, especially as dusk fell. On the pulsating gyration of their wings they would carry the thick humid air of the prairie summer.

We drove over the familiar long bridge that spans the Platte River between Omaha and Lincoln. I had a strange lack of any real consternation. I believed that nothing bad would happen to me here. I just knew it was true. We got to Lincoln a half-hour later as the towering monolith of the Nebraska State Capitol Building came into view on the horizon. At around four hundred feet, it was by far the tallest structure in the region. I have always thought it was the most impressive of all the capitol buildings that I had seen, rivaled only by the Nation's Capitol in D.C.

We drove across town to Bryan Memorial Hospital, where Clarke worked as the Hospital Chaplain. The place had grown from the small brick building I remembered from when Dad worked there to a huge medical complex. I was impressed. The little city of my youth had really come of age.

We walked into the hospital and met Clarke at his office. We chatted with him and he bought us lunch in the cafeteria. We ate and told him of our plans and I talked about the circumstances which brought me there. After giving us the directions to his house and telling us in true Nebraska style to "just come on in," we let him get back to work, and sauntered out into the sunshine again.

That evening, we were going to go to the Lincoln Composite Squadron Civil Air Patrol. I knew that the Civil Air Patrol, or CAP, had led the search for us that night, so it was likely that they would have some record of what happened. I hoped so anyway.

Within a day I got a response back from the CAP Information Officer, Kathy Hubbell. True to her title and word, she found some information for me. I continued to correspond with her leading up to my trip and when she heard I was really coming out, she invited us to come and talk to the squadron.

That night we went to the CAP headquarters at the Air National Guard base near the Lincoln airport. It was interesting to be in the building where the search for us had started so long ago. Other than new technologies, I doubted that much had changed. I met Kathy and she greeted us warmly and escorted us to the meeting room. A number of cadets, some just young kids, some in their late teens, and a few adults sat at the tables as the squadron commander talked to them about housekeeping and other items. Then Kathy introduced Kim and me.

I had thrown together a little presentation about the crash to show to the cadets as a way to thank them for their service and what they could someday do themselves. It seemed like the least I could do. It was a photo collage of several pictures of the wreckage that I had. They watched in total silence, disbelieving of what they saw.

I spoke briefly and told those cadets that they might go after that kind of crash too, someday. They asked a lot of questions, but for many of them I did not yet have answers.

Afterwards we went into a huge hanger connected to the building and watched the cadets drill, marching back and forth under the shadow of the big Air National Guard KC-135 refueler jet that was parked there. It was neat to see them marching so sharply, when most were still just kids.

Then we said goodbye and headed back to Clarke's house. We crept up to our respective bedrooms, whispering a hushed goodnight so as not to awaken our hosts. I entered the small room and sat on the bed, removing my shoes and staring out the darkened window on the opposite wall. I was tired, but determined.

I glanced over to a pile of boxes stacked neatly in a small cubby beside the bed and spotted a guitar case tucked on top of them.

Curious, I stood and gently lifted it and set it on the bed, popping open the brass clasps that held together the shaped vinyl halves. I recognized the instrument immediately. I had seen Clarke play it many times back at our church during the '70's. The distinctive "e" shaped

Epiphone symbol was still emblazoned near the black pick guard, just like I remembered. I liked that Clarke would play it at the services. It made hearing the word of God not so ominous, unlike organ music was to me sometimes. It was heartening to realize that my mom had heard the music from this same guitar herself.

I picked it up and carefully cradled it across my leg, roughly tuning it up then quietly strummed a few chords. The thinly grained wood had aged nicely and the tone was deep and warm as it resonated through my fingers. I closed my eyes and listened to the vibration as it gently faded into the air of the room. After sitting in silence for a few seconds, I replaced the instrument back in the case, setting it all gently back where I found it.

I clicked off the light and lay back on the little bed and stared at the darkened ceiling for a long time before fading off into sleep.

Soon, we would go to Hebron.

*   *   *   *   *   *   *

The roar of the silence that entangled Dad rang from the depths of him and was accompanied by dull throbbing sensations from all over his body, canceling out all other sound as if he were in a vacuum. Every piston-like pulsation initiated blunt undulations through his head, each pulse radiating down his neck through his torso and out into every limb. Each move was emphasized by inexplicable stabs, tweaks, pinches and thuds. Every neuron was inundated as the impulses jolted him through ragged nerves, flowing from so many spots that they were indistinguishable in their midst. Their sum total was a swirling, beating numbness that held his body fast in a haze.

He couldn't tell where it hurt first. But, he knew he was breathing, so he wasn't dead.

That was a start.

The right side of his face was resting against the planes control wheel and his cheek and head on that side felt numb and wet. Very slowly, he reached the dead weight of his arm up and ran his hand across his face, smearing sticky oozing goo that pulsed from a gash in his head. His side throbbed numbly causing the dark behind his clenched eyes to flash with each pulsation of his heart.

He tasted acrid blood in his mouth and gritted his teeth, aware of the welling of potential pain that surged just on the other side of the thin veil of black numbness. By force of will, he pulled himself through it to emerge into the cold, dark reality beyond.

With all of his might, he opened his eyes.

The darkness beyond was infinite. Bright pulsing flashes of light swirled on the surface of his eyeballs dancing upon the flat black of space. The world had lost all dimensions. He was effectively blind. He waited for a long time until the flashing subsided, gradually breaking up into glowing dots that drifted in the blackness before him every time he blinked or moved. He became aware of a loud, high pitched hum in his ears, and wondered what part of the plane would make that noise before realizing its source was from deep inside his own brain. It resonated in his skull with an intensity that shut out all other sound. His head swam. He closed his eyes again.

He slowly took a deep and ragged breath, as deep as he could bear it for the stabbing that shot through his side, cutting it short. Very slowly he pulled his leaden arms up to rest his hands against the control wheel. The action took way more effort than it should have. He gripped the wheel for a moment, wrapping his trembling fingers around it.

With what seemed like all his strength, he gritted his teeth again and slowly lifted his face off of the wheel, then pushed his body back into the seat. The jolt of settling back wracked him and caused him to freeze in a grimace while the sharpness flared up, then slowly dulled to numbness again. Once it subsided enough he opened his eyes again, again to a shroud of total darkness.

He wasn't really sure what the nature of the reality he now found himself in was. All he knew for sure at that moment was that he was in the plane, and the plane was on the ground.

How?

He racked his frazzled brain, but could not make sense of the jumbled memory of the chaos that had just occurred and whose violent and flashing images were still splashing randomly across his mind. He couldn't remember how this had happened. It now seemed almost like a dream. He lolled his head to the side and tried to wake up to some different version of reality, but he stayed right there.

His other senses began to resolve around him and he became aware of the smell of the plane, and other things, too. The fabric, the cold air drifting in from somewhere, the faint waft of fuel…

His eyes shot open. Fuel!

FIRE!!

Panic gripped him with the realization that he was about to be burned to death. His heart began to pound and he clawed for his seat belt. In his mind, he could clearly smell the acrid and choking smoke as it began to waft up from behind him, becoming thicker and thicker. His heart raced and his head screamed as he finally got the lever to operate, releasing the canvas strap across his waist. He jerked himself forward.

He could almost feel the fire begin to lap at him and the smoke burn his eyes as he clawed at random objects to pull himself instinctively to the right toward where the cabin door used to be. He lurched through the opening, stumbling and wracking his ravaged body with every movement, casting himself from the wreckage and into the darkness - to safety.

Suddenly he stumbled over the right engine and dropped forward, falling towards the ground. But his fall was cut short as he was whipped across his face by a sharp thread suspended in the darkness. The pain and surprise of the impact flashed explosively through his head as the thread wrapped around his face and dug into his torn flesh. He rebounded from it and was then flung backwards, drawing the breath from him with a ragged snort. He dropped on his back against the buckled engine, and sprawled out across the jagged stump where the wing used to be, clutching his face. He sat stunned and shocked, completely caught off guard. The sensation erased all other thought. He waited as the pain slowly faded and the darkness resolved around him before he could even move.

Holding one hand on his face he used the other to claw the darkness until he swatted the impediment. A thin strand of barbed wire hung suspended invisibly in the black air in front of him, and bounced off of his fingers. He grabbed it with both hands and stared at the dark space it occupied unseen for a second as the stun left him - before suddenly becoming succinctly aware of the lack of the plane exploding behind him.

Realizing that it hadn't, he turned to peer at the plane disbelieving and gazed into its darkened interior. There really was no fire. Nothing had changed. It had been in his head.

He was losing it.

He slumped over and closed his eyes.

"Jesus, Styner, get a hold of yourself!" he muttered, but his brain was too fuzzy. The pieces were still slowly dropping into place.

He pulled himself upright a little more and rubbed his left shoulder. He had injured it skiing a few weeks earlier and it had since frozen up. He was going to get it looked at when they got back to Lincoln after the trip, but now it was not too useful. He had over extended it as he got out and now it was throbbing and immobile. He could hardly lift his arm at all.

With his other hand, he reached up and grabbed the wire again. He couldn't see anything beyond a few feet and his vision was getting progressively worse due to the blood that oozed into his eyes from what seemed to be everywhere. He wiped it away as best he could. Hues of grey began to emerge blurrily from the darkness in his left eye. He was completely blind in the other. He probed at it and in feeling the puffy skin that squeezed around it figured it was destroyed and useless.

He tugged at the wire again and could feel that it ran around and away from where he was and there was a lot of it. It seemed like it was tangled all around the plane, giving it its own metal crown of thorns. Apparently the plane had picked it up at some point as it slid.

He was still reeling from the shock of the enormous magnitude of the whole crazy thing and wasn't quite sure what to do next. In his wildest imagination he had never pictured himself there, like that. The reality now quite overloaded his senses. He just couldn't quite get his head around it yet. His brain seemed to have seized up.

He moved his hand from the barbed wire to his forehead and gingerly felt around the flap of skin that hung loosely down, slowly dripping thick and sticky blood. It oozed over his head and face randomly, and made his head feel as if a bucket of oil had been splashed across it. It was most uncomfortable.

He picked at the wound absently for a moment as he tried to get his brain to work, but then suddenly he was shaken like a whip by the sound of a small voice coming from the still and inky darkness of the plane. He recognized it immediately.

It was the voice of his son. He sat bolt upright as it penetrated his ears causing his whole body to tense.

"Dad..?" The boy said meekly from the depths of the wreckage, his voice tentative and shaken.

Dad lurched himself up and onto his feet, pulling himself toward the gaping wound that had been torn into the side of the fuselage.

The kids! Charlene and the kids were still in the plane! His ragged thought process had not gotten to that realization quite yet and now it came as a shock, and snapped his brain into action mode once again.

Even if there was no fire yet, there easily could be. He still had to get us all out before a fire really did happen, which it could at any time.

The smell of highly flammable 100LL aviation fuel still lingered in the air. He peered into the darkness toward the gash in the plane, but could barely make out anything in the interior through the trauma of his swollen face.

"I'm here, son," he called hoarsely as he made his way back onto the shattered wing, trying get a look inside to see Chris. "It's okay, I'm here."

Suddenly he focused at a point just inside the darkened gap. An icy hand gripped his heart causing his body to stiffen, the buzz in his head increasing in intensity at his discovery.

Mom's seat was askew and was empty; he had not encountered her as he quickly exited the plane, he now realized. He waved his hand into the empty darkness of the devastated compartment, pawing the air for one hint of her, but quickly realized that she was gone. He reached down and grabbed the seatbelt hanging limply off to the side of the seat. Somehow it had been taken off. He didn't remember at that moment that Mom had handed Kim back to Chris. When she had sat back in her seat, he hadn't noticed that she had not put it back on.

He thought instead that perhaps she had taken it off after the crash and had evacuated the plane. He stood erect on the wing and looked hard into the night, rotating his body to scan the darkness that ran infinitely away from him in all directions. He may as well have been standing in the middle of outer space. If she had gotten out already and was hurt, she may be somewhere nearby. But he couldn't see her anywhere. He couldn't see anything.

He glanced down at the ground just behind the crumpled flap of the wing and was hit by yet another shock. Behind the wing he could make out the small cargo door. It had been ripped open by the impact, and now hung tweaked on its hinges. He knew Rick and I were back there. Concerned, he moved toward it and could just make out something protruding from it. Something that was not part of the plane, he could tell. He made his way off of the wing and stooped down to examine it.

My right leg had been pulled from the plane on impact, and now was bent under the plane. He placed his hand on the knee and positioned himself to look through the hatch. The leg was ice cold. He could see my limp body slumped unnaturally just inside. He couldn't see my wounds, but my leg lay jutting out of the opening, curved at the knee, then disappeared into the churned up mud under the plane. All practical experience as a doctor told him that it was mangled under there, and he tugged at it, finding it stuck and unmoving. I wasn't moving either. The leg was so cold that for the moment he could not tell if I was alive or dead. But he knew there was nothing he could do about that yet.

"I'll have to get to you last," he thought. If the plane did catch fire, he knew I was going to die. He felt a tinge of guilt at the thought, but he had to save the ones he could first. He stood. He needed his wife to help him.

"Char!" he called out again. "Charleeeene!!" He was met only with total silence, save for the moan of the breeze through some nearby trees. If she was not in the wreckage… he realized that it was useless to worry.

He had no way to tell where she went and he had to get these kids out right now.

Blocking the horror of the empty space where she had just been sitting a few moments before, he turned his attention to his newly defined mission. Resolved for the moment to do so, he pulled forward the seat where Mom was not, and worked his upper body into the fuselage as far as he could to try and survey Chris.

He could barely make out his shape sitting there in the deep dark of the interior. He appeared shrunken, small and helpless. The boy's wide and terrified white eyes blinked out of the darkness up at him. He clutched the limp body of his little sister tightly to his chest.

"Kim is hurt," Chris said, fearfully. "She's not waking up."

Dad reached out for his son. "Hand her to me," he said gently.

Chris tried to rotate his body towards his father, but quickly found he was unable to budge. His sister seemed to push him back into the seat with her limp weight. He jerked his body again trying to get free. The fear of being trapped began to rush up from his stomach, manifesting in sudden panic.

Dad could hear the grunts from his struggle.

"Son, the belt…" he said as gently as he could. "Undo the belt first and hand her to me."

The seatbelt! Chris reached around the front of Kim and found the buckle that held them both into the seat. He hadn't unbuckled it yet. He fumbled with it for a moment and suddenly it clicked loose, popping away from them. He drew a deep breath, unaware until that instant how much he had needed to breathe.

He regained his composure then turned toward Dad again shifting Kim's dead weight across him as he went. Her body flopped to the right and he caught her fall with the crook of his arm. He gripped her tightly and began to lift her toward Dad when he became aware of a grating crack coming from under her. Suddenly, with a sharp snap, his hand and wrist popped and shifted down, just as Dad grasped Kim and pulled her into him.

Chris grabbed his arm with the fingers of his other hand, and felt his wrist. It felt as if an additional joint had been placed just about half way up his forearm. He moved the finger on his injured hand and was aware of the way the jagged bones grated at the muscles in his forearm. It was distressing, yet he felt no pain. But he was scared by that. His eyes shot across the darkness toward his father.

Dad stared briefly at his son's twisted arm. He had clearly heard it break, and felt Kim's body shudder under it as he gripped her. Chris meekly folded the arm across his chest and wrapped his other arm around it, holding it in place. The lack of Chris yelling in pain was a good indicator that he was numb from shock, but Dad knew he couldn't do anything for him until he put Kim down.

"It's okay, son," Dad said, trying to reassure him. "Just hold on."

He lifted Kim into him, lowering his ear onto his daughter's tiny chest. Somewhere from deep within he heard the faint beat of her heart. A brief jolt of hope lurched into him. He looked back at his son. "I'll be right back. Try to get out, okay? It's really a wreck out here, though, so be very careful."

Dad looked around to pick his way carefully backward through the hole in the plane and then stepped gingerly off the back of the wing onto the frozen ground. The contrast of stepping out into the cold breeze was momentarily painful to experience and made him shudder.

He negotiated a path through the jagged debris and the barbed wire halo that was wrapped around the plane, and then stumbled across the rough dirt to a spot roughly 30 feet away where he thought Kim would be safe from any fire or explosion. Once there, he knelt down and gently laid her there on the cold stiff dirt.

He stood, then paused for a moment to consider his options. The ground around him was clear of debris or junk and only a few patches of icy snow covered it. Still, the air was very cold, and was getting colder quickly. In a few hours it would be dangerously so. She couldn't stay this way for long, exposed completely, or she would certainly freeze to death. They all would.

But at this point, that was better than burning to death instantly in the plane if it caught fire. He didn't have a lot of options. He knew that their survival in this mess would be calculated in terms of moment by moment for at least for a while. And at this moment he, Kim and Chris were alive, and that was all that mattered. He'd take the problems one at a time. It was all he could do.

As fast as he could in the shape he was in, he made his way back to the broken corpse plane. Chris was slowly emerging through the yawning gouge in the side of it as he arrived. Dad helped him down off the front of the wing, and directed him towards Kim, but then he had an idea and told him to wait a second. He turned to face the nose of the plane. Even in the pitch darkness, he could see that it was completely destroyed; a tangled mass of aluminum and wires and other debris. The baggage compartment door on top of the nose was ripped wide open and a couple of suitcases had spilled from it and were now laying in a pile on the ground off to the side of the nose.

He needed clothes! He snatched one of the cases and ripped it open, dumping it over and spilling the contents onto the ground. He stooped down to gather up all of the clothes he could carry, then turned to Chris who was standing behind him.

"Can you hold these?" he asked. Chris held out his good arm and Dad carefully hung the clothes across it.

"Kim is right over there," Dad said, pointing in the direction of his little girl lying on the frozen ground. "She's alive, but she'll be very cold soon. If you can, you need to wrap her in these. Keep her as warm as you can, okay?"

Then he grabbed the shoulder above the boy's good arm and gave it a reassuring squeeze. "I'll need your help, son. Put some of those clothes on, too," he said. "We have to stay warm and strong to get out of this. Go ahead. I'm going to get your brothers."

Chris nodded and carefully made his way through the debris and wire over to where Kim lay, disappearing from Dad's sight into the dark and fingers of fog that still clung to the ground. The clouds overhead were very low and made the scene impossibly black. Dad was frustrated. He needed light, but knew there were no flashlights on board. He had thought about buying one, just in case, but never did. One of those things...

But then he had another thought. He went back to the pile of items from the bag he had just opened. They were now piled at the front of the plane in a jumble. It turned out it was his suitcase, he realized. It was only by chance that he had grabbed it first. He poked around and retrieved his small leather shaving bag from the pile. He quickly unzipped it, and after some rummaging found what he was looking for.

He produced a small pen light; the kind the doctor uses to check your eyes. He had packed it only as an afterthought years ago and had pretty much forgotten about it until that moment. Now it was the only source of light he had.

He depressed the small pocket clip and the tip illuminated the scratched white and orange paint of what was left of the nose with a small halo of dull white light. For a moment, it was the brightest light he had ever seen. He swung it across the plane in the vicinity near him and the scope of the damage it revealed was beyond his ability to appreciate right at that moment. Barely noticing it anyway in lieu of his other concerns, he stooped and waved it around the interior of the suitcase until he spotted his old flannel shirt wadded up inside. He pulled it out and painfully put it on. It hardly stopped the chilled air at all, but was better than nothing. Then he turned toward the plane again.

He waved the tiny light around the jagged opening that had been torn into the copilot compartment. Something had ripped away the door, taking a large section of the roof and the passenger fuselage with it, as well as the passenger side of the windshield and the connecting fuselage in front of it. The whole side of the plane had been wrenched wide open, like the serrated claws of some monster had grabbed it and torn it away, and was now a ragged and treacherous orifice – the only way in or out.

He moved his upper body cautiously in, pushing Mom's seat back, and briefly glanced around the cockpit. It was hardly recognizable as such; it lay completely destroyed and was splattered with gobs of mud and clods of dirt and other debris that had flown around it at impact. The plexiglass windshield on the pilot side was cracked and jagged as well and many of the instruments were askew and jarred about. The entire console was dark. He fiddled with the radio for a few seconds, but it was dead.

However there were no sparks or smoke from any of the numerous wires and component in the console, so hopefully nothing would catch fire while he was in there. Considering that, he reached painfully across the seats to flip off the master switch on the console and kill the power altogether, just in case. There was no indication that the batteries were even functional, but the last thing he wanted was for something to short out and spark as he was stuck in the plane. The effect of that would be catastrophic should the fuel vapors still hanging thickly in the air be ignited. The resulting fireball would consume the plane completely.

As he began to extract himself from the cockpit, he spotted the emergency beacon box next to his seat, the ELT. It had its own battery. A small orange light flashed at him telling him it had been activated. That was good. Even at that moment it was pulsing a signature whoop-whoop signal into the air. Without radios or any other signaling device, it was the only thing that would tell anyone that we were even there, if they were tuned to the right frequency.

He squirmed backwards across the seats and pulled Mom's seat forward again, then worked his way back into the middle section of the plane to focus his attention to Rick and me in the very back two seats of the passenger compartment. We were still concealed in darkness and hidden from view by the high backs of the middle seats.

He steeled himself. He could not imagine what he was about to find back there. Cautiously he approached the seatbacks. The seats did not fold down so he pulled himself up to where he could get a good look, shining the tiny beam of light across the limp and twisted bodies of his two youngest sons.

I lay contorted in my seat slumped over in a tangle of limbs on my left side, legs splayed out in unnatural and opposite directions. My right leg was jutting out the open hatch and disappearing into the dark beyond, while my left leg was pointing straight out in the other direction and bent at the knee, causing me to look like I was doing some kind of grotesque gymnastic split. The seat belt, which had somehow kept me from getting pulled out of the plane altogether, was pulled up across my chest and my lower body had been compacted into the space in front of the seat by the force of the impact.

My head and face were awash with blood and lying in a crimson pool on Rick's leg. The blood ran across my brother's lap and soaked into his pants. A large flap of skin from my forehead had been flayed back, and was draped over my scalp exposing the glistening tissue underneath. My eyes were closed. Dad had no way to tell just then if I was even still alive either, but knew it didn't look good.

Beside me Rick was slumped against the blood smeared bulkhead of the plane. He began groaning and gurgling and a steady ooze of blood ran from his forehead and over his cheek. It had stained the entire front and shoulders of his white tee shirt dark red. His eyes darted unseeingly around, and he limply lifted his right arm and flopped it down again over my face, splattering our commingled blood across the seat back and bulkhead behind and beside him. Dad reached over the seat for him.

"Ricky!" Dad said to him loudly, trying to get him to snap out of it.

Rick only lolled his head and blinked unseeingly into the penlight. His pupils stayed as wide as saucers even as the beam danced across them. Dad could see he had suffered a severe head injury…and he was in deep trouble. The look in Rick's eyes was one he had seen in the emergency room hundreds of times. It was not a good look, and made Dad very concerned. Even as he sat there, Rick's brain was swelling in his skull and creating massive pressure which might start killing it at any moment. Once it was bad enough, the rest of him would follow.

Dad was seriously worried about how long he had to live if they didn't get help very soon.

He reached out to grab Rick and try to extract him from the cramped space, but it was difficult between his side injury and his frozen shoulder to get any leverage. Rick had inherited Pappy's physique and was a stocky kid for his age, so it wasn't easy to budge him. Finally, Dad adjusted himself to lean on a part of his side that wasn't broken, and using his bad arm to reach down and grab Rick's shirt, he reached over the seat back with his good arm toward Rick's lap, fumbled with the lap belt and popped it loose. Rick slumped forward.

Dad grabbed him with both hands and with a heave, pulled Rick up to rest his head on Dad's shoulder. He held it securely there, in an attempt to protect Rick's neck as much as he could. Dad then reached under his arms and with a grunt, pulled him the rest of the way over the seat, struggling against his dead weight. Rick's limp legs flopped over the seat back and onto the middle seats, and Dad gently set him back to rest across the cushions. For a moment they lay there together motionless, Dad panting from the pure physical exertion of the task.

After a second, he took a deep breath and looked around to get his bearings again, then readjusted himself and cradled Rick in his arms. He moved him as carefully as he could in the cramped fuselage, working his way out of the plane again, off the wing, and over the tangle of barbed wire. Once clear of the hazards, he made it over to where Chris sat with Kim, and laid Rick down next to her, pausing to insure Kim was still alive. She was.

He turned back to the plane, and took a deep breath. One more to go, he thought. Again he gingerly stepped through the debris and found his way to the outside of the cargo hatch where I lay silently. With my leg firmly pinned under there, he would have to get me out of the plane from the outside. He pulled out the penlight and examined my leg. It was stretched out of the hatch and folded under the fuselage at the knee. The lower leg was completely buried under the plane.

He wedged his arm and shoulder into the compartment and felt for my head. His hand brushed against my hair and he traced the side of my face to my neck. He felt carefully for a pulse. Through the tips of his fingers he could feel it. The placement of his hand was awkward, so he couldn't get a read on how good it was, but at least I was alive. He worked his arm out of the plane and adjusted himself to consider my leg again.

There wasn't much blood, which was odd, but he quickly figured that the pressure from the weight of the plane was pinching whatever was left under there tight like a vise, acting as a crude tourniquet. When he relieved the pressure, it would probably open up like a gusher and I would have very little time before I simply bled out.

How to do this, he thought?

He went to the suitcases at the nose of the plane and dumped out another one, grabbing a handful of clothes and selecting a couple of t-shirts that he could use as a tourniquet once the pressure from the plane was relieved. Then he returned to the hatch and slumped to his knees, setting the shirts off to the side. He held the pen light between his teeth and began to carefully remove the dirt around my knee and shin, trying to dig it out a little.

The earth came out in chunks and cold, clay-like clods. He continued to remove the most prominent chunks until they stopped coming and turned instead into slick, muddy soil created by the friction of his frantic fingers. He scraped it away from my leg as best he could, scooping it out of the excavation handful by small handful until he could see under the plane a little.

Under there the jeans I had been wearing had been completely ripped away from my leg, and the flesh he revealed by his excavation was bare and exposed. He saw some large scrapes and gouges on my shin, but the initial look indicated that the leg had not been overly stressed during the crash. This surprised him. He had expected it to have been torn clean off.

After some more fierce digging, he got to where he could look at my calf pressed tightly into the riveted underbelly of the plane, and could see that my leg appeared to be impaled just below the bend of my knee by a stump of metal on the belly of the plane. When the plane was still intact, it had served as a step to get up to the wing and the main hatch. That had been ripped mostly off and the 2-inch wide stump of solid aluminum that was left now protruded deep into my flesh and held it firmly in place, snug against the fuselage. He could not yet see my foot, or even tell if it was still attached.

Dad renewed his digging, reaching as far into the excavation as he could, until he could finally feel my bare foot. My sneaker and sock had been pulled off too, and my entire leg was bare, wet, and cold as a dead fish, but seemed to be all there. He gripped the front of my knee and shoved his shoulder against the plane. It groaned and budged slightly. He felt the leg loosen on the impalement behind it. He carefully pushed again, lifting the plane ever so slightly while he gently worked the leg off of the metal that stuck deep into it. With one more hard shove my leg dropped off of the jagged chunk of metal with a sickening sucking sound. Holding the fuselage with his shoulder, he grasped my leg and pulled it towards him. The limb slid limply out of the hole from under the plane like a wet piece of thick rope.

He grabbed one of the shirts from beside him and prepared to tie it tightly around my knee to stop the spurting blood he knew was about to erupt like a geyser. He could now see the ghastly gouge that had been ripped into the back of my knee from the bottom of my thigh to half way down my calf. He watched and waited, adrenaline pumping, waiting to spring into action to attack the bleeding like he was back in the emergency room.

But the bleeding never came.

His immediate thought, and shockingly so, was that I had already bled out while he was working to extract me, so there was no more blood to bleed. But when he reached through the hatch and grabbed my wrist, he could still feel my pulse - which was not only strong, but wouldn't have been there at all in the absence of blood.

I simply wasn't bleeding. He was amazed. He'd seen people die from less severe looking wounds in the ER at Lincoln General Hospital. But he wasn't going to question it right now. He unfolded the rag and wrapped it loosely around my knee and shin to cover the worst wounds, then secured it the best he could.

Dad then reached into the plane to pull out my other leg and position it next to the injured one. He reached around me and gently unbuckled my seatbelt, grabbing my limp body by my hips and sliding me through the hatch and onto my back on the cold ground. As I lay there, he placed his hand on my neck and could feel my pulse again.

It was good and strong. He bent down and listened to my chest and could hear my thumping heart. My breathing was regular and deep. I was deeply asleep, but I was alive. He was amazed. He thought for sure I was either dead or would be shortly. But I seemed to be stable for the time being.

He quickly looked over the wound on my head. Three large flaps of skin flopped off in different directions. It looked bad, but could be superficial. He couldn't see any sign of skull fracture. It hadn't killed me yet, at any rate. But all of this could change.

He gently positioned the flaps of skin back into place on my head and wrapped another shirt around it to hold them there, then cradled me in his arms and lifted me up. Finding and negotiating the same path he had used to exit the mess before, he carried me to the relative safety of the pitch black field to lie beside what remained of my family.

When he found them, he set me carefully down next to Rick and draped clothes over both of us. He stood and looked around. Chris sat on the ground next to Kim and stared wide-eyed at him. Dad took a deep breath, and surveyed the limp bodies of his children illuminated dimly by the pen light. Mom was still out there in the dark and he would have to look for her now. He didn't want to leave us alone but he had no choice. He looked back at Chris, centered in the dim beam. Dad had him, at least. He was just a boy, but he'd have to be a man tonight.

"I'm going to look for Mom." He said. "You stay here and look after the kids, okay?"

Chris nodded toward the light and Dad turned back toward the plane again, took a deep breath and trudged away. As he staggered toward the wreck, he rubbed his hand across his face. His finger pierced a hole in his right cheek that he hadn't even noticed before. It had been punched through presumably when he had slammed into the instruments on the initial impact. He thought for a moment that it was strange that it didn't hurt, but in reality he wasn't acutely aware of any of the serious pain he should have been experiencing from a multitude of injuries.

He just wasn't thinking about pain. The truth was that it was masked by the surging adrenaline that was flowing through his veins and was actually all that was keeping him going now. But he could have cared less about all of that at the moment. He had other things to worry about besides pain.

He wiped the blood out of his good eye again and felt his head wound again. He could feel the small flap of skin half way up his scalp was loose and flopping around, releasing a steady flow of oozing blood over his face. It didn't feel really severe, but it seemed to bleed a lot. Annoyed with the pestering sting of the slick fluid in his eyes, he pressed it firmly back into place, holding there as he walked until it stuck. He was aware that his left side dully throbbed with something uncomfortable jabbing around inside his abdomen.

He knew what that was…he was a doctor after all. His rib, or maybe more than one was snapped off and floating around in there. The jagged ends still connected to his rib cage were now in physical contact with his internal organs, most significantly his spleen, and were rubbing across it with every movement he made, making it a very dangerous injury indeed.

It didn't hurt too bad, masked by the adrenalin and shock, but he knew that if one of those ends poked the spleen hard enough and it ruptured he would be immediately immobilized and would die most horribly within a matter of hours.

And as he died, so would his kids out in that field without anyone to help them. He couldn't do anything about the injury now except try not to aggravate it, and he also knew that there was nothing that he could do out here that would stabilize the effects of his bursting spleen it if it did go anyway. It was a matter of chance, he supposed. He didn't particularly like the odds, but he shook off the thought. He couldn't think about that right now.

Right now, he had to find his wife.

He stumbled along until he reached the wreckage again, and then scanned the darkness around the plane, out of the small range of his light. He could see nothing.

Where was she, he thought? She couldn't have gotten far.

He thought again for a moment that maybe she had gotten out right after the crash, maybe while he was dazed. She may be injured and wandering around in the dark, but she should still be close. He picked his way out of the tangled barbed wire wreath that circled the wreckage and made his way to the tail, scanning the darkness in that direction; the way he assumed we had come from. He had no idea how far the plane had slid, but it had seemed at the time like miles.

Mom was nowhere to be seen. He held his hands up to his face.

"Char!" He called out. "Charlene!!"

He scanned the sky above him. The low clouds obscured all celestial landmarks and helped hide the landscape around him under a curtain of black. All he could see in any direction was a few far off pinpoints of light that he assumed were farms or outbuildings scattered here or there. His good eye was still swelling, further blurring things. The perpetual ooze of blood from his head into his eyes didn't help either. He felt like he couldn't judge distance at all, and was in general feeling very much disoriented.

His current concern was that if Mom had gotten out of the wreck somehow, she may be wandering in the cold and would very soon be in grave danger of freezing, especially if she was wounded and losing blood. He had to find her soon. If she hadn't gotten out by herself then she had fallen out. He figured that if Mom had fallen out of the plane on impact, she would be back that way, behind them. He stumbled along the rough and bare dirt ground, scanning off to either side as far as he could see, waving the little light before him as he went, calling her name.

The churned up earth of the field appeared grey before him as he ventured farther into the darkness. He walked in as straight of a line as he could for what he was sure was 50 or so yards before stopping at the edge of a parcel of dead grass. He strained his eye, trying to pierce the darkness and see his wife.

He did not want to lose track of the kids or the plane by getting too far away. He hadn't seen a road or track or any other sign of the way to some kind of safety or help beyond the icy grip of this place, but wasn't surprised. He had been in and around plenty of these Nebraska cornfields over the years and knew how big and vast they could be. With no means of keeping a fix on the plane, he could easily get disoriented and wander off in the wrong direction, not being able to find his way back until sunrise. By then, we'd all be dead.

The prospect didn't sit well with him. Then he thought about Mom. If she were able to move or walk, she would be in the same dilemma and be in danger of getting lost, too.

But the nipping at his ears reminded him it was the middle of February in that field. The kids, whose status he at least knew, needed shelter of some kind. The search for Mom would have to wait for the time being. He figured the odds of her being mobile were in reality pretty slim anyway, and she probably wouldn't be going anywhere. But she was out there somewhere, and he would find her, just not yet. He took one more intense look into the night, then executed a careful about-face, and made his way over the churned up earth back towards us.

Squatting from his cold perch of earth, Chris looked through the blackness toward Rick, Kim and me. He then stared through the darkness that enveloped Mom and Dad and the plane somewhere beyond, for the moment unseen.

We were neatly laid out, tucked together side by side on the bare ground. Chris' eyes had adjusted to the dark so he could see a little, but not much. He had to look close to see the shadowed features of our still bodies laid out there. Every few minutes, he blindly felt our faces to find our mouths and then bent close to listen and make sure we were all breathing, although he wasn't sure what he was supposed to do if one of us stopped. Pound our chests, like on T.V., he figured. Luckily, right now it didn't seem to be an issue.

His hand was stained and sticky with blood from touching us. He didn't like the blood. It made everything messy.

The scant pieces of clothing he and Dad had tried to tuck around us seemed purely ornamental and didn't seem to provide much protection from that increasing cold. He shivered in the icy breeze. At least we were out, he thought, and not having to feel it. He gazed toward the plane.

He could spot Dad's location on occasion off in the field, whenever he turned on the little pen light that he had gotten from somewhere. Chris was cold, but he was growing quickly accustomed to it. He wasn't really even scared. He just felt…numb. It all felt like a dream, but he knew he was not dreaming.

Chris looked towards us again. He knew my leg and my head were ripped wide open, but could only make out the wound to my scalp from where he was. My viscous leg wound was hidden beyond his view by darkness. When Dad had finally wrestled me out from under the wreckage and brought me over, he had removed the shirt from my leg and looked over the wound with his light. Chris thought it had looked like raw chopped up meat, glistening and dripping red. Now all the blood was blackened by the darkness. He could not believe I was even alive. When he felt my skin, it felt ice cold. But I was breathing, so I wasn't dead.

Rick was bleeding from his head pretty good, too. He alternated from being dead still to moaning and flopping around. His breathing went from deep sighs to rapid staccato breaths. He would twist and turn every few minutes, but for now seemed calm. Chris was afraid of what to do about him if he got worse.

Kim lay still as death; only the fog whispering from her lips in staggered and ragged breaths betrayed the life she struggled to keep. He wondered if she would die. She wasn't bleeding too bad, but had a large cut on her eye, and her face was darkly bruised and felt puffy and swollen.

He hoped Mom was okay, but he already figured she probably wasn't. He knew that the more time passed the worse it probably was. He was trying to hold out hope, but he wasn't overly hopeful.

But he could still hope a little. Kids can always find hope.

He rubbed the sore part of his arm, and examined it as best he could in the dark. It didn't hurt too badly, but sure looked funny. On his way over to our refuge he had discovered that a large flap of skin had been pulled away from the back of the hand on his injured arm. He figured it all happened while he and Kim smashed into the seat back where the oxygen tank was strapped in. It had ripped his hand and broke his arm.

The skin had slumped back into place somewhat, but still dripped blood. He didn't show it to Dad. Dad had other problems to worry about. Instead, he had taken a shirt from the clothes Dad had given him and wrapped it around his hand. His entire arm was numb, so at least he wasn't in pain. The rest of him felt okay. He wasn't sore or limping or anything, but he was worried.

He wondered if he'd get a cast. All of the kids at school would sign it. The thought made him smile, but the smile quickly faded. The thought of all those kids suddenly made him sad. They were all home in bed safe and warm, and none of them knew about him stuck out here, wherever here was. No one anywhere did.

Then there was a sound being carried on the cold breeze which caught his attention, and connected with another memory.

He had been with our friend Paul, out at the end of Old Cheney Road near the little brick school we all attended, messing around one night. It had been a dark night like this, too, although not as dark. This was the darkest he had ever seen. The memory was of a sound that had been coming from behind a rise in the dark distance of Rural Route 1, almost like a distant sigh which approached with greater and greater intensity, building and building, and turning into a breathy roar.

That was the sound he heard now. It was the sound of tires on asphalt, far in the distance!

A car! Actually, it sounded like a truck! He whirled his body around to look behind him and scanned the darkness. In the distance he locked onto the sound, but he couldn't see anything. His view of the truck was blocked so he was unable to fix on the two distant specks of light that had just cleared an unseen hill and were now moving down a distant road. At first he thought that the sound was coming right toward us and his hope for rescue surged. But quickly the trajectory of the whoosh took the truck on a straight path from right to left that never even got close to them.

He could continue to hear it as it crossed in front of him. The cold air carried the sound even at the seemingly great distance, but the whoosh of the travel became slowly muffled. His hope began to fade. The road it traveled didn't sound like it was impossibly far, but, as things were, it may have been on another planet. All traces of the sound disappeared a few moments later, gone under the low groan of the freezing breeze that wafted around him.

He stared at the last place he had been able to hear it for a long time, gripped once again in the embrace of the cold and dark silence of the field. No more cars came. Nobody on that road was looking for them, or even knew they were there.

But at the same time, at least there was a road somewhere out there.

He listened for a long time but all was silent. He felt a little crestfallen as he knew that truck wasn't coming for us, but maybe there would be more and one of them would somehow know we were there. He settled back beside us and again looked at the darkness toward the last place he saw where Dad had been.

Dad had heard the car too, but it took him awhile to figure out where it was. He couldn't see the road either, but the sound of it was unmistakable, although he had to concentrate on it to know it was even moving. It was a long way off but if he had to, it was somewhere to go for help.

That wasn't an immediate concern of Dad's yet. The ELT in the plane still sent a signal pulsing nonstop into space. It should continue to work for 12 hours, if what they said was true. Dad knew that any planes nearby would hear it, and probably already had. Help would come, he was certain. But for now he had to keep his family alive and wait it out. He knew the ELT wasn't a precise mechanism, just a beacon. They would have to lock on to it, and then follow it to its source. It could be a while.

He arrived back at our little safe area and stooped down next to Chris.

"I can't find her," Dad said upon seeing Chris's hopeful and expectant expression in the dim little circle of his penlight. "She's not back there."

He reached for Chris's arm and examined it for a couple of silent second. He poked around the edges of the swelling.

"Does that hurt too bad?" he asked, fixing the pen light on the break. He saw the makeshift bandage Chris had put on his hand and gently unwrapped it. The flap of skin had slid back into place roughly, but was still askew. Dad hadn't noticed the injury before then, and Chris hadn't mentioned it, but it must have hurt like hell. He pressed the edges of the skin back into the periphery of the wound and gently wrapped the shirt back around it.

"That okay?" he asked.

"Not too bad..." Chris said, with a slight grimace at the slight sting from Dad's examination.

Dad nodded and turned toward Kim. He knelt beside her, stroking her forehead and checked her breathing and pulse. Then he went to Rick and then to me, checking our injuries and vitals the best he could.

We were still alive, but that was all he could tell at that point. He waved his tiny light at Chris and motioned for him to come over and sit down. Dad held one of the shirts he had taken from the wreckage and now struggled with it, pulling and tugging then finally ripping it into a few long strips. This, he fashioned into a sling for Chris' gnarled arm, securing it tightly around his neck and holding it close to his body. Although Chris still wasn't aware of how much pain he should have been in, the act caused some throbbing to go away in his arm, and it felt a little better.

"You're okay," Dad said, after checking his work. "You'll be okay, son."

Dad looked back toward the wreckage once more, thinking of Mom. Could she have been ejected when we impacted, he thought? How far would she have gone? The plane must have slid after the impact a long ways, at least 100 yards. Would she have gone farther than that, and was in front of the plane? It didn't seem possible.

He considered going back to search again immediately, but quickly remembered the cold. He glanced over at us and then turned again to consider the plane. It was all they had left. If they were going to make it through the night, they had to use it.

"We need shelter." He announced resolutely after a few seconds. "I'm going to check out the plane, and see if it's safe and if we can we'll hole up in there. You stay here with the kids, okay?"

Chris nodded, and Dad patted his good shoulder then rose to his feet. He turned again and just before he returned to the dark void, he stopped to look at Chris once again. The kid had to be terrified, although he sure didn't show it. Still, Dad reassured him.

"We'll be okay, son." He said. "We'll get out of this."

Chris nodded silently at him again and tried to look confident. Dad turned away and faded again into the darkness. Chris traced his movements by the little pen light bobbing up and down in the black of the night as he stumbled.

The rough plowed up ground would reach up and painfully trip Dad as he made his way back to the wreckage, but he slowly got there, the little dot from the pen light his only defense against total darkness. As he approached the crushed and twisted wreck, he paused and wiped the blood out of his eyes from the oozing wound on his head again. It did little to improve his sight. He considered the crash as it lay before him.

He studied the breeze. It was blowing gently on his face against the intact side of the plane. The interior of the plane was sheltered from the breeze and that was a plus. The wind was relatively light, maybe eight or ten knots at its worst, but was cooling quickly, dragging the temperature of the entire environment quickly down with it. The wreckage might be adequate shelter if he could pack us up into it and bundle us up enough. It was better than the exposed ground, at any rate.

He believed the danger of fire was no longer an issue as all the fuel had been left back there…wherever the wings went. The smell of fuel wasn't very prominent at the main wreckage anymore. Most of the loose fuel had evaporated already.

He began the task of pulling out the rest of the luggage from what was left of the nose and then moved to the aft luggage compartment and unloaded the bags from there. He proceeded to open all of the suitcases and bags and dump them into a pile on the ground. He quickly separated the useless junk like shower bags and toys, tossing them to the side, and presently had a fairly sizeable cache of clothing that he could use as bedding to keep us warm.

He made his way outward from the wreckage, stomping down the tangles of barbed wire that ensnared it to clear a sort of path around the right wing and into the large hole on that side. He worked his way into the fuselage and pulled forward Mom's seat and pushing the seatback down as flat as he could. He then crawled into the middle seats and looked around. It was definitely warmer in there than it was outside. He breathed in the air and could not smell a lot of fuel fumes, so it appeared that the fire danger had indeed passed. He hoped he was right.

Satisfied for the moment, he climbed back out of the plane and gathered an armful of clothes from the pile. Then he made his way back into the center of the plane and placed them evenly over the seats in a few layers, forming a nest where his injured children could lie and hopefully fend off hypothermia.

Once he was finished he climbed back out of the wreckage, and turned to make his way back to Chris and the rest of us. Without thinking about it he glanced at his wrist - but paused in shock. He hadn't noticed his watch before, that being the first time it occurred to him to check the time. The face of the piece was pulverized, like it had been smashed by a hammer. The stainless steel case was warped and askew. He lifted his wrist and held the watch to his ear but could not hear the sweeping tick of the gears. It was completely destroyed. He carefully pulled it off expecting to discover yet another injury he wasn't aware of, but was further amazed to see his wrist was un-marked; not a single bruise or scratch was upon it.

Whatever had destroyed the watch had done so with incredible force, but the watch appeared to have taken the brunt instead of his arm. He didn't want to think about trying all of this with a broken wrist too, and he didn't understand how it was possible that the watch took all of the damage without any of the force transferred to his arm, but there it was. He wasn't going to question that now.

He held the watch in his other hand and flexed a fist a couple of times. His wrist felt fine. He was truly not injured there. Without thinking about it, he put it back on, as useless as it was at the moment and began his trek towards us again. He didn't bother to look at it again.

If the watch would have worked it would have said it was 7:15 p.m. We had been on the ground for about 45 minutes.

Helen Boman walked along the neat rows of tables in the common room of a small church in Hebron, Nebraska. The church was hosting their regular soup dinner and those always brought out a large group of locals from town. The soup was always good, and tasted even better on cold nights like that one was. She enjoyed these occasions, which were really as much social times as dinner. Some of the people would come and leave cranky, but most of them enjoyed just spending time with friends.

Helen had moved to Hebron from Cuba, Kansas, after she had married her husband Loren. She loved the slow pace and the laid-back lifestyle the country life provided. It suited her. She enjoyed her job as a nurse at the hospital, and doing it gave her the opportunity to get to know most of the people in the town. She really felt that she made a difference in the town. She was glad that she and her family had decided to settle here. Hebron was her speed.

Helen smiled at the thought and paused to sip a cup of punch when she overheard some of the conversation coming from a small knot of ladies talking excitedly nearby. Curious, she listened in.

"It was a huge boom, like a massive explosion." one of them said in a hushed tone, like she was telling a secret. Helen listened closer, intrigued.

"It seemed like it was right next to the road, but I didn't see any fire or anything. I couldn't even tell where it had come from, so I just kept driving" she continued.

"Just the strangest thing!"

It was an odd sounding thing, for sure, Helen thought. She wondered along with the other ladies what the woman could have possibly heard. She wasn't particularly worried or concerned. If there had been any kind of big accident or incident, she would have known. The hospital would have called her. Just something about the words…they made her feel a little strange.

Helen walked away from the group toward her table, and focused on her warm bowl of soup. It was good, but she couldn't turn off the alert switch that the conversation had tripped in her brain. For some reason, she kept thinking about what that lady had said.

Chapter 6

I awoke at dawn and opened my eyes, a little disoriented, until I realized where I was. Kim and I were at Clarke and Sharon's house in Lincoln on our trip for the truth.

I pulled myself to sit upright and stretched. Sunlight glistened outside the window. I rose and walked over to it to peek out. Clarke and Sharon lived in a sprawling development of big houses on a beautiful lake south of the city. The water sparkled as the sunlight danced across it. It was a nice spring day. I went back to the bed and sat down, reaching for a binder in which I had sketched out my itinerary for the trip. I reviewed my notes.

A few weeks before, I found a reply to my email to the Thayer County Health Services. It was just a day after I acknowledged Joyce's first email, which shocked me. I hadn't expected anything so soon. I opened it excitedly in anticipation of the news it would bring.

"Randy, I found two nurses and a doctor who remembered the incident immediately! They are thrilled that you took the time to get in touch with us. They will be very willing to meet with you. We will also look for rescue workers who might remember you from the accident. Please keep in touch. Joyce."

This was like hitting the jackpot! I couldn't believe that there were still people around who would know about it, yet alone several people! I can't say that I was 100% believing of what I was seeing. And it was that same day I got my first email from Helen.

"Hi Randy," she wrote. "My name is Helen Boman and I am the nurse who rode with the injured in the helicopter to Lincoln. I am contacting people I know who were there and remember that tragic night. All are interested in visiting with you."

To say that I was awestruck would be an understatement. I felt a surge of motivation and excitement that I could actually learn the real story. Maybe even learn about the whole thing! It was an incredible rush.

Helen and I emailed each other a lot in the days leading up to Kim's and my trip to Lincoln, and had become very close. Now I looked forward greatly to meeting her. Over the next couple of weeks, she managed to bring together Gary and Dick, Blanche, and Evelyn, and Doctor Bunting, and would arrange a meeting for me to talk to them all.

It was really happening. I was beginning to think the whole story really was out there. I could not have known then where it would end up taking me. Quickly, I made my travel arrangements, and in what seemed like an instant, yet painfully long, I arrived in Lincoln.

Kim and I met up with Dr. Bruce Miller at his home in Lincoln later that night. It had been a while since I had seen him, but he still looked the same. I was quite sure he had stopped aging around 1983. His wife Patti greeted us warmly and made sure our glasses were full all night. He never forgot the crash and was glad that we were trying to figure it out.

Like everyone else we had met who were associated with it, he really only knew his role in it all, and was just as curious as everyone about what everyone else had done.

I had brought along a bottle of 16 year McCallen scotch. Bruce was a single malt man like me. I poured some of the amber liquid over the ice in our glasses and handed his to him. We toasted and I sipped the peaty scotch that warmed my throat as I swallowed it. We both sat for a moment savoring the drink then set our glasses down.

He listened as I told him about our trip so far and what we had discovered. Then I asked him what he knew. I had brought along some photos of the crash which he now looked through and shook his head. Then he began to tell his story.

Bruce glanced at the clock in the office of his spacious home on the outskirts of Lincoln. His best friend and business partner was late. He hadn't heard from Jim yet, and was growing increasingly concerned. He had expected a call over an hour ago.

He and Jim Styner had met as residents together at Denver General Hospital, and had quickly come to realize that they had many of the same ambitions. They were both gifted orthopedic surgeons, and during the last term of their residency, had arranged to join a private practice in Lincoln.

Together, they brought their families across the plains and set themselves up in the little capital city of Lincoln, Nebraska. They joined the Lincoln Orthopedic and Rehabilitation Center with four other doctors in town. It was tough at first. They were so busy that they were immediately inundated with cases. Many of the doctors who had been working months without breaks took much needed vacations, leaving the two new doctors to sink or swim.

They swam. Between their practice and their respective stints at the local hospitals, they quickly integrated themselves into the medical establishment of Lincoln, and then the rest of the Midwest.

In the winter, Bruce and Jim skied together in Aspen, Breckenridge and Winter Park. The rest of the year, they traveled together all over the country, both for business and, with their families, pleasure. Even their wives had become very close in the pastoral setting of rural Nebraska. The two families purchased adjacent land in the country and built their homes together. They had kids around the same time together, and each had a daughter born in Lincoln.

Bruce was my godfather, and, not surprisingly, Dad was the godfather of Bruce's kids. Bruce's son Greg was the best friend of my childhood, and to this day, my unofficial brother.

Bruce had always thought Dad was cocky, but in a good way and he respected that. Surgeons needed a certain element of that. And Dad could back it up. Actually, both Bruce and Dad were as good a surgeon as any one there.

Bruce remembered a good story about my dad one winter night early in their careers. They were working together in the ER at Lincoln General Hospital when a big Cadillac driven by a Texas oilman had skidded off of Highway I-80 and hit a pole, crushing the pelvis of the man's 17 year-old son. Dad consulted with the man about the necessity of the surgery, but at one point the oilman, very much a Texan, began to get agitated and loud about what Dad was telling him.

"Boy, don't you realize I can get the best doctor in the country for this?!" he proclaimed in a loud Texas drawl. "Just one phone call and it's done!"

Dad was undeterred. "Call all over if you want," he shot right back. "But I'll save you some time, because the best doctor in the country is already on the case!"

The oilman, apparently impressed with Dad's spunk calmed down, and Dad did the surgery and fourteen hours later had completely repaired the boy's hip. The father was genuinely happy and by the end of the ordeal had become like a good buddy to all of the staff at the hospital, who received his bear hugs and slaps on the back with nervous chuckles.

The kid recovered.

Bruce had served in the Air Force as a young man, and had always loved to fly. He had introduced Dad to it. They flew all over the country to all of their various professional functions and on vacations. He had flown next to Dad at the controls over countless hours of flight. They bought the Baron together and loved it. They flew it on every excuse they could. He thought Dad was a skilled and capable pilot.

That was why Bruce now glanced at the clock and again noted with growing concern that his friend was overdue.

The two of them had an airtight agreement that if either of them was flying without the other, they would call the other as soon as they landed, and if they were ever late or grounded they would let the other know their status ASAP. He thought about it for a moment, and then shook his head.

Nope, Dad had never neglected that end of the agreement that he could remember. And it was something he'd remember. Like most pilots, neither took anything about flying lightly.

He walked across the hallway from his office to a window oriented toward our house, a few hundred yards away. The interior lights all appeared to be out, and the place looked closed tight. He had a slightly uneasy feeling, but immediately shook it off. Jim had called him from the airport in Farmington around lunchtime and said they were just getting ready to leave, but that didn't mean they left right away. Maybe something got forgotten, or they decided to have a long lunch…any number of things.

Hell, Dad had probably run into the low clouds that had been over the plains all day, and put down in North Platte. Or turned back to Farmington. Either way, Bruce was sure it was a long day, with his wife and four kids in tow, and he had simply forgotten to call.

He ignored the elephant that had come into the room as he gazed at the space where our house stood outlined in darkness under the low clouds.

Dad had plenty of IRF experience in case he had run into the clouds and found them to be too low to go under, even though he wasn't officially certified. He knew what he was doing, and there had been no severe weather or turbulence over the state that he had heard about. And Bruce knew Dad would never intentionally fly in IFR conditions unless he absolutely had to. He was just...delayed somewhere. Bruce figured Dad would wake up around two in the morning realizing he had forgotten to call and wake him up then in a flurry of apologies and a good story or two.

Oh well. All he could do was wait anyway.

He considered calling Betty Lou or Grandma in California for a moment to see if Mom had called them. He knew she would call them at some point, or at least they'd be expecting a call. He decided against it. He didn't want to cause anyone to worry unnecessarily.

Outside it was getting cold. He was suddenly very much aware of the cold, even as he stood in the comfortable warmth of his house. He turned and left the living room toward the kitchen. Diane was making Hungarian goulash for dinner and the aroma filled the air of the house with tomato-based spiciness.

He liked goulash.

Around the same time as Bruce was wondering about us, at the Lincoln Federal Aviation Administration Flight Service Station the manager checked the flight log, right at 7:00 p.m., as he did every hour. One entry had immediately caught his attention and he quickly glanced over at the clock on the wall. Beech N3600H had not cancelled their flight plan and was now 30 minutes overdue. He picked up the telephone and called the tower at the Lincoln Municipal Airport to see if anyone knew anything. No one there had heard from the aircraft or its pilot that day. They most certainly had not landed at Lincoln at any rate.

After checking to make sure he hadn't missed anything, he had to list us as missing. As was protocol, he then ordered a series of radio calls to be sent out to stations along our flight plan to determine if anyone had heard from us, or if they could establish contact.

Eventually one of those calls reached Minneapolis Flight Service who confirmed they had communicated with Dad as he flew over the dust storm in Kansas around 5:30 that afternoon and had provided him with a weather briefing, but that was all.

At that point the Flight Service manager contacted his bosses who began to send requests to all airports and landing strips along and in the vicinity of the flight's planned path to confirm that our airplane had not in fact landed at one of those and that the pilot had not just neglected to cancel his flight plan. Many airports were able to answer back right away, but many were closed or not staffed at all.

At the time, the Midwest contained hundreds of small farm-supporting airfields with very limited communication. For those places local authorities, generally State Troopers, were dispatched to visually ensure that missing planes were not at any of them. Unfortunately, this took several hours, and a search would not be launched until they knew for sure.

The manager probably didn't like doing it that way. Nobody did, but it wasn't his call. No one with the authority to do so was willing to mobilize a full scale search for what would likely be a false alarm. Not without an emergency beacon being reported.

Still, he did what he could. He sent a notice to all flights over flying the last known flight path to request that they monitor the emergency frequency to see if any could hear an emergency locator transmitter, or ELT, signal. So far, no one had.

But no one was listening, yet.

* * * * * * * * * * * * * * * *

Dad emerged out of the darkness to where Chris sat with his forlorn brothers and sister. He started to gather all of the loose clothing that lay around them.

"Let's get these kids back in the plane." Dad told Chris. "It's going to get colder and we may have to wait it out for a while. I think the plane is our best bet to stay warm."

Chris glanced over towards us and then nervously at the plane. Dad saw his hesitation.

"Hey," Dad said, prompting Chris to look back at him. He walked up to the boy, and put his hand on his shoulder. "If there was going to be a fire, it would have happened already. Look, the wings are gone...that's where all of the gas was. It'll be okay. We'll be okay."

Dad looked for confidence to return to Chris. Chris silently stood and began to help him gather the loose clothes. Dad patted his son's head.

"Let's get back into the plane and figure out what we're going to do next," he said. "I need your help, son. Okay?"

Chris nodded and sheepishly turned toward the plane. He really didn't want to go back in there. It had become a scary and foreboding place. Dad gently lifted Kim and followed Chris slowly back toward the wreckage.

The gash across the copilot side yawned in the darkness before them as they approached. Chris stopped at it and stared anxiously inside for a moment hesitating, but then he gingerly stepped into the pilot's seat and sat down.

Dad appeared at the door with Kim. He worked his way into the fuselage and placed her gently on the farthest seat behind Chris. Then he left and returned a short time later carrying me and laid me next to Kim. Once finished he disappeared again and returned this time with Rick, who he set nearest the opening.

He went to the pile of clothes he had made next to the plane and filled his arms with shirts, pants, underwear, and any other clothing items that could provide warmth, and then crawled back in the cramped compartment to tuck them around us in several layers.

A few minutes later he finished tucking one last article of clothing then he stepped back through the opening and surveyed his work with the pen light. He was for the moment satisfied. We were now nestled together and seemingly snug and relatively warm. If it didn't get too cold, at least we wouldn't freeze.

We all appeared stable, and that gave him a little comfort. He was fairly amazed that one or more of us wasn't dead yet by that point. At any rate, he knew that even as an experienced surgeon if there was a massive internal hemorrhage or other problem with one of us, there wasn't anything he could do without an operating table anyway. But for now the field first aid he had done was good, and all signs were for the moment positive. There wasn't any more he could do with us but hope and wait.

He didn't like to just hope and wait. It wasn't really his nature, to go with the whim of a situation. He liked to be in charge. But for now he saw no options. The emergency beacon was still functioning. Someone would come soon and rescue them. He just had to be patient. Besides, where was he going to go?

Dad pointed the light at the pilot's seat. Chris had settled in there, pulling a thin jacket they had rummaged around his shoulders.

"Let me see your hand," Dad said. Chris worked his arm out of the sling and held it out using his good hand to support it. Dad reached in and examined it once more. The make-shift work he had done was effective. He had wrapped it and it was about as well supported as it could be out here. The bandage seemed to have stopped the bleeding on his hand, and his arm was well immobilized.

He looked Chris over with the light. He was dirty, and covered in smears of blood and mud, but didn't seem to have any other injuries. Dad wished he was in as good of shape as the boy. He wasn't in pain, but his body throbbed. He knew his shock was masking the pain. He had assessed his own injuries and he was hurt. But he was not yet willing to let that stop him from protecting his kids.

He'd have to be dead first.

"You're sure you're okay?" He asked. "No new pain anywhere?" Chris shook his head and positioned the sling around his arm, then folded it to his chest again.

"Okay," Dad said. "You stay here with the kids. I am going to look for Mom, okay?"

Chris nodded, and Dad stepped back out of the plane.

Dad made his way back to the tail and headed out again. He walked in more or less the same direction as last time, but not quite, just in case she was off to the side. When he reached the grass again he waded into it a little way. She could have been covered down in it and out of sight. He searched around a little more before he realized something else was missing.

There was no scar from the impact and subsequent slide across the grass, as there would have been if the plane came through here. There was no debris, either. There was nothing.

He couldn't immediately figure out how that was possible, until he considered that we may have turned as we slid, which he hadn't considered. If we had, then the way the tail was pointing wouldn't be the exact way we came from...it could just be pointing in some random direction. That meant Mom could be anywhere! He calmed himself down at the thought and began to make his way back to the plane again.

When he got there, he examined the wreckage scattered on the ground around the plane, and began to see where the debris appeared to be extending in a straight line away from the plane. The main concentration of debris appeared to be heading in a direction slightly forward of the right wing.

If that was the direction from which we had come, the plane had rotated almost towards the opposite direction. He had no idea. He couldn't remember. But it appeared from the debris that it was almost facing backward from whence it had come. It was pointed in the same direction as the distant road where he and Chris had heard the car before.

That direction was where she would have fallen. At any rate, she couldn't be far off, unless somehow she had walked away. Even if she had, she still couldn't be far.

"Char!" He called through cupped hands in the direction of the debris trail. "Chaaaar!" No answer came from the breeze floating all around him.

Dad took a couple of steps forward toward the clumps of wreckage and twisted metal that the tiny light danced over and which lay strewn along our path of travel. The earth had been freshly churned up here, confirming to Dad that this was in fact where we had come from. He peered into the dark, scanning the area before him as best he could with his one good eye, which wasn't doing so well. He took a few more steps, when suddenly he caught a glint of soft color on the ground that did not appear to be just wreckage. Curious by the sight, his mind didn't let him think about what it could be.

He took a few more steps, until he could barely make out the shape first appearing as a lump lying on the earth. He didn't comprehend what he saw at first as he moved closer and waved the small beam of the penlight over it.

But his brain began to grip the image as it resolved, then like a sledge hammer the reality hit him, spinning the freezing, dark world that engulfed them both. For a moment, all else around him was shut out.

Mom lay on her abdomen, her upper body rotated over onto her left side facing away from him as he approached in a contorted and unnatural way. Her legs were spread shoulder-width apart, with the left leg bent at the knee at about a 45 degree angle and draped across the back of her other ankle. Her left arm extended out from under her away from her face as if she reached to touch something just beyond her grasp. Her right arm was wrapped around her face, cradling her head. Her fingers from that hand protruded from her hair which was all messed up and obscured her face so all he could see of her features was her exposed ear.

There was what appeared to be blood on her hair, but he could not tell from where he stood the extent of the injury. The powder blue suit she wore was tattered and smeared with mud and other stains.

Dad realized in that instant that she must have been ejected on the plane's initial impact with the ground and flew all of the way out here, traveling through the air at the same rate of the plane until her momentum was lost and she pummeled into the ground behind the rest of them as they spun.

She had not so much been thrown from the plane as she had been flung from it, and then plunged into the cold fertile earth like a projectile, into a place she could have never imagined.

He was consumed in the moment by the physical incarnation of his worst fear.

"Char!!" he cried as it became clear that what he saw was indeed his wife. He stumbled over and dropped to his knees beside her.

He raised his hands to her, but for a moment hesitated to touch. He already knew she was probably dead, although he would not allow the thought to enter his head just then. He gently took her arm and pulled it away from her head to get a better look at her face and try to ascertain how badly she was hurt. Her eyes were closed, he could see, and he was suddenly struck by how peaceful she looked.

Like she was only sleeping.

He gently brushed the matted hair out of the way, caressing her cheek and whispering her name, but she did not move. Even so, he felt that she was still slightly warm. Still hopeful, he turned her head to roll her over so he could open her airway and see if she was breathing, and to attempt CPR if she wasn't, but that hope was quickly obliterated as he reached under her head to move it around to where he could do some good.

As he began to lift her, his fingers slipped on her blood and slid into wet, soft tissue on the other side of her head. He held her head there, and with his other hand gently rolled her over onto her back. His fear turned to horror as he realized that his fingers had entered a ghastly hole where left side of her forehead should have been. Most of it was now gone, and her deformed skull turned her lower face on that side into a twisted and unnatural mask where it been pressed against the ground. It now grimaced at him and was rigid and purple with trauma. The beginnings of livor mortis could be seen as her blood began to settle.

He recoiled as the reality of the image gripped him. The blood from the vicious wound clung to his fingers and began to cool as he pulled them away. He could not even try to save her. She was gone. He could now only stare at her. Gently, with trembling hands he laid her head back to the ground.

He slumped backwards to sit on the ground beside her, stunned. He squeezed his eyes closed, and clutched his face. He was overcome so completely that he ended up with just a sort of numbness by it all. He subconsciously reverted to the cold defense of his profession and forced him to now look upon her like any patient – limiting his actions to analyzing her injuries, assessing her condition, and developing a diagnosis.

But deep down he knew that if he gave into the horror of the reality, he would be reduced to a blathering slob unable to function at all…and then we would all die.

And he wasn't going to let that happen.

He could only hear the thud of his pulse in his ears. He attempted to move her into a more dignified state, what dignity there was to be found here. He took very little comfort in the knowledge that from the looks of her wounds she had died quickly, probably instantaneously.

He would find little comfort later when he found out it was a piece of the left prop that had been torn off when we hit the first tree that killed her. It turned out it had spared his own head twice by mere centimeters as it ricocheted like a bullet around the interior of the airplane before it had ripped through her head just before she was ejected.

Now he held her still warm hand and squeezed his eyes, trying to maintain some speck of composure, trying to not think about what the hell he'd do now. Trying not to comprehend the extent of the hole that had just been torn into our lives, like the hole in the airplane. He took a deep breath of the cold dead air that mingled with the vapor of her cooling blood, soaking slowly into the ground. It would soon freeze her solidly to it.

He snapped himself together as best he could with a shake of his head and opened his eyes again, looking down on her. There was nothing more he could do. He gently placed her hand back on the frozen ground beside her, and bent down till he felt the press of her cheek on his lips. He would have cried, would have stayed and mourned here, but there was just no time for it now. He still had a family and they needed him, now more than ever. He would not let them down now, for Mom if no one else.

"I'm sorry," he whispered close to her face, and then raised himself painfully to his feet, turning his attention to the task now at hand. He made his way back to the plane.

As he climbed back into the passenger seat, painfully aware that it was the last place he saw her alive, Chris looked at him hopefully. Dad said nothing. He just slumped back and stared out into the darkness. He had to think.

Chris looked back out into the darkness too. They both sat in silence. Time ticked away.

The big EC-135 called Looking Glass rumbled through the sky far above the prairie and way above the clouds that concealed our wrecked Beechcraft in the field. A young pilot sat at the controls, staring into the starry sky that rose limitlessly above him and extended off to the horizon. They were on the last leg of their mission and would be landing at Andrews Air Force base in a few hours.

The intercom crackled: "Flight Deck, Comm," came the voice in the pilot's headset.

"Go ahead, Comm," the pilot replied.

"Hey, Sir," came the voice of his communications chief coming from somewhere back behind him, deep within the electronic bowels of the plane. "Message just came over CTAF from Lincoln Flight Service. They say they're missing an airplane somewhere in the sector we're approaching. A little civilian one. Last heard from by Minneapolis around seventeen thirty hours."

The pilot looked at his watch. It was creeping up on 10:30.

"Roger that, Comm," he replied. "Go ahead and monitor the emergency frequencies, and report all contacts."

"Roger, standby," The airman said back. "Out."

The airman rotated his seat to face the emergency radio, which monitored the 121.5 MHz frequency, the international civilian emergency locator transmitter frequency, and switched it on then fine-tuned it in. All was silent so far.

The fuselage of the EC-135 resonated with a steady vibration that the airman had long become accustomed to. He was hardly even aware that he was in a plane at all anymore, he'd been at this job for so long. This airplane had become a second home to him. These flights were good duty.

The mission of the Looking Glass program was simple: To have airplanes in the air at all times that were equipped and capable to electronically direct missile bases on the ground, whose control centers were destroyed or otherwise inactive, then launch their nuclear tipped ballistic missiles anyway. It was all part of the mutually assured destruction of the Cold War.

The big plane wasn't ugly, but definitely not the sleekest thing in the sky, for sure. Lots of Air Force planes were sexier, what with their maneuverability and high-speed weaponry and such, but Looking Glass crews never took too much static at the Officers Club. The airman always laughed at the fact that although they carried no actual weapons on board, the big Looking Glass planes were simply the most deadly things in the sky. So to hell with the jet-jocks, with their little guns and rockets – this was real power.

He settled back into his seat sedated by the drone of the plane and rubbed his eyes. They were flying back to Andrews and some time off. He closed his eyes and lost his thoughts of some future drink, or a girl, or just the sleep he'd get to catch up on. He stayed like that for a long time.

Far below, Dad had gone back to check on Mom two more times. He had sat beside Chris for a very long time in silence after he returned to the plane from finding her the first time. But he was agitated and after a while had convinced himself that he had missed something somehow. He convinced himself she may still be alive, that he hadn't checked her breathing or pulse. She was still warm, after all. Besides, he didn't want to tell Chris his mother was dead until he knew for sure.

He made his way back to her and examined her once more. Nothing had changed. She was indeed dead.

He had come back to the plane after that and after some more rummaging found a small blanket, and then he went back and covered her head and upper body with it. He certainly didn't want Chris to see her like that, to see what he had seen and dream about for the rest of his life.

He touched her once more that last trip and she was cold. All doubt and hope he may have still had for her was erased. It was just us now.

He returned to the plane once more but stopped outside the constricting barbed wire perimeter. He decided that he wanted to see what shape the plane was in, in case it had to remain their home for a while. He slowly walked around it, taking in the extent of the devastation for the first time.

The wings on both sides were gone, just past each engine. The fuel was in the wings. When they had been ripped off, the fuel must have drained before they hit the ground, before it could be ignited by a tiny spark or sufficient friction which would have caused us to become a rolling fireball as we advanced across it. We all would have been immolated with no chance of survival, he thought rather matter-of-factly.

The rest of the plane appeared to be fairly intact, except for the huge hole where Mom had been sitting. It was a wreck, and was buckled and bent, but had held together. It held them in…mostly. He pulled himself back in the plane and slumped down to sit by Chris.

He still didn't tell Chris about Mom. He wasn't sure how. It didn't matter now, anyway. And judging by his reaction, Chris already had figured it out. Dad sat in silence and tried to think.

He had to figure out how to get out of there. He looked up beyond the horizon, and was suddenly heartened.

For the first time he noticed that the cloud layer had risen significantly and the cold air seemed to have begun to break up the clouds that covered the sky above us. At first he thought that the pressure was merely changing slightly and the elevation of the clouds had just increased a little, but then Dad became aware of the twinkling of stars through the thin grey veil as it dissipated.

Creeping, the overcast began to disburse into several large sections that then had begun to float apart in dull gray clumps, gradually evaporating into thin, frozen air. Dad and Chris watched them slowly dissolve in silence, and stared at the widening swath of dark sky beyond, twinkling with bright stars.

That was much better than the alternative. He had been worried that it might start to rain or storm, and that would make life, and living, very, very hard. It was still freezing cold, but the clear sky heartened him.

Now, it was the frustration caused by the distinct lack of rescue that was heavy on Dad's mind. It had been hours, for Christ sake! How could they not have found us by that point? He fumed and wondered about it bitterly.

He looked over at Chris. The boy sat staring out the cockpit window at the fresh field of stars. His arms were wrapped around himself and he looked cold. Dad wished he could do something for him. The kid was a real trooper.

"They'll be looking for us by now," he said trying to reassure them both. "It just takes a little time, that's all. The worst is over." He thought about that and hoped it was true. He gently rubbed his side and hoped his spleen would hold.

Chris didn't say anything. Dad figured he was deep in mental shock over all this and didn't press the issue. They had to be ready to spot the rescue team and help them find the wreck once they got close, and he didn't want to depress the kid and make him useless. Dad knew he needed him. He turned his head to look back out the hole in the plane, into the night towards what he now knew was the northern sky. He lifted his gaze to the star field and scanned it for any sign of hope.

He suddenly locked his body as his eyes clicked on just that hope, blurrily tumbling across the dark sky.

"There!" Dad exclaimed excitedly, and pointed to the high northern sky. Chris pivoted to look and adjusted his stare toward the area of sky at which Dad pointed, high over the distant horizon. At first he saw nothing but low dark clouds and patchwork clumps of stars, but then his eyes locked onto it; a tiny pin dot of red, thousands of feet up and many, miles away. It appeared at first to shimmer like a star in the sky, but then it was obvious that it was moving in a straight line across the night. It wasn't shimmering after all, he suddenly could see. It blinked.

For the first time since realizing they were alive, Dad felt a flash of hope. It was a big plane way up, probably around 25,000 feet. It didn't matter because it would pick up their beacon, even at that height! They would have to report the location of the beacon and then we'd be saved!

Dad and Chris watched the light move until it began to hide behind the remaining puffs of clouds, and eventually disappeared. Dad was heartened.

"They will see us, son." Dad said with more confidence than Chris had heard all night. "Help is on the way."

The Looking Glass communications airman bolted upright and lifted a hand to cup the headphone on his ear and push it tighter to his head. He intently concentrated on the slight sound coming into his head.

At first it was like a static surge over the dead silent airwaves, but it began to materialize and melted into a distinct tone, like a ghost materializing from the ethereal plane of radio space. It sounded like it was barely there at all. He adjusted the frequency knob on the radio and suddenly the tone filled his head much louder, with a distinct woo-woo siren which he recognized immediately.

An ELT signal.

His heart began to pump a little harder. He hadn't expected this! Missing planes almost always turn up somewhere safe. He certainly had never actually found one. He toggled the switch of the microphone extending down from his ear.

"Flight deck, comm.," the airman said. "I am monitoring a weak signal on 121.5 MHz, sir! I'll bet you it's the distress signal you were looking for."

"Roger that," the pilot replied. "See if you can lock it down. I will advise Scott," he said, in reference to the Air Force Rescue Coordination Center (AFRCC) in Scott, Illinois. After a few moments the Captain came back on.

"Scott is advised. Do you have a fix?"

"Standby," the airman said. He made some calculations, then pulled out a map of the landscape below and poked around at it for a few moments, trying to get an approximate location based on the signal's direction and intensity. If he could get them close, the ground teams would find it no problem.

"It appears to be somewhere southwest of Lincoln, sir" he said. "Near the…Lancaster County line, maybe fifteen to twenty miles from the airport."

"Roger," the Colonel said. "Scott is rolling the CAP. We'll stay on station awhile and see if we can help out, over."

"Roger that," the airman said.

He took off his headset and rubbed his eyes. He thought for a moment about the source of the signal. Someone down there was having a bad night, that was for sure.

Beech N3600H a couple of months before the accident. Dad was piloting when Bruce Miller took this shot from his plane while flying over the Nebraska prairie.

The Styner family, circa 1945. From left to right is my aunt Mary Lou, my uncle Jerry, Dad, Grandma Hazel and my Pappy.

Arriving in Hebron for the second time in my life, standing beside highway 81. The crash site was about two and a half miles southeast of this spot.

Kim, Helen, and Gary near the entrance of the Thayer County Health Services hospital during our visit.

Deputy Larry Russell standing beside the helicopter he searched for us in. This photo was taken behind the little school I attended as a child during a demonstration, and I am one of those little heads, but not sure which. This was only a few years after the crash.

-Photo courtesy of Larry Russell

The Trinity Chapel church in Rokeby, Nebraska outside Lincoln. We attended this little church when I was a kid, and my mother's funeral was held here. I have heard the crowd of people was out the door and into the parking lot.

A photo taken by the NTSB during the accident investigation showing the point of impact as seen from the field. The bushy plum thicket took the brunt of the impact and saved us. To the left, you can see the right wing in one of the trees. The writing on these photos was made by whomever took them.

Another view from the trees looking out onto the field. With our wings gone, our fuel was drained and probably saved us from burning up as we slid.

NTSB investigators at the corpse of Beech N3600H. The plane traveled approximately 294 feet after impact. My dad found Mom's body near the debris seen in this shot to the right and beyond the plane.

Another view of the impact. In the center of the gap you can clearly see the farmhouse where Charles and Cara Braun lived that we passed over just before the crash. The position of the house makes one wonder how we could have missed it.

Our sanctuary from the cold. The seat folded down was where my Mom was sitting during the impact. You can see she had no chance of staying in the plane without her seatbelt. Most people I have talked to agree that her seatbelt was probably a moot point, judging from the damage.

The chunk of metal that killed my Mom. This was a piece of the prop that was sheared off from the first tree we hit. It had barely missed my dad's head twice as it ricocheted around the plane before lodging in bulkhead beside the unoccupied seat behind Mom.

The rear hatch. I was trapped here, my leg pinned under the plane. You can see the barbed wire in the foreground. This stuff was wrapped all around the plane. Looking at this picture always makes me wonder how Dad ever could have gotten me out.

The engines.

The lower picture shows the prop missing the piece that killed my mom.

This picture was used in a CAP communiqué that came out after the crash. The caption read "How could anyone have survived this?"

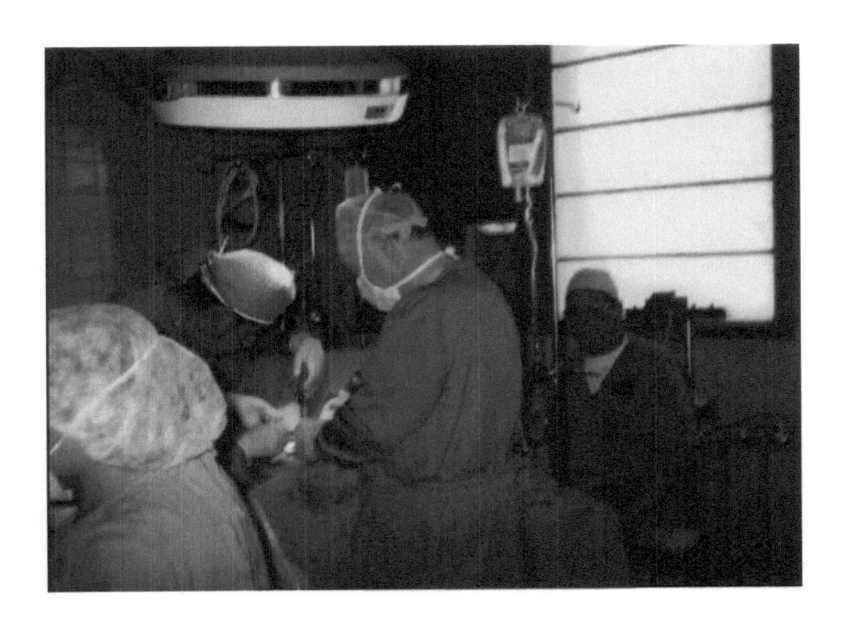

Dr. James Styner in Cusco, Peru and Orange County, California.

At peace in Lincoln Memorial Cemetery.

Chapter 7

My sister Kim and I drove over the black asphalt stretch of interstate 80 that connects Lincoln to North Platte. A weather front was washing over the Midwest from the west, and rain splattered loudly on the roof of the rental car most of the way. It reminded me of many other trips I had taken down this road, toward Denver to ski, toward California to spend summers from college, toward home. It always seemed to rain.

I liked the rain. It washed away the smell of the interstate and the corporate farms that rolled away from us to the horizon in all directions. It made the air smell fresh and clean and earthy.

After doggedly hovering directly above us almost the entire drive out there, the rain finally stopped. Like always, the air had an almost electrical ozone smell right after, copper-like, the way a penny tastes on your tongue.

That sensation hit me as I climbed out of the car once we reached our destination. I stretched, working the road out of my spine and breathed deeply of the damp and cool fresh air. I was momentarily lost in the memory of a thousand other times smelling that same air. A rush of images of children splashing carelessly through puddles, running home on rainy days, or just sitting on the porch, watching it come down, maybe comforted by a mug of hot cocoa.

That energy from the storms still flowed through my veins, and now that same energy rejuvenated me and oxygenated my blood, finding its way to old and familiar parts of my brain. It was part of me. I had almost forgotten about it.

We came all the way out here, half way across the state, to see one man, the man Kathy had found for me. I had gotten a message from him only a few weeks prior and had set up this meeting.

Jim's message had said simply:

"Mr. Styner, Kathy Hubble passed on your request to me regarding the aircraft accident near Hebron. I was on the CAP ground team that night in February. I would be happy to talk to you about the incident."

When I read that, I could hardly breathe! This man had been there, actually been there, on the ground! Maybe he had seen the plane. Maybe he had seen Mom. It was more than I could have possibly hoped for.

I arranged to meet with Jim Nitz during this trip. Jim then gave me information to contact two more searchers, Jon Morris and Larry Russell, who he knew through CAP.

Walking across the parking lot now, I had to keep my inner child in check to keep from jumping into the new puddles with both feet to see them splash. We entered the restaurant called the Whiskey Creek Steakhouse. There weren't very many people sitting around that day. The rain kept them home, I guess. A young and pretty hostess greeted us and showed us to a big red vinyl clad booth surrounding a sturdy wooden table in a quiet end of the restaurant. We slid in and looked over the menu, sipping ice tea. The flat iron steak called to me.

I spotted Jim immediately when he walked into the restaurant. He looked very much like I had pictured him. He was an older man now and he carried himself with a humble and nondescript air. He looked around and I waved when I caught his eye. He ambled over and we rose to meet him. He greeted us with warmth and friendship and we easily chatted for a little while.

My steak came while we made small talk. I cut a small piece of it and popped it in my mouth. I immediately remembered why Nebraska beef is known as some of the best in the world. The succulent juices spread across my tongue, reminding me what I left behind when I left here, so long ago. I still remember that steak, from that little roadside steakhouse.

The waitress came to check on us after a bit, cutting us away from the small talk. When she left, I took the opportunity to get to the point.

"What happened?" I asked him. He shifted his eyes down for a moment, and shook his head slightly.

"I'll tell you," he said, looking right at me with dead seriousness. "It was no night to crash an airplane…"

Jim opened the front door to his house in Lincoln as he got home from the Tuesday night Civil Air Patrol, or CAP, meeting, weary from the long day. A full shift at the tire shop where he worked as an assistant manager starting at 8 a.m., combined with the evening CAP meeting, took its toll a bit, but he wasn't complaining. He took off his coat, hung it on a hook on the wall, and made his way toward his bedroom and his calling bed.

CAP meeting nights were always long, but he enjoyed them. He had been involved with the Civil Air Patrol for many years, but never got tired of seeing the eager young faces of the cadets who had joined, fueled by the dreams of adventure and hopes of making it out on a real search some day.

They were good kids. The group was good, in general. After more missions than he could count, he never got tired of it. Their job was important, and he knew it.

It took a particular kind of person to be a CAP cadet. Some of these kids were really young, as one could join at age 12. But they all had a common pride and professionalism about them, regardless of their age. Even the youngest ones had it. They put effort into their uniforms, they worked to become good in drill, and they participated equally in events, all with a full measure of enthusiasm. They were fascinated by all aspects of aviation and would listen intently to everything they were told. It was really something to see, and it made him proud.

The CAP was originally sanctioned by the Air Force primarily to help locate downed planes. More and more however, they had been getting involved in disaster relief and aerospace education as well, plus community service projects. It kept them busy. Over 95% of all aircraft searches in the inland United States were performed by CAP teams, and a fair number of those crashes occurred in the Lincoln Composite Squadron's sector. For an all-volunteer group, they were exceptionally well equipped and well trained to do their jobs. Even the younger members who had been around for awhile had a feel of "veterans" to them.

Jim climbed into his bed and switched off the lamp on the table. It seemed that his head had just come to rest on the soft warm pillow and he was drifting to sleep when he was startled awake by the telephone next to him.

He reached over and picked it up, fumbling a little in the dark.

"This is Jim," he mumbled.

"Commander, we have been requested to assemble the teams," the voice on the other end said. "Scott says they've located an ELT in our sector."

Jim switched on the lamp again, and shook off the cobwebs. An ELT signal? That wasn't atypical but also was no joking matter. Most of them were just hard landings which caused unnoticed activations of ELT's, but not all of them were.

"Hold on," he said. He found a piece of paper in a drawer on the nightstand and made some notes as the caller spoke. He repeated the information back to the speaker, then hung up. He sat up and hung his legs over the edge of the bed and stretched his neck back and forth for a moment. It was an ELT report all right, and there was a missing plane.

He looked at the clock. 11:30 p.m. The night had just started.

He got up stretching, and put his fatigues back on. They were still warm. He grabbed his gear bag, pulled his field jacket back on, and headed out the door into the cold night, back toward the CAP Squadron headquarters at the Lincoln Air National Guard Base from where he had just come an hour ago.

About midnight, Jim pulled into the sodium arc-lit parking lot outside the CAP headquarters. Jon Morris was there when he pulled into a spot by the door. Jon, a Lincoln cop and CAP veteran, was one of the search team leaders. Jim killed the engine and slid out of the car and into the cold night. He and Jon greeted and walked together into the cinderblock building and up to the operations center.

Jim had telephoned Jon after he had learned of the ELT signal, so Jon was already up to speed. A family was missing. The night brought back a familiar feeling for Jon. Several weeks prior he had been out on another search for a family. It was complicated by the fact that the airplane's owner had loaned the plane to his friend. The friend had a wife and three kids with him on the flight - the same make up as the owner's family, who also had a wife and three kids.

They found the plane quickly, just off a highway. It had impacted a tree line and burned. Inside they found the charred remains of the pilot and his family – five bodies in all. Based on the FAA information, they had thought it was the owner and his family and had begun to list them as the victims, but of course they turned up alive in short order.

It was a weird sensation – the joy at knowing the people you thought had been killed were alive, then the realization that there was still a dead and burned up family out there in the trees. It was a common kind of sensation in that line of work, however. One he never got used to. He didn't figure tonight would be much different.

Jon and Jim made their way up to the briefing room. Team members were arriving and waiting for their orders as they assembled their gear and checked equipment. Harold, the Squadron Commander, came in and made his way over to the table where Jim and Jon were going over their communications protocols for the search. He rolled out a map on the table.

"We have been informed by Scott that they received FAA notification of an overdue private plane en route to Lincoln earlier tonight," he said.

"An Air Force SAC EC-135, code-named Looking Glass, just picked up a distress signal about 45 minutes ago which may be our guy," Harold continued. "It looks like it's along the same flight path. The CAP search plane is up and in communication with the 135. They offered to stay on station for a while to support us. They have the crash site to be somewhere just southwest of the County line."

He slid his finger on the map along our route and Jon and Jim quickly scanned the map for possible search areas. They agreed that 15-20 miles away along the flight plan would put them at right around the Lancaster County line near the border with Saline County. That seemed like the best place to start. They scanned the map some more, making note of roads and other possible access points.

"I contacted Don in Omaha when I got here. He's on his way down," Harold said. "He's probably 15 or 20 minutes away."

That was good, Jim knew. Don had a DF unit. The DF, or Direction Finding unit, could locate the precise direction of a beacon, and was very handy to have, particularly when your search area is darkened fields and woods accessible only by farmers' roads. It didn't have a really long range, but once you were close, it'd bring you right to them. Without it, they'd have to rely on signal strength as detected from the CAP plane which would be flying above the search area. It could nail down the general area, but wasn't good at telling you exactly which way to go.

Jim looked at his watch, and then made a loud announcement to the team:

"Okay, listen up!" he loudly said. All of the search members immediately stopped what they were doing and focused on him.

"This is the real thing, people," he said. "We estimate that the wreck is somewhere near the Lancaster/Saline county line, so we will initiate our search in that area, near Crete."

He surveyed the teams. The looks were anxious, but motivated. For some of these cadets, this was their first mission. But he had trained these men, and knew they were ready to go.

"Team one and two is with me," he said. "Team three will be with Mr. Morris." He pointed at Jon.

"Maintain good contact at all times and watch out for each other. It's going to get past freezing out there, so make sure you have all the right gear." He made one more look at the teams, and then looked at his watch.

"Do one more gear check. We mount up in fifteen minutes!" He concluded.

He and Jon went through their own gear quickly, then descended the stairs and out to the parking area where the trucks sat. They fired up the trucks to get them warm and did radio checks. Everything was working. Don had shown up by that time carrying the lunchbox-shaped DF unit with its T.V.-looking antenna. He took his place in Jim's truck, which would act as the lead vehicle. The rest of the team divided up into their assigned vehicles and waited to go.

Jim had decided to first head towards the small town of Crete, just inside the Saline County line to begin the search. With the help of the CAP plane, they should be able to find the signal by the time they got down there and could be brought closer to the vicinity of the crash, at least. The DF would tell them right where to go after that.

Jon walked up to Jim.

"I called my buddy Larry Russell at the Sheriff Department." Jon said. "He is standing by with his chopper if we need it."

Jim was heartened. All the help he could get on a night like this was appreciated.

"Yeah, tell him to come along," Jim said. "He can meet us in Crete."

"Will do," Jon said, and went to his vehicle.

Jim got a radio check with the CAP search plane. The pilot still couldn't see anything from up there, but had begun to hear the signal. He couldn't tell where it was exactly, but was on it.

That was the start of a mission that he liked to hear.

"Let's mount up, people!" he hollered to the teams. Time to go.

Kim and I drove back to Lincoln and walked into the Lincoln Police station. I sat on a vinyl couch in the small foyer across from Kim and waited for Larry to receive us. It was a little creepy. I had been a law-abiding citizen at least since my days in the Corps, but here I kept wondering if anyone recognized me. I knew it was impossible, but to that troubled youth of my past, it still felt a little unnerving.

Larry, dressed in the olive drab uniform of the Lancaster County Sheriff, eventually came up and greeted us. He was a Deputy from the old school. There was no nonsense coupled with an easy and casual way about him. He was a man who had been around and seen many, many things alien to most of us. But he remembered that night, and here I was. His handshake was warm and firm. I felt immediately safe and at ease with him.

As we walked toward his office, he stopped at a picture on the wall and tapped it.

"That's her," he said. "That's the same chopper I went after you guys in."

I studied the photo of the bubble nose chopper with Larry as a much younger man standing in front of her. It was a strange thing to see, considering the circumstances.

Kim and I sat down in Larry's office for a few minutes until Jon came in. He introduced himself and, with Larry, began to tell us the story of that night. The two of them had been friends for many years, since the time Larry began to fly for the Lancaster County Sheriff and Jon had become a Lincoln Police Department officer.

Larry had flown Piper Cherokees for the sheriff for years before he segued into choppers. He flew prisoners all over the country from jails to courts, dealing with extraditions and such. He loved to fly, and was a good pilot. He knew about the Beechcraft Baron, too, and had flown them many times.

"You really had to fly that plane," he said. "Especially on instruments, or it'll get away from you." He talked about landing one in IFR conditions at St. Louis once many years ago.

"We got into some rough weather on the approach," he said. "I was almost upside down at one point as we came in."

"But I was the only one who knew," he said with a wink.

After a while, Jon Morris walked into the room. He worked in the adjacent section of the Police building and was in his blue Lincoln PD uniform. He greeted us in the same manner as Larry, and seemed very happy to see us. Jon had known Jim Nitz since they were both kids. He had been with the Civil Air Patrol most of his adult life and had seen a lot of missions. It had been interesting to talk with Jon in the weeks leading up to our trip. He had sent me an email just prior to me leaving that left me excited. It read:

"When we meet, I will tell you why it's important to know as much about this situation as you can. It will have a much greater meaning later in your life."

I had been thinking about those words since I first read them. It turned out that one of his wife's parents was killed in a car accident, and it had bothered her for many years. She finally went back to the scene and that act became a pivot point in her coming to terms with the event. Now that was happening to me, although I did not know it yet. Jon was right. The meaning of me being there was bigger than anything I could have ever anticipated.

I was distracted for a moment. Seeing the picture of the chopper on the wall had transported my mind briefly back many years to when I was in grade school.

I went to school in a small brick building near the outskirts of Lincoln, an area people who live in Lincoln refer to as "the country." The school was what most people would refer to as a one room school house, but I took exception to this throughout my youth, as it actually had three rooms. The place finally closed in 1979. Greg Miller, Kevin Anderson, and I were the sum total of the last graduating class. Now it's someone's house.

Before then, a year or so after the crash, the Sheriff department flew a helicopter into the field behind the school to give us a presentation about the use of helicopters in police work. The pilot, a young and good-looking cop, asked at one point if anyone had ever been in a helicopter. From the back of the knot of kids packed around him, I meekly raised my hand. I was the only one.

"What kind of helicopter was it?" the pilot asked. I didn't know, I had said, because I was knocked out. He studied me for a moment and then to my surprise asked me if my name was Styner. I said yes.

The pilot, Larry Russell, nodded at me. "I remember you," he had said.

The air was near freezing as Larry quickly walked across the dark tarmac that night, tinted dull yellow in the glow of the industrial lights surrounding the airport. He approached the bubble nose of the Bell 47S helicopter waiting quietly for him. His baby. It was the Sheriff's bird, he knew, but to him, it was his.

He unlocked the pilot door and crawled in to begin to conduct his pre-flight checks of the aircraft. It was a small helicopter that reminded everyone who saw it of the opening of M*A*S*H. But it was a nice helicopter. He had set it up military style, and had even equipped it with a beacon locator antenna. That would come in handy tonight, if he could get close enough.

He was going up to support the CAP search for a downed plane was all that he knew. The CAP was already en route to Saline County, and he would be coming up behind them. He had heard that the plane was missing a few hours ago through communications with the Sheriff's dispatch over his scanner, and had been anticipating that CAP might call to use the chopper.

He admired the machine as he walked around it, checking the entire craft. The chopper really was a beautiful bird. Its big plexiglass bubble nose gave him an excellent view of the world as he rode across the sky in it, making it a true pleasure to do his job. It let the good guys know that help had arrived and made sure the bad guys didn't get away. He felt like no matter what, he always had a good day.

He wondered how this day would go.

After being thoroughly satisfied with the air-worthiness of the chopper, he climbed into the cockpit again to finish the preflight checks, and put his headphones over his ears. A few seconds later another deputy named Bruce, his observer for the flight, opened the door and climbed in. Larry had requested him to act as an extra set of eyes. He'd need them.

"Ready?" Larry said as Bruce buckled the seatbelt around himself.

"Copy." Bruce said flashing two thumbs up and pulling the headphones onto his head.

Larry flipped the master switch. The turbines whined as the bird flipped into life. All of the gauges kicked up to normal, like a lean dog, snapping alert and quivering, waiting for the word. Larry activated the ignition.

With a labored whine, the rotors slowly begin to spin, quickly bursting to life as the big engine fired up, filling the air with the distinctive chopping sound as the blades whirled around.

"Check, check…nice and cold out there" Larry said over the intercom as he gave another quick look at the gauges. He gently eased the collective forward as he pulled the throttle arm, and pitched the blades. The combination of actions gently lifted the little bird effortlessly off of the deck. Once clear, he revved the engine and launched the bird into the western night, toward the Lancaster/Saline County line.

He flipped the frequency knob on the radio to get on the common channel of the 39-99 radio system, which allowed him to communicate with other agencies all over the state.

"CAP-1, this is Sheriff-1," he said. "Do you read, over?"

"Sheriff -1, CAP-1" came Jim's voice. "Got you Lima-Charlie. Please report your position, over."

"Roger, CAP. I am presently two miles southwest of Lincoln Municipal Airport, heading toward the Lancaster County line. ETA roughly…fifteen minutes, over."

"Roger that, Sheriff-1," came Jim's reply. "Be advised that we have a report of a distress beacon in that approximate vicinity. Our CAP plane is in orbit over Crete and trying to lock it down. Please advise when on station, over."

"Roger, CAP-1. I will advise. Out." Jim released the radio button on his stick. He glanced over at Bruce.

"Give me some of that damn coffee!" He said over the intercom with a smile. Bruce grinned and twisted the top off of the thermos.

"After me." he said.

Jim stared into the dark as the CAP team raced down highway 77, south of Interstate 80, toward Crete. The crash site had to be nearby, but they hadn't picked up a thing on the DF receiver. The CAP plane was circling the area above, but had yet to nail down the beacon. He could hear it all right, he just couldn't tell which direction it was coming from or how far away. He certainly couldn't see it. The air outside was quiet, and, at times, left Jeff wondering if the ELT was defective somehow. It wasn't.

Looking Glass, who was still in the area, was monitoring the beacon, or so they were reporting from their slow flight on the northern horizon. He knew there was no such thing as a pinpoint location of an ELT signal, but they were usually close. The EC-135 was so far away that the words 'close to them' could still mean miles off. Jim hoped that wouldn't be the case tonight.

If it was, they'd be able to use that helicopter. He could get close to the ground and support them visually and with his tracking equipment. He knew the chopper had locating equipment on board, which was both rare and good, but it would only be effective if he got within range of the signal transmission. The power of his receiver was nothing compared to the C-135. So for now they just had to guess. He hoped they guessed well.

The small convoy turned west onto State Route 33 following the banks of the Big Blue River. After a few more minutes the trucks rolled into Crete. The little town was quiet, and no one stirred. Jim decided the best course of action would be to circle to the north and then head south, and if they didn't pick up the signal, cut east near the tiny town of Kramer, directly adjacent to Crete, hopefully by then, the CAP plane or the chopper could get a lock on the signal.

Jim radioed the other teams to follow and headed out on the small roads that ran around the town. Beside him, Don listened on the headphones of the DF, but only heard silence.

Chapter 8

The Jamaican sun had caressed her skin as she napped under it, next to the bay of a little resort near Kingston. Dad and Mom went there the year before, and it was wonderful. They had looked so forward to it, and shot frisky looks across the dinner table at each other in the days leading up to it when we kids weren't looking. They had not had a vacation of just their own in a while. They had danced and listened to calypso music and steel drums and snuggled while they watched the sun set.

Another chilled draft shook Dad and washed away the memory, returning to him in its wake an empty and numb feeling.

This was sure as hell not Jamaica.

Dad rubbed his shoulders and scanned the sky. The black tapestry above our airplane was filled with bright stars. The sky was dotted with them, sparkling clearly. But he had not seen an aircraft since the distant blinking light he had pointed out to Chris with such enthusiasm what seemed like hours ago.

On any other night Chris would have noticed the beauty of the stars, but he couldn't care less now. Now they were just stupid stars. But he didn't feel the same way about the moon.

The moon began as a dull yellow lump behind the clouds but peeked out once or twice as the last remnants of the front broke up and floated around it.

Then all at once it seemed to suddenly burst into the open sky. It was two days after the full moon, so it came out big and white and radiated a bright light that splashed across the landscape around them, bringing for the first time that night figures and substance from the dark. For the first time in what seemed forever, he could actually see a little.

To the front of the plane, Chris could now clearly make out the tree line that we crashed through. Beyond that, still a long way off, was the road he had heard earlier, but it was still out of sight. There wasn't a lot of traffic on it at this time of night, but what there was he could hear. A handful of vehicles had gone across his front with the familiar whooshing sound during the hours that they had waited. They were so close, but none of them had any way to know we were out there, just out of their sight.

Dad saw the moon too, although it was blurry and dim through his swollen eyelids. His vision had gotten progressively worse to the point that he could hardly see at all, his face was so swollen. The blood had slowed it's flowing into his left eye, but still impeded it.

He had considered more and more about the possibility of going for help. When he had seen the airplane fly above them, he had thought that there would be a rescue soon if not immediately. He hadn't wanted to try and make the journey for help if he didn't have to.

For one thing, it was so dark that he was sure he'd get lost, particularly with no guidance, even from the stars. For another, he was feeling very lucky that he hadn't ruptured his spleen yet with the broken rib that floated in his side. Whatever path led to that road from this field was sure to be rough, and he was worried that a single stumble or trip would finish the job. He had enough experience with this exact type of injury in the ER numerous times, and knew that if his spleen went, he most likely wouldn't even make it back to the plane before he died in agony somewhere in the dark and frozen night.

So there was that. Not to mention he could hardly see. At any rate he was getting pretty sure that if help wasn't on the way now, if it wasn't here yet, it might not be coming at all. The thought was infuriating and made absolutely no sense to him.

1976, and no one even knows when a plane crashes??

He didn't buy it. They would have noticed immediately that we were overdue, he would have thought. All they had to do was come this way. Why were they not here? Why were they not looking for us?

The thought suddenly made him feel very alone.

Dad snorted it off. He didn't even know who 'they' were. He certainly had no knowledge of the intense search being conducted only forty or so miles east of us. He only knew it was beginning to look like he was on his own.

Kim and I were still asleep and hadn't moved since he had placed us in our patchwork nest of clothes behind him, but Rick was becoming a problem. He was going through bouts of excitement and thrashing about. Dad was worried he would hurt himself or one of us during a violent fit.

Moreover, he was worried about Rick's brain, which he knew was continuing to swell in his head even as he lay there, and that it could kill him at any time.

It had gotten very cold, too. Beyond just uncomfortable. The tingling in his fingers and toes told him it had gone toward dangerous, even deadly if they didn't get out of it soon. He had no way to tell the exact temperature, but had been out in it enough in his time in Colorado and Nebraska winters to know it was near freezing. This was emphasized by an occasional shudder from Chris beside him.

He began to really worry that none of us would make it till morning, and even if we did, this was Nebraska in the wintertime. Plenty of people had died in cold like that in the middle of a crystal clear and sunny day. Here, he knew sun would not necessarily equate to warmth. And God forbid if the clouds returned bringing a storm with them in the next hour or two, which was also not unheard of.

The old joke was that if you didn't like the weather in Nebraska, wait a little. It wasn't a joke to Dad now. It scared him. Dad knew the joke was based on very real weather phenomena that occurred over the plains all the time. Violent storms could grow from seemingly nowhere, in the middle of a clear blue sky. Dad had seen it many times. Every Nebraskan had.

All of this weighed on him now as he tried to work out what he had to do. He had been eyeing a distant point of yellow light glowing from a darkened rise in the land to the northeast for some time now. He thought it could be a farm building. And a farm building is usually located next to a house...but not always. It could just be a light on a pole at the corner of a field. He had no way to know. He didn't trust his eyes.

Then there was that road. He had heard the cars on it the several times Chris pointed them out, and he thought the road might be closer than the building, or whatever it was.

But he couldn't tell for sure; his blurry vision made judging distance to either point impossible. Not to mention that wandering out into the prairie with no landmarks to guide him would be roughly the same as walking into the desert. People can get disoriented and lost and freeze to death in the fields on nights like this, the distances between aid being so great and the cold so bitter.

The moon changed that. He knew the road was his best bet for eventual help if another car came, but an occupied farm house would mean more immediate help. The darkness of the night had made either option too treacherous, but he could now make out the contours of the ground around us, and knew with the light of the moon, he had at least a chance.

Either way, he also knew he had to make up his mind quickly. The last thing he wanted was for the clouds to come back when he was a long distance from the plane, storm or not. They would obscure any landmarks he could see and very possibly cause him to lose his way and not be able to find his way back. He would most likely not survive that.

Now was the time either way, he decided. He turned to Chris.

"Son," he said, "How far away is that light way out there?" he pointed to the speck on the horizon over his shoulder that he thought might be near a farm. Chris turned to look at it and stared for a long time.

"I don't know," he said. "It seems to be a long way."

Dad faced forward toward the road.

"How far to the road?" he asked. Chris thought hard. Judging by the sound, it wasn't far, but without seeing it he just couldn't tell. He knew what Dad was thinking. Dad had muttered about going for help a few times in the hours they had been waiting. He didn't want to make a mistake now, but it was up to him. He clenched his jaw and made his decision.

"I...I think the road is much closer," Chris replied, trying to sound confident.

In an instant, all doubt was gone. Dad had the answer he needed and knew what he had to do. He formulated a quick plan in his head. He turned to look at Chris.

"Listen, Son," he said. "I don't think we can wait any longer. I don't think anyone is coming just yet and we have to get the kids help now. I am going to try and get to that road and hopefully flag someone down."

Chris had locked on to him with his stare, but said nothing. He only nodded. The thought of really being left alone was terrifying.

But Dad continued. He hadn't really thought about what he should say if this point came, but there was no time for stoicism.

"I think we can get help there." He paused to gather his thoughts. This was getting difficult, but Chris had to know everything, in case something happened to him out there.

"If I don't come back, you need to wait here with the kids, okay?" Dad said. Chris nodded, wide-eyed.

"Someone will come sooner or later." Dad tried to sound reassuring. "You just need to stay strong. But don't come looking for me, no matter what happens. If I don't come back, you need to stay here. Do you understand that?"

Chris nodded. He didn't know what to say. His impulse was to beg Dad not to leave him, but he knew Dad was right. Chris had to trust him.

Dad went on, and began to pull himself together to get out of the plane.

"Keep an eye on Ricky," Dad said as he got up, glancing toward us in the middle of the plane. "Try to keep him calm, but try not to move anyone."

Chris watched as Dad worked his way up and out of the plane, using the ripped up fuselage to balance himself. The breeze hit Dad as he stood. It was now really cold.

He surveyed the ground around him. It seemed so bright now, bathed in the moonlight. He could see the tree line we had crashed through, silhouetted in the moonlight, which to his injured eyes appeared as a dark blur against a slightly lighter one. To the right of the trees, he could make out a slight rise in the contour of the ground that he thought looked like it could have also been a road or a path. Near that, there was probably a road. Probably a small road, but a road all the same, and that would lead somewhere, hopefully to the bigger road. He decided to start out that way.

He scanned the remainder of the area around him for a second and his eyes rested on a moonlit spot of lightness against the dark earth on the other side of the plane. He stared at it for an instant before realizing with a tinge that it was the blanket that covered Mom. He gazed at it for a moment more, and then stooped down to look at Chris.

"Look, son, your Mom is right over there," he said and pointed to the approximate direction of her broken and dead body. "You can't go over there, understand?"

Chris shifted his eyes away and looked down. Chris knew where she was. He knew she was dead. But Dad was horrified at the thought that Chris might look for her and see what he had seen. He was adamant.

"Son," he said trying to be gentle but stern. "You have to listen to me. There is nothing we can do for her, okay? You have to believe me. She is…gone."

He waited for a response, but Chris just looked away from him and stared at the busted instrument panel. Dad tried a slightly different approach.

"The kids need your help," he said. "I am depending on you to watch out for them and take care of them, Okay? Chris??"

Chris looked at him again and nodded once. He knew. Dad reached in and patted his head.

"It's going to be all right. We'll get out of here soon," Dad said, then stood again and began to move.

Chris watched him as he stepped carefully off of the shattered wing, and toward the front of the plane. He paused to gain his bearings for a moment, and then walked in a straight line across the rough ground of the field toward the right hand edge of the silhouette of trees. The moon played off of his form as he went, bobbing and weaving his way into the moonlit darkness of the cold night. Gradually his form dimmed until it blended with the dark backdrop and faded completely out of view.

Then he was gone.

Chris stared at the empty space where he had caught his last glimpse of Dad. He was aware of the whispery moan of the icy breeze that washed across the plane in irregular intervals. Behind him, we were all still. He sat cold and alone. He wasn't scared. He had never really been all that scared. There was simply no point. If he was supposed to be dead, he knew he would be. We all would be. But he wasn't now. Not yet.

To the side of the plane through the dirty plexiglass, he could now clearly see Mom.

Dad reached the tree line. The forest was surrounded by the dense brush of a plum tree thicket. He had come across a long strand of barbed wire which he followed to the forest, presumably from the fence we took out on impact. Dad couldn't penetrate the thick brush of the plum thicket, so he followed it around to the right. It ended abruptly and he suddenly found himself standing on an earthen dike that circled gently away from him to the north and around what appeared to be a pond before bending toward the west and in the direction of his objective. As he stumbled along the dike, he could make out the ruts of past trucks and tractors that had traveled over it, and was heartened.

After a few steps, he could see that the dike abutted what was indeed a large pond just off to the left as he walked over it. He felt fortunate we had hit where we did, or we might have ended up in there. We would have sunk without a trace. No one would have ever found us.

He continued to make his way when he stopped abruptly and squinted into the dark. Fifty or so feet before him he could make out a light swath of ground running toward the east and west as far as the moonlight would allow him to see. He immediately recognized it to be a dirt road. As he reached it, he was excited, so much so that he stumbled and was compelled to focus again on his broken rib, which jabbed him rudely.

He bent forward, grabbing his side tightly, and the stab faded slowly back into the steady throb he was used to. He was reminded that if he wasn't careful, he was as good as dead. The thought was punctuated by a fresh curtain of breezy cold, which numbed him further.

Dead as dead can be.

But not yet. He composed himself and gathered his strength, then stepped gingerly over the dirt curb of the road, turned west, and began to stumble slowly toward his hope for salvation and deliverance from this hell.

Chris turned around to survey us, laid out in the middle of the plane. No one had moved, not even Ricky. Chris felt very restless since Dad had left. He didn't want to just sit there anymore.

He needed to stretch.

He worked his way out of the plane again and slowly stood on the cold earth, shivering against the freezing breeze. He adjusted the sling around his neck and looked at the make-shift bandage on his hand. It was darkly stained in the moonlight from being soaked with his blood. He surveyed the blue tinted landscape around him until his eyes locked again on the body of his mother, so clear now in the icy moonlight.

Up to that point, he had held the impulse at bay, but seeing her and being separated by only a small distance was overpowering. Suddenly he didn't hear Dad's warning. He wasn't worried about us, either. He just knew he had to go there.

He slowly made his way through the debris and barbed wire and walked past the buckled nose of the plane and across the moonlit void between him and Mom. He felt like he wasn't walking to her as much as being drawn, and was now merely submitting to the force of it.

When he reached where she lay, he stood motionless for a while taking her in. He wasn't sure what he was supposed to do. He was completely spellbound by the sight.

The blanket covered her head and upper body and most of her torso. Her lower body and legs protruded from it still. Her feet were bare; she had lost her shoes. The pants of her light blue suit that she wore were colored monotone in the moonlight and stained with dark patches. He couldn't tell the difference between which were dirt and which were blood. He didn't really care.

The tips of the fingers of her left hand extended from the edge of the blanket. Her diamond wedding ring sparkled softly in the moonlight. Chris stared at it. She was a prominent person in Lincoln society. My family was considered fairly well off by the day's standards. She could have had a big huge diamond to show off, but she didn't. She had this small modest one. It was lovely and the epitome of her.

Chris lowered himself to the ground to sit beside her, and then reached out to touch her hand. It was like ice, and frozen stiff by the cold and rigor mortis. He withdrew in shocked horror.

It wasn't what he had expected. It was the first time he had ever touched a dead body. He sat for a moment and considered her. He shook off the horror, then gently took her hand again. It wasn't so bad this time. Wrapping his fingers around hers he slowly leaned over, lowering himself to his side until he was laying next to her on the frozen stiff ground of the field, his head next to hers. He looked at the shape of her profile under the dark stained blanket but he didn't lift it. He didn't need to.

The decision to go to sleep came to him like a logical conclusion. He was suddenly very tired. He didn't mind anymore if he had to die. He preferred that it would be here, with her. If he wasn't supposed to, he wouldn't have come out here. He didn't feel cold or scared or in pain. The sanctity of the darkness behind his closed eyes brought with it the promise of delivery from this place, one way or another. He didn't know if Dad would make it back or not, and suddenly he just didn't care.

Darkness began to wash over him. Then he felt peace.

The road rolled up and down before Dad, and seemed to go on forever. He had to stop often to catch his breath and get his bearings. He didn't feel overly tired at that point, but he didn't want to push it. If he could get to the main road, someone would see him sooner or later, even if he dropped dead when he got there. Hopefully they would be able to tell from the condition of his corpse that something dreadful had happened nearby and at least go looking for that. With any luck they would find the wreckage and the kids before they all froze.

He only had to make it to the road.

He paused again in a trough between two small rises for a moment, and then began to climb once more. As he reached the crest of the hill, he abruptly stopped again. He was stunned to clearly see the octagonal glare of a stop sign glinting in the moonlight just at the bottom of the rise.

The asphalt of State Highway 81 appeared black before him as he stumbled down the small grade over the thirty yards to get to it, like a man finding water in the desert. When he reached it, he slowly wandered slightly dazed into the middle of it, looking up and down the long black and empty moonlit ribbon of road. He stood in silence for a few seconds to consider the new scene around him.

To the south he could make out the lights of what appeared to be a small town in the far distance. He had no way to know what town it was as he still wasn't sure where the hell he was. To the north, west and south, there were no obvious signs of life or activity. If no one came along, he decided to make toward the town to the south.

Just then, as if on cue, he was spun around to look south again. He heard again the familiar whooshing that suddenly emanated from that direction. Over a far off rise in the road, a halo of light faded up brighter and brighter simultaneously with the rising pitch and intensity of the whoosh, until its source suddenly burst into view with a flash as the high beams of a big truck crested it, rushing straight toward him!

For the first time in the last fifteen hours, his cracked and puffy lips slowly curved upward into a smile. Finally, they would be saved! He lifted leaden arms and waved up and down at the still distant truck excitedly, stumbling desperately toward it.

"HEY!" he yelled as loud as he could, even though it hurt his side. He was too overcome with joy. If he could have he would have jumped up and down. "HEEEEEY!"

The truck raced toward him, and he moved to stand in middle of the northbound lane where he was sure it would see him. He could quickly tell it was a big 18-wheeler. He continued to wave and the truck continued to come.

Fast.

Suddenly, the reality that it wasn't stopping gripped Dad. Could the driver not see him? He waved his arms over his head frantically and with all his might and screamed at it as loud as he could, but it wasn't stopping. He waited till the last possible second then dove off of the road as the massive truck careened by with a long blast of its horn, kicking frozen dust and rocks at him as it rumbled by without so much as a pause.

Dad landed on his good side in the deep ditch beside the road, smacking the half-frozen trickle of water that was gathered at the bottom of it. It quickly soaked his clothes.

His head swam in a swirl of throbbing pain and angry amazement as he struggled to catch his breath. He closed his eyes, and waited for something to happen.

Slowly it did. Focus began to return and the pain of the dive began to dissipate. He forced himself to sit up disbelieving, and tried to catch his breath and make sense of what had just occurred, but was cut short.

The whoosh of another big vehicle was approaching from the same place as the last, heading north. Again its lights broke the crest of the hill and bore down on his spot. He struggled to his feet and hauled himself out of the ditch and onto the asphalt once again, once again waving and hollering with all of his might.

And once again he was forced to dive into the icy bottom of the ditch a few moments later to writhe in pain on his back as the second truck rumbled by as if he were invisible.

What the hell? Dad thought, blinking at the starry sky above him, utterly baffled.

Chris lay next to Mom without making a sound or moving for a long time.

It wasn't really a voice that shook him away from the edge of peace and caused him to open his eyes again. It was more like an impulse. Like a feeling.

Don't go to sleep, it softly nudged him.

He lifted his head, and listened, only capturing the sound of the icy breeze. He laid his head on frozen ground again, and again he felt it.

Don't go to sleep, my sweet boy…

He could make it out clearly. It rang through his mind, although its origins were as foreign to him as this field. It spoke to him from somewhere deep within him, a place he couldn't quite finger.

Go back, he felt. It will be okay. The kids need you. Go back…

He looked at Mom once again, and thought he understood. She was still, but suddenly he felt like he could sense her around him. Suddenly he realized that even in her death he knew what it was she would have wanted him to do. It wasn't to die out there next to her, either. She would have never had that. It was to live. It was as if she were in him and speaking to him, even in death. He knew what he had to do. He had to live – for her.

He slowly worked his way to his feet, and looked down at her again. He was taken that she looked as if she was at peace, too. That was enough for him right then. The thought that it would be the last time he would ever see her didn't ever cross his mind. If it had, he may not have left after all.

He turned and walked through the cold and dark toward the plane. He never looked back, and he never saw her again.

Chapter 9

Jim pulled the CAP truck to a stop on the shoulder of a dirt road running by the south side of Kramer and got out. The other CAP search vehicles rolled up behind him. He looked up and down the dark road. They had completely circled the town but there had been no sign of the beacon on the ground. He never thought that it would be an easy search from the lack of specific location info from Looking Glass, but this was beginning to feel like he was looking for a needle in a haystack.

He unfolded a map and put it on the warm hood of the truck. They had drawn a red line of the planned flight path of the missing plane and were standing right on it, but the DF was completely silent. It was frustrating. They just weren't here.

Larry thudded by in his chopper just above the trees, shining his spotlight through their leafless forms as he passed slowly overhead. Larry had flown an orbit around the entire area and had come up with nothing on his locator. Jim picked up his Radio.

"Sheriff-1, be advised we are going to take a second to get our bearings," he said. "No sign of them yet."

Jim gazed up and back down the road, figuring out their next move. The next town along the lost plane's flight path was Hebron, about thirty-five miles due southwest. He decided to move that way and see if they could pick up anything. Above them, the CAP plane circled. It had been monitoring the beacon, but it was still very weak, meaning it could still be a ways off. He called Larry.

"Sheriff-1, CAP-1." He said "We're going to move toward Hebron. Can you move in that direction and see if you can get anything?"

"Roger, CAP-1." Larry replied. "Give me a minute to get a vector."

Larry adjusted the pitch of the rotor blades, gunned the engine of the chopper, and quickly shot up to 4,500 feet above sea level. As he gained altitude the siren-like squeal of the ELT signal began to creep into his headset. It had been blocked by the terrain as he flew low, but now he had it. It was just a matter of finding the right direction and if he did, it would get louder as he approached. He adjusted his radio and raised Minneapolis tower.

"Minneapolis, this is Lancaster County Sheriff Helicopter-1. I am at 4,500 feet above Crete, Nebraska conducting a search, I am squawking 1200 and will ident…now," he said pushing the identifier button on his transponder which he had quickly tuned to 1200. "Do you see me?"

A few seconds passed then a voice came back.

"Roger, Sheriff-1," came the reply from Minneapolis as he appeared as a blip on their radar. "We have you."

"Roger, Minneapolis, can you give me a vector to Hebron?" Larry asked. "We're trying to locate an ELT out there somewhere."

"Roger Sheriff-1," the voice said. "Stand by."

A few moments passed, then the reply:

"Sheriff-1, fly to magnetic bearing two-three-five. Squawk 4342" Minneapolis replied. "That'll put you right there."

"Thank you much, Minneapolis," Larry said back, adjusting his transponder to the code he received so the radar would identify his blip as him. He pulled the stick and moved the helicopter toward the bearing until his compass read 235 degrees. Then he called the CAP search plane.

"CAP Search, Sheriff-1, I am flying on heading Two-three-five, do you have a signal?"

"Roger that, Sheriff-1," came the reply from the CAP plane that orbited above him somewhere in the dark. The little Cessna was still picking up the weak signal, but still couldn't tell where it was coming from either, although the pilot was beginning to suspect it was in the direction of Hebron, too. "Go ahead and travel in that direction and I'll see if I can get a fix on you. I am at five-thousand, right above Kramer."

Larry began to fly to the bearing he had gotten from Minneapolis. In the CAP plane the pilot leveled his wings and brought the plane into a straight and level flight. He was listening intently to the beacon coming weakly from his headset, as he watched the lights of the small helicopter head away from him to the southwest. The downed plane was out there somewhere. If he could get to a place that put the helicopter between the

CAP plane and the crash, the signal would be blocked, and he could extrapolate a bearing right to it.

Suddenly the signal went dead, just for a moment, and then popped up again. Larry had flown through the beam!

Larry, unaware that he had just tripped the beam, was looking at his gauges. He was becoming more and more aware of his slowly sinking fuel indicator. This would have to wrap up soon, or he'd have to cut off to refuel. He flew and waited for a signal from CAP. Then the radio crackled.

"Sheriff-1, hold your position right there!!" came the cry from the CAP pilot. Larry eased back the yolk and brought the chopper to a dead hover. The CAP plane banked sharply to come around and fly the opposite direction. As he passed the path of the helicopter, the signal died again. The CAP pilot quickly turned 90 degrees, flying away from Larry. The signal stayed silent. The CAP pilot did a quick azimuth calculation. A moment later the radio crackled again.

"Sheriff-1, you are blocking my signal to the beacon. That puts you directly between me and them. Continue on heading two-three-five. I'll continue to circle behind you and let you know if you get off course."

"Roger that!" Larry responded, excitedly.

Now he had them! He turned the chopper to the right heading again and pulled the throttle to full open slinging the chopper full tilt toward the signal, gradually descending as he went. In his head set, the whoop of the ELT signal continued to grow louder and louder.

At his truck, Jim listened intently to the radio transmissions from the two aircraft. The search teams were indeed in the wrong place. He began to plot a route to move further southwest, toward Thayer County. He and Jon ran their fingers along the black lines on the map, finding the roads to take them there. He radioed to Larry.

"CAP 1, this is CAP Search Actual," he said. "See if you can lock down that signal and we will start our move that way. Do you read, Larry?"

"Roger," Larry replied. "Let me see if I can get you an escort."

Larry flipped frequencies to the State Police band and was greeted by a patrol officer cruising a nearby highway. Larry quickly explained the situation and the officer promised to meet the CAP team at a nearby intersection to escort them full speed to Hebron.

The CAP teams jumped back in their vehicles and roared south toward the officer. They'd find them now.

Dad hunched on the side of the highway impatiently waiting for the next vehicle which was now coming over the hill. He wasn't as excited now, and was, in fact, getting pretty fed up with being run off of the road. He considered picking up a big rock to throw at them if they tried to go past too, or making some other means to make them stop, but thought better of it. He was in no condition to get into a fight.

As the lights crested the hill, he could see this one wasn't a large truck but a passenger car. As it approached speeding towards him, he began to wave and shout again. He thought with building anxiety that it appeared it was going to pass him, too, but then, to his surprise, it swerved to the side of the road, grinding to a stop on the rocky shoulder twenty feet away from him. He stood for a moment squinting into the bright headlights washing over him, temporarily blinding his one eye that could blurrily see, and then began to lurch toward the driver side.

Ricky Arnold and David McLaughlin sat stunned in the car. They had barely caught a glimpse of the man on the side of the road, but they both knew something was very wrong. It caused Ricky to slam on the brakes and pull off before him without a second thought. They could immediately see that the man wasn't dressed for the cold at all. His face appeared to be disfigured and twisted, like he was wearing some kind of mask.

"What the hell?" David muttered as he pulled up to the shambling figure. The man stood there for a few uncomfortable seconds, washed bright in the beams of the headlights, then began to stumble toward them. For a moment, they were both a little nervous.

Dad reached the driver's door and looked inside. Slowly the window rolled down and Dad saw David looking up at him.

"Man…" David said. "Are you all right?"

Dad hunched down, and leaned on the door, trying to catch his breath, then lifted his head to look at David and Ricky inside the car. They could see that it was no mask on his face. He was really messed up. He was covered in dark stains, bruises, blood – both dried and fresh. Dad took a few deep breaths, trying to find some words. He felt awkward all of a sudden and out of place before these two. Finally he spoke.

"I just crashed an airplane…" he said. "Can you give me a hand?"

Kim and I sat excitedly as we drove west on I-80 out of Lincoln, toward the highway that led to Hebron. It was right around 10 a.m. and the rain clouds that had come around that morning were beginning to clear up.

We had been anticipating this part of the trip the entire time and now the excitement of it was overflowing from us. At the small town of York, we turned south on Highway 81 and the conversation tapered off. We soon sat in silence and spent our time looking off into the distance of the road, towards the clumps of trees that dotted the landscape, wondering if they were the place. Neither of us had any idea as to where the crash had actually happened. Only that we ended up in Hebron.

Eventually a big red billboard appeared announcing to all that Hebron was just ahead. We stopped to look at it for a few seconds, perhaps to consider what our being there meant. I stood and looked at the sign. I was nervous, afraid of what I was about to find. I shook it off and got back behind the wheel of the Pontiac, and we continued, eventually turning off of the highway and into town.

The main street was brick and unassuming, like it had been there forever. We drove slowly through the little town, taking the place in as we followed the blue signs emblazoned with a big white H that guided us toward the hospital.

The town was neat and clean. All of the houses had neatly trimmed lawns and freshly painted fences. American flags fluttered proudly in the spring breeze everywhere we looked. The place wasn't at all what I had pictured it would be; rather it defied every image I had kept of it. It was actually beautiful and peaceful.

We rounded a corner and saw the hospital up ahead on the left. I wondered if this was the same road we had come up on that night, and if Dad saw the same things then that we saw now. It was a strange sensation, like déjà vu.

We pulled into the parking lot of Thayer County Health Services right on time for our appointment and found a place to park. The hospital was small, but modern looking and clean. I felt suddenly dizzy as I strode towards it. It was a surreal, dream-like dizzy. There was no way I could know this place, but yet I knew I did.

We went through the sliding glass of the entrance doors, and immediately saw an older, pretty lady standing there, beaming at us widely. She immediately reminded me of my grandmother, and I felt an instant bond to her.

I knew it was Helen. With barely a word I went to her and gave her a long warm hug, and she hugged me back, like we'd known each other for our whole lives, which I guess we had.

When I pulled away, there were tears in her eyes. Surprisingly to me, there were tears in mine too.

"I have thought about you so often all of these years," she told me. "I am so glad to see you now."

She took us around the corner and into an office where we were greeted by Joyce, who hugged us both and offered us a seat.

We told Joyce and Helen what we knew, which at that point wasn't much. They both shook their heads in disbelief the entire time.

"That poor, poor man," Joyce had said repeatedly as I told her the story of Dad's ordeal that night. I had never thought of it that way. I never saw my Dad as the victim until Joyce said that. Hell yes, he was a victim. He'd survived a plane crash!

I turned to Helen. It was strange to finally meet her. She had cared for me so long ago, and I never even knew who she was, now here she sat, next to me. I felt very privileged.

Presently, she took us into a small conference room. Around the table sat Dr. Bunting, Blanche and Evelyn, and Dick and Gary. They had all been there that night, and now they were all here. It was truly amazing to me. I could see that Kim felt the same way. It was almost like a dream.

I looked at Dr. Bunting. He was 82 years old now, but still held a sparkle in his eye. He had long retired and he and his wife had moved into a retirement home directly across from the hospital. I felt warmth and sincerity coming from him. I liked him immediately, and now hoped I could get him to talk about me and my family.

"What happened that night, sir?" I asked him.

He looked at me for a moment, sizing me up. Then he asked:

"Do you want the watered down pleasant version, or do you want to know what I saw?" He said. I was taken with his honesty.

"I just want to know what happened," I said.

"Well, I'll tell you," he said. "Throughout my entire medical career, I had never had a more frustrating night than that…"

Blanche stood chatting quietly with Evelyn, sitting at the small desk in the emergency reception area of the Hebron Hospital. It had been pretty quiet that night. Outside, it was cold, but the fog and clouds had lifted.

She was glad that there weren't a lot of people out on the highway tonight. It would have been a lot worse.

The hospital was empty of most staff, except for them and a few others, as usual. Not enough going on to warrant paying a doctor to hang around doing nothing. Besides, Dr. Bunting was right down the street should the police scanner near the desk or a phone call report a bad accident or other emergency that might be headed their way. Then they would call him and the on-call staff and have everything ready by the time the patients arrived. That was how it was done.

As usual, they had locked the big sliding doors overlooking the emergency driveway just after dark as soon as Dr. Pumphrey went home for the night. It wasn't long ago that that wayward goat had gotten through the automatic doors and into the reception area. In a panic, it had run amok and made quite a mess. It took them almost an hour to get it out! They had had other visitors in the past as well, including cows, snakes, and even a deer once, which had tripped the automatic door mechanism before it scampered away into the night.

Besides, nights like this had a foreboding nature about them. Blanche had heard stories lately of armed drug addicts bursting through emergency room doors of small hospitals elsewhere, and terrorizing the night staff as they rampaged to find something to get them high. It was just safer to keep the doors locked. The second someone called, they'd call the emergency staff, and unlock the doors, just like always. But, so far that night, the scanner and telephone were silent.

According to David and Ricky, Dad directed the car back up the road he had just walked down to get to the highway. He had mentioned the woods, and Ricky seemed to know where it was. As they approached the dike, Dad recognized the spot where he had found the road.

"There is a path along that dike," Ricky said. David swung the car off of the road and carefully directed it along the narrow abutment finding his way around the pond and the woods. Suddenly they emerged onto the frozen field. Dad pointed the way he had come and David maneuvered the car to rumble over the tilled-up soil in that direction. As he turned the car, the headlights splashed over the wreckage in the near distance, illuminating the forlorn hulk of our little airplane.

"Holy mother of God!" Ricky exclaimed, totally stunned by what he now saw.

The headlights fully illuminated the wreck and for the first time Dad could see the extent of the damage clearly, and it shocked him, too. The plane was totally destroyed. For a moment, as the reality hit him, he was taken by how they had survived at all.

David pulled the car to within several yards of the plane keeping the headlights oriented on it and stopped. He caught a momentary glimpse of a young boy's face in the pilot window. Dad and Ricky got out of the passenger door and headed over to the hole in the other side. David threw the car in park and quickly followed them.

A dirty little boy emerged from around the plane as they approached. The sight of him shocked David and Ricky both. Dad got to him first and could tell immediately by the look in his eye that Chris had seen her.

"Oh, son," he said to him, bending down and grasping Chris' good arm. "Why didn't you listen to me?"

Chris looked down and didn't speak. Dad hugged him, horrified.

"Go sit in the car," he said. "These men are going to take us to a hospital."

In the meantime, Ricky and David began to pick their way through the barbed wire and debris to get to the plane. Dad followed. David gingerly climbed into the wreckage and looked around, immediately spotting the little kids nestled in there. He was stunned. He had never seen anything like this.

All he knew was he had to get these kids out.

David gently reached down to pick up the little girl, and then carefully turned to hand her to Dad. Dad stepped around Ricky to get her, but suddenly as he reached, his body was wracked with intense pain, causing him to double over in agony. All night he had no real pain when he was digging me out and carrying us all around.

Now he suddenly, and much to his dismay, found he could barely even stand upright anymore. There was no way he could lift. Ricky saw his pain and grabbed him to help support him as the pain slowly subsided.

"Take it easy, man!" Ricky exclaimed. Dad leaned against him.

"I-I can't lift...I..." he grabbed his side again.

"Let's get you to the car," Ricky said, pulling Dad's arm around his shoulder to carry him away from the wreck. He was suddenly very worried that this guy was going to keel over and die right there. He was in bad shape. How he even made it to the road in that condition was beyond explanation.

"We'll get these kids, don't worry." Ricky said. He helped Dad over to the passenger seat and sat him down.

Ricky jogged back to the wreck. Dad turned and thought about Mom. He couldn't leave her like that. The flash of pain had subsided a little. If he didn't have to lift anymore, he'd be alright. He pulled himself to his feet, and patted the pocket on his flannel shirt where he had put the little pen light that had guided his way all night. It was still there, and he pulled it out.

When he depressed the button, the light dimmed. He pointed it towards his face and watched the light fade out and finally die. He looked at it for a second a little baffled by the timing, then flung it away. It had done its job. He knew where to go anyway. He called to Ricky and David:

"I'm going to see about my wife!" he shouted in a hoarse and raspy voice. Ricky called out an acknowledgement and Dad staggered across the dirt once more to where she lay. When he reached her lifeless form, covered with the blanket he had placed there and frozen to the earth, he knelt down beside her and gently took her cold, stiff hand.

In his wildest imagination, he had never thought it would be like this. He was trying not to think about what life was going to be without her; how he'd raise the kids, how he'd take care of things the way she had.

She believed in God, he knew. Even though he had always had his doubts about all that, he needed to say something, hoping that if her soul was still out there somewhere, he could bring her comfort. Sitting there in that field, there was no sign of God. But still he brought her hand to his lips, pressing them against her cold flesh. He began to whisper, and a tear trickled from his eye, falling from his cheek to mingle with her frozen blood.

"Our Father, who art in Heaven, hallowed be thy name…"

Ricky and David had gotten us placed in the car as Dad re-emerged from the darkness. Somehow they packed all of us in, including Chris, into the back seat, leaving room for Dad up front. Dad took one last look at the plane, feeling a tinge of gratitude for it. It had saved them, in its death. It was a strange thing to feel for an inanimate object, but still he did.

David slid in next to Dad and Ricky put the car in drive, slowly guiding it bumpily away from the plane and out of the field. Dad glanced once more in the direction of Mom, and slumped back in the seat, closing his swollen eyes. He was exhausted and suddenly in intense pain but grateful the ordeal was almost finally over. Ricky pulled the car onto the dirt road and sped down it, trying to avoid the jolts of the potholes the best that he could.

Eventually he reached the highway intersection, gave a quick glance in either direction and screeched onto it, heading south back toward Hebron. He punched the accelerator to rush us to the Hebron Hospital, which was the nearest one for many miles. A few minutes streaking down the highway and the turn off to it approached. Ricky screeched the tires as he thundered around the corner.

From the opposite direction, the lights of a small helicopter appeared over the horizon, bearing down on the beacon that silently pulsed from the shell of our airplane, the only sign of life left there.

Blanche was startled by the screeching of the tires coming roaring off of the street and into the emergency drive, and turned her head to face it. The car whipped around through the driveway, its lights flashing briefly into the room through the glass, and ground to an abrupt halt just outside the locked doors. The passenger door of the car burst open and a figure leapt out. It came rushing to the door and pulled on it.

When the person found it was locked they began to hit the glass repeatedly with an open hand, slapping loudly and rattling the whole thing in its frame. From a voice muffled beyond the glass she could hear the cries of the man to let him in. She could see his eyes widen when he saw her and Evelyn inside, a desperate look in them. He looked dirty and she could make out his long hair.

Both she and Evelyn stood and faced the door, trying to make sense out of the commotion. This smelled like trouble.

"That's Ricky Arnold," Evelyn said, suddenly recognizing the young man from town. "What in God's name is he doing?"

Behind him, a car door slammed and another figure approached the glass. David appeared beside Ricky and also banged his hand on the glass and waved them to come over to the door. Blanche approached carefully, trying to make out their muffled and excited speech. She wasn't sure what to make of this. She thought about the Davis boys just a few months ago who did this same exact thing, getting them to rush to the door before they ran off in a prank! That had scared Blanche half out of her skin, and neither of them were about to fall for those shenanigans again.

"Ricky, David, what's going on?" She asked from a few feet away, trying to sound stern. "What do you boys want?"

Both of them began chattering so loud she could hardly hear either of them. But she distinctly heard the words 'plane crash.'

"Plane crash??!" Blanche asked bewildered. She turned around to look at Evelyn standing by the desk. They both glanced at the scanner which still sat surrounded by eerie quiet. Evelyn shrugged befuddled. Blanche looked back at Ricky and David angrily.

"I don't know what this is about, but we didn't hear about any plane crash, or any other kind of crash," she insisted. "Is this some sort of joke?"

She was truly annoyed by now and a little frightened.

"Please, let us in!!" David pleaded. "There's a whole family here, and they need help! Lady, please!!"

Blanche stared a cool glare at him. "Well I am going to call the Sheriff! We'll just see about this!" She turned and hurriedly walked toward the phone, but was stopped in her tracks by Evelyn's startled cry.

"Blanche! My God!" Evelyn gasped.

A sudden enraged smash against the glass of the door prompted Blanche to wheel around. She gasped and grabbed her chest in shocked horror. The hand that had pounded the door slowly slid down, leaving a streak of blurred crimson where the fingers touched the glass. Beyond the smear she could make out a shambling figure beyond. She suddenly was too frightened to move. Evelyn was motionless. Then he spoke to her in a loud and angry croaking voice.

"Listen to me! I have crashed an airplane and my family is in this car and needs emergency care!" He barked. "Open this door! Please!"

Blanche slowly approached the door again. His face was covered in glistening blood. He had a ragged cut across his forehead. His clothes were tattered and covered in mud and blood. His one eye that she could see, obscured through swollen lids, was dark red and crazy looking.

"I...I..." she tried to say, but he slammed his hand into the door again, spattering more blood across the glass, making her leap. Her heart began to pound in her throat.

"OPEN THE GODDAMN DOOR!!!" He shrieked.

"Call Dr. Bunting!!" she turned and screamed at Evelyn, snapping her from her trance, and causing her to scramble at the telephone receiver. Blanche turned back to the man. She was now very scared.

"You have to wait for the doctor to come for us to admit you!" She said, hoping he got there quickly. The man pressed his face up to the glass glaring at her.

"A doctor is here!" He glowered. "NOW YOU OPEN THIS GODDAMN DOOR RIGHT NOW!!!"

He emphasized each of the last several words with a further pound on the glass by his bloody hand, causing her to gasp again. Suddenly the reality of the moment collided with her, and she realized what it really was that she was looking at. This was no joke! Something horrible had happened, and they hadn't heard!

"Oh my God! I'm sorry!" she hollered pleadingly, and turned to run to the desk and grab the keys to the door. She could see Evelyn was shaken to tears as she dialed Dr. Bunting's number with fingers trembling so bad she could hardly get them to work at all.

Blanche raced back to the door and quickly unlocked it. It flew open, nearly knocking her over as the man burst through. He had pulled a bloody little girl from the car. He was wild and agitated. He looked around the emergency room with a quick glance, then turned to glare at her. She stood immobile, and this seemed to enrage him further.

"Gurney?!" he barked. She jumped startled and immediately pointed to the hallway beyond the door where the ER gurneys were. He rushed in that direction. She went out the doors to the car, and was again horrified. Three more young children, all boys, remained in the car. She reached in and slowly lifted the one closest to her. David and Ricky hurried to the other side and began to extract the others. Carefully she entered the emergency room and made her way to another gurney near the door. The man had begun rummaging through the drawers of the ER, pulling out bandages and other items.

She slowly lowered the boy down on a second gurney, but his head was slick with blood and slipped from her grasp. It lolled backwards before thumping onto the smooth surface. She was shocked by the man's enraged bellow, and shrank in terror as he steamed into her.

"What are you doing!!?" he screamed. "Be careful!!!"

He roughly shoved her backwards from the gurney. She could feel the tense strength that pulsed through him as she staggered back. Instinctually, she stepped toward the boy again, but the man snapped at her. Even in his broken state, he exhibited enormous strength, which did not seem tempered by his rage. She was truly frightened of him.

"Get away from us!" he screamed at her, bloody spittle splattering her face and shirt.

She burst into tears and ran toward the reception area where Evelyn had gotten Dr. Bunting on the phone. Meanwhile Dad had found a fresh penlight in one of the drawers and was pointing it into Rick's eyes for a few moments. Then he tenderly stroked his head before going to the other children one by one, lying on gurneys now strewn about the hallway.

He ignored Blanche completely after that. Ricky and David stood in the waiting room and watched the scene unfolding in tired disbelief, having no idea what they were supposed to do. This was not what they had expected. For the moment, they just stood in silence, the blood of my family stained on their clothes.

The ringing of the telephone late at night was not a strange sound to Dr. Louis Bunting. He had been doing this work for a long time, and this seemed to be a common time for people to get into trouble. He'd seen a share of trouble during his time here as a doctor in Hebron, which was all of his life, save for his childhood. He grew up in Belvedere, a few miles up the road, and had gotten his MD from the University of Nebraska. Then he settled back down here where he could work at the little hospital in Hebron and enjoy the life of the country physician. He was a pilot, too, so he got to fly around and had seen the world, but the road had always led right back here - and probably always would.

He had seen Highway 81 change from a dirt road to a two lane highway, and had watched many a family farmer come and go as life whisked them into and out of the life of this town. Times around him had changed, but he was always here.

He reached into the darkness to pick up the phone. He could hear Evelyn's excited voice chatter in the headset as he lifted it to his ear.

"Dr Bunting, Dr. Bunting!" She shrieked.

"Slow down, Evelyn," he said calmly into the mouthpiece. "What's going on?"

"Oh God, Dr Bunting," she gasped. "A man just brought his family in here! Said they were in a plane crash and forced his way in. Now he's going crazy and has taken over the ER!"

Dr. Bunting took a moment to process the information, then sat up with a start, grabbed his glasses, and switched on the lamp on the table beside him.

A plane crash?? What the hell was going on?

"Where is he now, Evelyn?" he asked. "Is he injured?"

"He's in the hallway with his kids! They are all injured!" she cried. "There is blood everywhere and he won't let us do anything! What do we do??"

Oh my god, he thought, this wasn't a joke. There were wounded people there, and by the sounds of it, it had caught Blanche and Evelyn completely off guard. How was that possible?

No time to worry about that now.

"Okay, Evelyn, okay, calm down" he tried to reassure her. "If they are all breathing, make sure their airways are kept clear and control the bleeding as best you can. I am on my way. Call the Sheriff, and everyone else on call. Better call Pumphrey, too."

"Yes, Dr. Bunting," Evelyn whimpered. "Please hurry!"

"I'll be right there," He said and hung up the phone. He hurriedly shook of the remnants of sleep and quickly got dressed. He said a quick goodbye to his sleeping wife with a quick kiss to her cheek and left the house, emerging onto his big front porch. He trotted down the stairs and into his car, backed out of the driveway and gunned the engine, aiming the car toward the hospital a half mile up the road.

Evelyn spoke in hushed tones to Blanche behind Dad. She had just got off the phone with Dr. Pumphrey and he was on his way too. Rick was beginning to thrash about and was getting very agitated. Blanche tried to calm him.

"I'll do this, you go call Marilyn and Helen," Blanche said to Evelyn, trying to regain control of the situation. "And call the Sheriff and tell them what we have."

Evelyn hurried off and passed Dr. Pumphrey coming into the ER. He walked up to Dad and touched him, speaking gently. Dad wheeled to glare at him, but calmed down once he became aware that he was a fellow doctor. Dr. Pumphrey spoke to him about what happened for a moment. Dad wasn't very happy. They argued briefly about what was to be done.

Dr. Pumphrey wanted to stabilize us and admit us to the hospital, but Dad was still shaken by not being let in right away. Dr. Pumphrey knew Dad, although in his state it took a while to recognize him. In fact, Dad had been in that very hospital many times. He had flown the same Baron that now lay crushed in the field to the Hebron airport on several occasions to consult on surgery cases. If he knew where he was now, and who it was he was talking to, he didn't show it.

He was adamant about getting us to Lincoln, where he would be comfortable with our care. Dr. Pumphrey chose not to argue the virtues of the various facilities and told Dad that for the time being they should at least get x-rays of our injuries. Dad relented and Dr. Pumphrey called one of the staff to warm up the X-ray, which was in a little room next to the ER, and walked away.

He ordered Blanche to put an IV in Rick, whom he was most concerned about due to the closed injury he had suffered to his head. He gave Rick valium to calm him down. Seeing that someone was now actually in charge, Dad calmed down a little, but was still very on edge.

Dad turned to look at a nearby mirror. It was the first time he had gotten a look at his face. It was dirty and bloody and disfigured by swelling. He could still only see somewhat out of his left side. His right eye was still swollen and caked shut with dried blood. In the mirror, all he could see was a blurry smear where his face should have been.

Still, he could see enough. The hole in his cheek wasn't bleeding any more, but the side of his face was black with a massive bruise. His forehead was covered in dried blood from the gash he had suffered. He lifted his shirt and took a look at his injured side. A dark purple bruise spread across it, up to his armpit and disappearing into the top of his jeans. He gently lowered his shirt and turned his attention back to his face.

He gingerly picked bits of dried blood and bits of debris from the wounds, carefully probing tender spots and cuts to try and determine how thrashed he was. Then he noticed Dr. Pumphrey approach Rick.

He saw Dr. Pumphrey lift him off of the gurney, cradling him by his shoulders and knees. Dad saw Rick's head loll back and wobble side to side. Dad had learned that kind of lifting done to a patient with a head injury was dangerous. Rick's neck appeared to be completely unsupported. Dad quickly became quite upset by that.

"Doctor, you need to support his neck!" Dad shouted. Dr Pumphrey ignored the outburst and carried Rick into the X-Ray room. Dad shook his head. He was starting to get very agitated again. Dr. Pumphrey returned a short time later and laid Rick back down. He produced an X-Ray and held it up to the light. He and Dad studied it for a moment.

"Well there's no skull fracture," Dr. Pumphrey said. "We can clean him up."

"What about the cervical spine?" Dad said. He knew the cervical spine should always be considered when head wounds were involved. But that wasn't necessarily how everyone did it.

But Dr. Pumphrey stared at him. "I don't see any reason to do a cervical spine. He hurt his head, not his neck." He said, slightly annoyed by this other doctor.

"You should always…" Dad began. He cut himself off when he saw Blanche approach me, lying on my gurney. She held a suture kit. Dad turned his attention to her.

"What do you think you're doing?" He snapped. Blanche shrank back. "I was going to clean his leg wound and head," She said.

"What? Why??!" Dad shouted. "He's not bleeding anymore! The bleeding stopped out there!" He thrust his finger toward the door.

"He has to have these wounds totally irrigated!" Dad yelled and moved toward us. "He'll need surgery to close that, not a goddamn suture!" He swiped his arm and knocked the suture kit to the floor.

"Get away!" he yelled. Blanche burst into tears again and ran out of the ER. She was only trying to clean the child up so the doctors could stitch up the smaller wounds. She had done this a hundred times before, and she knew my wounds needed more than a suture. She knew what she was doing and was only trying to do her job, but this man didn't care.

Dad was now really mad. He lost it.

"You people don't know what you are doing!" he announced to the emergency room, stopping everyone in their tracks.

"We were stable for hours in that goddamn field and I am not going to lose one of these kids in an Emergency Room!!" he hollered, almost screaming.

Dr Bunting pulled up to the hospital just as Helen arrived. They greeted and walked into the hospital together, right into the middle of Dad's tirade. The entire ER was in chaos.

"Oh my Lord!" Helen murmured under her breath. Dr Bunting, shocked and taken completely off guard by all he saw, slowly approached Dad speaking as calmly as he could. Marilyn, the hospital Administrator had since shown up as well.

Dr. Bunting and Dad talked briefly. Dr. Bunting knew Dad, too. At that moment though, Dad didn't seem to recognize the place or any of his staff. Instead, he kept shouting and carrying on about nobody knowing what to do, and that they needed to just leave us alone. Dr. Bunting relented but tried to shift the focus. He was a pilot too after all, and knew there were procedural things Dad needed to do. If nothing else it would serve as a momentary distraction and get him out of the way for a second, and maybe give them time to restore some sanity to the place.

"You have to call and cancel your flight plan, Dr Styner." He said. Dad calmed down for a second when he knew Dr. Bunting was right and agreed to go to a phone in an office. He gave one more shout for nobody to touch us and left the ER. Dr Bunting followed Dad, but paused at Helen and Marilyn.

"Keep up on vitals, and let me know if anyone starts to slip," he said. "Nothing else, understand?"

Helen and Marilyn nodded and Dr. Bunting hurried to catch up with Dad. Helen went over to me, lying there next to Kim. She took our vitals and looked us over. She had been a nurse here for several years now, and knew all of us were in trouble. She touched my skin. It was still all wet and ice cold.

Her heart went out to us, and seeing us there so helpless she felt it start to break. She was very frustrated she could not be allowed to do more. She knew she could help us, if she was allowed.

Meanwhile, Chris was sitting near a small table in the corner of the room. He was quiet, and just sat watching the whole scene. Marilyn saw him and went over to him.

"How are you feeling?" she said. Chris looked at her and shook his head.

"I don't know what Dad's going to do," Chris said to her. "Mom pays all of the bills."

Marilyn was taken aback. In her frustration with Dad and his rant, she had forgotten in that moment about the tragedy of the whole thing. This boy's Mom was still out there, dead. She sighed deeply and patted the little boy's head. It was a very hard night.

Chapter 10

Larry eased up on the collective of the helicopter, slowing it as he passed over a small road and then over the northeast corner of a huge field. The whoop-whoop of the beacon was now screaming in his headset, so much so that he had to turn down the volume. He pulled to a hover and concentrated on a place encompassed by the darkness below them. He was close, he knew. He adjusted the helicopters big searchlight and flipped it on, and was immediately stunned. The wreckage of a small airplane appeared lit up exactly in the middle of the beam. He didn't even have to adjust it. He had hit the crash perfectly.

Then the realization of what lay before him settled on him. It was a terrible crash. He swung the light around and stopped as the beam washed over a covered figure several feet from the plane. He made out the arm and legs of the body lying there. He paused to point it out to Bruce, and then slowly set the chopper down.

When the skids hit, Bruce leapt out of the helicopter, gripping a hand spot light as he went and switched it on. Its beam pierced the hazy air and dust kicked up by the rotors as he swung it around, focusing from one thing to another.

Larry keyed the radio.

"CAP-1, Sheriff-1," he said somberly. "Looks like we got 'em."

"Roger that, Sheriff-1." Jim said. "Give us a location. We are almost there."

"Approximately three-quarter mile east of Highway 81, maybe three miles northeast of Hebron, just southwest of the intersection of two dirt roads." He said. "Approach on the dirt road to the east and parallel to the Highway and head north. You'll find it."

"Roger that," Jim said.

He could almost feel them screaming down the road toward him. At least this part of the mission was over.

Bruce first went to the body and lifted the blanket. Bruce shook his head and Larry could tell by his expression that whoever it was, she was dead. Bruce then moved to the wreckage and probed the interior with his light. A few moments later he emerged and began to look around the outside of the wreckage.

"CAP-1, Sheriff-1," Larry said. "We've got at least one dead here. We are searching for the others."

Larry switched to the common frequency to call the local Sheriff and report the crash, but was cut short. Excited chatter filled the frequency and told of a carload of badly injured people that had just gotten to the hospital in Hebron. Larry knew it was them.

How the hell was that possible?

The conversation with the words 'plane crash' was shocking of course, but when he heard 'all alive,' he couldn't believe it. He knew it was time to go there. He flipped the switch to activate the outside loudspeaker.

"Come back," he said. "They are in Hebron. Let's go there."

The light Bruce carried bobbed as he made his way back to the chopper in a quick jog. He appeared at the door and climbed in, pulling on the headset and clicking the seatbelt around him.

"There's one dead down there," he said breathlessly as they lifted off. "I couldn't find any more."

"There are five people that just showed up at Hebron," Larry told him. "I guess we'll know soon. CAP is on the way and will do a thorough search of the crash site."

"Roger that," Bruce said. Larry pointed toward Hebron and flew toward the green and white airport beacon there as it rose into sight beyond the horizon. He cut into the radio chatter and told the deputies who he was and requested a ride to the hospital. He wanted to get a look at them for himself.

A few minutes later, Larry set the skids of the helicopter down on the tarmac of the Hebron Airport, and shut the craft down. The fuel gauge read that that they were almost empty. Larry shook his head. There was something to be said for timing.

A local sheriff's car was waiting for them as they wound down the chopper and exited into the cold night. They quickly scrambled to the car and Larry got in, sliding beside the young deputy driving, while Bruce offered to stay with the chopper and get her fueled up.

The image of the crash was still burned in Larry's mind, and he could only imagine what these people, this family, had endured to make it this far. Anything he could do to help them now, he would.

A few minutes later, they pulled into the emergency room driveway and Larry hopped out of the patrol car, expressing quick thanks to the young deputy. He briskly walked through the cold to the same doors Dad had found locked only a little while earlier. He noticed it was smeared with someone's bloody handprints.

He fully expected that the scene would be chaos, and doubted this hospital saw much action like this very often. He pictured a flurry of activity as doctors and nurses rushed about trying to save the victims that had somehow been pulled from that airplane.

Instead, as he walked into the Emergency Room, he was struck dumbfounded, utterly baffled by what he saw.

Around the room stood several hospital staff, either in small groups or alone, some with arms crossed and frustrated looks on their faces, some nervously sipping coffee. A few caught his eye with restless glances as he entered, but no one said a word.

The room was practically silent. He looked past the fidgety staff towards the motionless forms of the patients lying on stretchers beyond them. Three small children were laid on their backs, each with blood stained gauze bandages wrapped around their heads. One had a bandage loosely wrapped around his leg, which was currently propped to the side. Over the boy stood a filthy man, bending down and appearing to inspect the wound under the bandage. He was the only visible person providing any kind of care to any of the victims.

It felt like something out of the Twilight Zone. Larry had been a cop for a long time, but had never seen anything even remotely resembling the scene that was laid out before him right then. He glanced around at the staff again. They muttered hushed but sharp tones at each other. Many slowly shook their heads side to side. None made any attempt to help.

A surreal feeling crept over Larry. The man was dirty and bloody from head to foot. His clothes were mud-caked and tattered. His head was bent forward, but Larry could clearly make out the open gash that extended from his forehead into his hair. He could see that his face was disfigured with swelling and other trauma.

Just then, the man glanced in his direction briefly giving Larry a good look at him. His face looked like a prize fighter after a very bad several rounds. It was grotesquely swollen and his eyes were mere slits recessed into red, bloody, swollen flesh. Larry was amazed he could see at all. He didn't move around the children so much as he lurched. Larry could not believe his eyes. Was this the pilot? From the looks of him it was amazing that he was even standing, yet alone providing care!

Why was no one doing anything to help him, Larry wondered intently?

He spotted an older lady who appeared to be hospital staff standing near another dirty and bloody young boy that he hadn't noticed before. He was sitting off to her side, and she stroked his hair gently as she stared transfixed by the spectacle along with everyone else.

Another victim by the looks of him.

He had a blood stained bandage on his hand and his arm was held in a cloth sling. He stared in stunned silence at the man as he worked around the other children. To his other side, two older men in long white coats were staring toward the man and quietly speaking. They appeared to be doctors.

Larry made his way to them and introduced himself. He was a little angry by all of this.

"I just found their wreckage," he said. "Can someone tell me why no one is helping that man?"

One of the doctors huffed a snorted and sarcastic laugh and turned, walking away from them down the hall. The other lifted his hands in an exasperated gesture.

"He won't allow us to treat them!" Dr Bunting said loudly, in an exasperated and amazed voice. He was clearly incredibly frustrated.

"He exploded on my staff, and now he won't let us treat them!" He waved his hand around the room. "Any of them! He is extremely agitated, and frankly I am afraid for my staff's safety!"

Larry couldn't believe it. Why would he deny his kids care from these people?

"Does anyone know his name?" Larry asked. The nurse by the boy spoke up from beside him.

"It's Doctor Styner," Marilyn said. "He's a doctor from Lincoln."

But Larry already knew where he was from, and the name struck him into silence. He had in fact known Dad for years, having seen him and spoken often with him at Lincoln General, where Larry was a frequent fixture in the course of his job. The realization of the discovery hung confusingly in the air as he watched this wretched figure before him feverishly working on his kids as the hospital staff looked on, unable to aid in any way. Right here, like this, Larry did not even remotely recognize this man.

Another pretty young nurse quietly sidled up to one of the little boys and began to fasten a blood pressure cuff around his bicep. The man shot a look around at her that made her freeze, but then he turned his attention back to the other boy and let her continue without a word.

Helen softly but quickly smoothed the blood pressure cuff over Rick's arm. He wasn't in good shape, she knew. Dr. Bunting had already seen he had a bad head injury, but Dr. Styner had shut them down early on, and no further diagnosis had been made or any more X-rays taken. She felt compelled to at least try to help these poor kids, though. She refused to just watch them die doing nothing. So far, Dad had not made any steps to stop her from checking vitals. So she did what she could. It was all she could do.

She caught the eye of the young policeman that had just walked in. He looked anxious, too. She was sure this had to look crazy to him. He nodded to her and she smiled nervously, and then shifted her attention back to the little boy before her. She felt helpless, like she was walking on eggs.

Larry slowly walked toward Dad, who defensively looked up as he approached.

"Dr. Styner?" he said softly. Even through the swollen face, Larry could detect the hostility in Dad's eyes. When Dad recognized him as a cop, his demeanor softened a little. He sheepishly looked back at the young boy on the table, and brushed his hair back from the bloody wound on his head. Dad didn't seem to recognize Larry as someone he knew, and if he did, it didn't show.

"Dr. Styner," Larry said again. "Do you know who I am?" Dad looked at him again. He was obviously in shock. He appeared to be operating on nothing but adrenaline. He didn't respond.

"What happened?" Larry asked. It was a silly question, but he had to say something.

"We...crashed," Dad croaked. "Out in the field..."

He looked down and stared at the boy for a few seconds. Up close, Dad looked even worse. His lips were swollen and cracked, slurring his speech slightly. Up close it was easy to see that his right eye was swollen completely closed and dried blood and dirt filled in every inflamed groove around it, sealing the eyelid shut.

A small flap of skin on the right side of his head had been peeled back, and was now stuck roughly back in place, held there only by the coagulated blood that still oozed down his forehead and over his cheek. Another deep wound was obvious on the same cheek, but wasn't bleeding so bad anymore, although the stains on Dad's clothes seemed to indicate that it did a great deal at some point. Larry could make out dark circular bruises on Dad's face and head, which he recognized had been made by the casings of the instruments when Dad's face was pummeled into them on impact.

His left shoulder was obviously immobile, and by the way he walked, Larry could tell he had suffered at least some level of internal injuries. In short, Dad was a real mess. Larry could scarcely believe he could even be on his feet at all in his condition, yet alone taken control of this situation.

Helen moved up quietly beside Dad. Larry could see she wanted to take the young boys vitals. When Dad became aware of her, he quickly shifted himself in front of her to head her off, defiantly glaring at her. Larry could see her fear, even if it was only for a moment. He was still a cop, and wasn't about to let the situation spin any further out of control especially into violence. He stepped between them, facing Dad.

"Look, doc, she just wants to take his vitals," Larry said.

"They don't know what they're doing!" Dad snapped, glaring at her over Larry's shoulder. Larry tried to calm him.

"It's just vitals, doc," he said. "Let's just let her do that."

He gently touched Dad's arm, not sure what he would do if Dad got pissed and decided he wanted to fight. Larry would have really hated to force him down and put him in handcuffs. The act of forcing him to the ground alone might just kill him in his state.

However, Larry was surprised that Dad moved with him as he led him a short way from the table. Helen began to fasten the cuff around my arm. The other staff didn't move.

Dad stared at the floor and began to tell Larry what he thought had happened. Dad told him a staggering story of the field and his search for the highway and the men who picked him up. Dad looked around for them for a moment, but didn't see them. Ricky and David had already left, not knowing what else to do. Dad never got to thank them.

He went on to tell Larry about the locked door and that he didn't think the staff at the hospital was able to provide us the care we desperately needed. He went on about Rick's neck, and things that they didn't do that they should have. Then suddenly he looked at Larry with desperation and grabbed his sleeve.

"Please," he said in a hoarse whisper. "Please, just get us to Lincoln."

Larry realized in that moment that if any of these kids were going to get help tonight, it would be up to him.

It had nothing to do with the competency of the staff here he knew; it had to do with getting them somewhere where the doc would let them be treated. He pressed his lips together considering his options and gently patted Dad on the shoulder. Dad turned and moved back to the table where I lay. He didn't yell at the nurse this time, but just let her do her thing. He was resolved, for the moment.

But Larry had a few tricks he could try and asked one of the staff if he could use a telephone, then followed him out of the room to an empty office just up the hall. Helen glanced up to see him go. She felt better when he was there. She tried to ignore the man glaring at her as she tried to work, but it didn't help much.

Jim spoke into his radio as his truck negotiated a quickly executed sharp right turn onto another dirt road a few miles northeast of Hebron and parallel to Highway 81.

"Where are you?" He said. The tin can tone of Jon's voice replied:

"I'm with the trooper. We're on some farm road in the vicinity of the main dirt road intersection," Jon said, referring to another intersection crossing the road he had just turned into. "I just ran into a dead end. I'll have to find my way around to get back to you, over."

"Roger," Jim replied. He glanced over at Don who was listening intensely at the DF headset. Without looking up, he pointed down the road, motioning Jim to keep going. They were close.

Behind them, the other CAP truck followed closely, obscured in the cloud of dust Jim's truck kicked up, tinted red by the tail lights as they barreled along the road. Jon and the trooper were behind them somewhere, and coming up fast, but Jim couldn't see them yet.

"Let me know when you're back at the intersection," Jim said into the mic. "The DF is almost pegged out. We're definitely in the right place, over."

"Roger, out." came the reply from Jon.

Jim stared into the blackness all around them, the brown earth of the dirt road zooming under them, each bit reflected for a moment in the bright yellow headlights. He tried to scan the area ahead, trying to pick up some sign of the plane. He was no longer looking for burn evidence, or a large debris field, just a wreck. If that plane had burned, there would be no one going to the hospital, that was for sure - unless it was for the morgue.

That was good, but it made the search difficult to do in the dark, but that's why they started putting ELTs in planes in the first place.

To his left he could see a stand of trees some distance off, silhouetted against the black backdrop. Another small road appeared on the left ahead. He began to slow as he approached it. Just then Don shouted:

"Whoa! Stop here!"

Jim hit the brakes and brought the truck to a skidding halt across the rough surface of the road. He grabbed the radio microphone.

"This is CAP-1! CAP 2, hold your position!" he barked into it.

Don jumped out of the truck as soon as it stopped, and stood in the middle of the intersection. He held the DF in front of him, swinging it slowly back and forth and listening to the intensity of the tone waver in his headset. He stared straight ahead, into the blackness beyond the roads, washed by the headlight of the other truck which was rolling up in a cloud of dust to stop on the side of the road behind Jim.

Jim threw the truck in park and jumped out. This road had to be the one Larry had identified, he thought. Don turned to face roughly southwest and stopped, standing perfectly still for a few moments. Then he lifted his finger and pointed to an unseen spot somewhere in the distance directly ahead.

"There it is," he said. Jim stared at the spot shrouded in darkness for a second, momentarily relieved.

They found it.

He turned to address the team members that were dismounting the two vehicles.

"All right team, let's form a line south from this intersection! Twenty-five foot interval!" he shouted. "Keep up good verbal communications! Report anything you see immediately! Stay on line and keep good visual contact with your right and your left. Understand?!"

A chorus of 'Yes, Sirs' was shouted from the team.

They quickly finished their equipment checks and the beams of several high powered flashlights popped on, one by one, piercing through the dust that was held suspended in the frozen air around them. They began to work their way down the road to their relative positions roughly 25 feet apart until they each stood in place facing silently into the darkness in front of them, waving their lights from side to side, each one in their own secret way hoping they would be the one to find it.

Jim hurried back to the cab of his truck and called Jon on the radio.

"We've got the signal strong on the DF, and are organizing the sweep right now," he said. "What's your twenty?"

"I'm still working my way to you about two miles south," Jon replied. "I'll see you there."

"Roger that. I am starting the sweep." Jim replied. "Out."

He made his way down the line to where Don stood facing into the dark.

"Move out!" Jim hollered. He watched as the team carefully made their way into the shallow ditch beside the road. Voices began to call out through the dark, warning others about the barbed wire fence bordering the field on the other side of the ditch and other hazards as they moved onto the plowed field.

They moved slowly, but with purpose. Everyone was trained here. They all knew what to do. After several long minutes, there came a startled cry from one of the cadets just off to Jim's left.

"Plane!" the voice shouted excitedly. "We have the plane! We have the plane!!"

Other voices called out excitedly in acknowledgement, and the rest of the team began to converge on the source of the call. Jim stood and called out:

"Everyone assemble on the plane!" he called out towards the team. "Watch for debris and be careful!"

"I've got something here..!" Another young voice yelled out from the darkness. "Jesus! I think I found someone!"

Jim quickly made his way over to the young man, standing still and staring at the dirty and bloody blanket spread across the top half and head of the woman, lying frozen to the ground. He picked his way over the debris that scattered around the area until he got to him. When he saw the body, he bent down and touched her hand. It was ice.

There was nothing they could do for her.

Jim turned to go toward the plane, but as he did he noticed the cadet who discovered the body was still staring at her, as if in a trance. Unfortunately, he had seen that before. The horror of death when a young cadet sees it for the first time can freeze him up. It just sucks you in like a vortex and won't let you go. Jim patted him on the shoulder. It was a hard part of the job, but an unfortunately necessary part, nonetheless.

"There's nothing we can do for her," he said gently. The cadet glanced at him nervously and swallowed hard.

"You did your part for her, okay?" he said. "You found her, and that's your job. That's what we do."

The young man nodded, the horrified look still embedded on his face.

"Let's assemble the team." Jim said, and took the cadet by the shoulder, guiding him away from the lifeless woman.

The young man nodded, his eyes still fixed on Mom for some time as they both walked over toward where the rest of the team had assembled near the motionless corpse of our shattered airplane. Their lights washed over the wreckage, illuminating it fully.

Down the road, Jim could see the blue and red lights of the State Trooper flashing through the fog of dust suspended on the road, coming toward them. It pulled in near the other vehicles and the Trooper and Jon got out, making their way to where the rest of the team stood.

Jim was awestruck. The area around the crash was littered with clothing, as if it had exploded from the plane on impact. The plane itself sat dug into the ground, and was completely twisted and ravaged. The entire empennage was buckled and bent down from the fuselage at a weird angle. Various chunks of assorted debris littered the path it had traveled.

The right side of the nose and the copilot compartment were peeled open exposing the gaping wound through which Mom had been flung. The left side was crumpled and shoved inward. Both wings were gone just past the engines. The propellers were still somehow connected to the engines but were bent into spirals from whipping into the ground as they impacted. The right windshield was shattered out, and the remaining plexiglass fragments hung jaggedly inside the frame.

The entire plane was wrapped in barbed wire. Near the rear, the small cargo door was open and bent forward. The plane was a mess, but somehow had stayed together and didn't burn up. How that happened was a miracle, Jim thought.

Don made his way toward the hole in front of the right wing and gingerly worked his way into the wreckage, sliding into the pilot seat. He shined his light around the interior of the cockpit pausing at the smears of blood and dirt that commingled all around him. Then he reached down to the left of the pilot seat on the bulkhead, to where the ELT silently pulsed its signal into the air. He felt underneath it for the override switch and flipped it.

The signal went dead.

Thousands of feet above them, Looking Glass disengaged, turned toward Washington D.C. and headed home.

Jim looked at the team moving slowly around the area as they searched for anyone else. Voices called out to each other as they systematically searched. They all knew what to do. They had done one hell of a job tonight that was for sure. He was very, very proud of them all.

Mission accomplished.

Jim continued to take in the scene as Jon made his way to him. They both stared in silence as the cadets continued to search around the plane for other victims.

"People survived this?" Jon wondered aloud. Jim nodded encompassed in his own disbelief of the fact.

"So far," he said.

Jon shined his light on the plane slowly looking over the paint and markings. He carefully walked around it, and then returned to where Jim stood.

"I know this plane!" he said, realizing that he recognized it from the Lincoln airport. He had seen it there often, and had talked to Dad on several occasions about it. It was a nice plane.

He shook his head. "I think it belongs to a guy named Styner…"

Larry came back into the Emergency Room. Nothing had changed. He walked over to Dad standing protectively over us, addressing him as he approached.

"Doc, I made a call to the Lincoln Air National Guard," he said. "They are aware of the situation and are making arrangements to get you to Lincoln." For the first time, Larry saw a hopeful look from Dad.

"It might be a while, but they are on the way," Larry continued. "They're sending a big helicopter. Is there anyone you need to call?"

Dad nodded and Larry asked one of the hospital orderlies to take him to a telephone. Larry told Dr. Bunting and Dr. Pumphrey of the arrangement, and they began to make preparations for the transport. Larry ordered people to move their cars so they could land the helicopter in the parking lot of the hospital. We would leave from there.

The telephone rang. Bruce Miller opened his eyes to the darkness of the room. His wife Diane slept peacefully beside him. The phone harshly jangled out from beside him again. He shook the cobwebs out of his head and reached out into the darkness to feel for it, then brought the receiver to his head.

"Hello?" he mumbled tiredly. There was a moment of silence. "Hello??" he said again.

"Bruce?" the creaking and broken voice said. It was Jim. Bruce immediately recognized him, but he sounded much different.

The bad feeling Bruce had been carrying all night had receded like the tide as he drifted to sleep, but it suddenly came rushing back at the sound of Dad's voice.

"Jim?" he said.

"Bruce?" Dad said again. "There-there's been an accident...the plane..." Tension wound down Bruce's spine.

Oh my god, he thought and his heart began to pound.

"The plane crashed..." Dad said, his voice quivering. "Char is dead, Bruce. I saw her. She's dead."

Oh no, no, no! Bruce pleaded silently to no one. He reached over to touch Diane. She felt the tension in his touch and woke immediately to sit up beside him. A million thoughts swirled in his head.

"Wh-where are you?" he managed.

"We're at Hebron hospital right now, but were coming there," Dad said. "They're flying us there..."

Flying them? An evacuation? Why not treat them there?? Bruce thought. He didn't get that one, but shook it off.

"Are you okay, Jim? The kids?" Bruce said.

"Char is dead." Dad replied. "I'm pretty bad, too. The kids...we're all bad...all bad..."

Bruce knew he had things to do. His heart pounded in his chest.

"Okay, you just get up here, and I'll make sure things are ready," Bruce said. "Just get up here."

"Can you call Clarke? Have him meet us at the airport?" Dad said. "The National Guard...they're sending helicopters...I need him."

"Of course," Bruce replied. "I'll take care of it."

Dad grunted a response and the line went dead. Bruce ears rang.

Jesus Christ.

Diane gripped his hand. Char and she were very good friends. He hung up the phone then quickly dialed another number.

"Lincoln General Emergency..." came the voice of one of the nurses. Bruce knew her, but couldn't remember her name just then. He asked for Ron and waited a few moments.

"This is Dr. Craig," Ron's pleasant voice came over the line.

"Ron its Bruce Miller," he said. "Listen, we need to get the ER ready. Jim Styner has been in a plane crash in Hebron. He and his kids are badly injured...his wife..." he trailed off.

Beside him, Diane tightly gripped his hand and her body began to hitch with sobs.

From the warmth of his sleep, Clarke Mundhenke was drawn to the ringing of the telephone next to his bed. He did not know what time it was but he sensed it was early. He felt Sharon stir beside him and without opening his eyes reached over and after a bit of fumbling picked it up. His job as a chaplain kept him up sometimes, but as a man of God he was obligated to respond. He was aware of the sleepy hoarseness of his voice as he spoke.

"Hello..?"

"Clarke..? Bruce Miller." The voice said. Clarke opened his eyes. Bruce? Why was he calling? His attention was suddenly focused.

"Bruce?" Clarke greeted him. "How are you? Is everything alright?"

"Clarke, Jim Styner crashed coming home," Bruce said. Immediately Clarke thought of an auto crash. The thought of the plane didn't hit him immediately.

"Crashed?" Clarke stammered, surprised. He would have to prepare to comfort his family…then he remembered that he thought we were on vacation…that we had flown to California in the airplane.

"Oh, my God…" he almost whispered. "The plane?"

"Yeah, he went down in Hebron." Bruce said.

Clarke refrained from babbling the myriad of questions that immediately flooded his mind. Jim's family was on that plane. It would be a big funeral, was his first thought. Then Bruce floored him again.

"He's alive. His kids survived too, but they're all in bad shape." Clarke could not believe his ears. They survived a plane crash? Then it occurred to him that Bruce hadn't mentioned the wife.

"Charlene?" he asked. The pause that followed was all he needed to hear. He imagined Bruce shaking his head.

"No," was all he heard.

The gravity of the news swirled into Clarke. Sharon had sat up next to him hearing Charlene's name. They were all friends. Charlene was a strong member of their church. They had all just been skiing together in Colorado just a couple of weeks ago, where Dad had hurt his arm in a nasty fall.

He was momentarily overcome, and then his thoughts went to Bruce. Jim was his partner. He knew they were great friends. Dianne Miller and Char were very close, like sisters, Clarke had always thought.

"Bruce, my God! What can I do to help?" he asked. "Are they at Lincoln General?"

"No, they are going to be moved from Hebron in helicopters." Bruce replied. "The Air National Guard is going to get them and bring them here. I have to go to the hospital and get things ready there."

"Okay," Clarke responded making mental notes.

"Jim asked for you, Clarke," Bruce said, which took Clarke slightly aback. Bruce continued. "He wants you to meet him at the airport when they get here."

Clarke immediately understood. He was their pastor, and they were coming out of hell. He needed to be there to comfort them and let them know they weren't alone. The souls of those kids might be in the balance. Suddenly, he realized how important his mission had become. He was compelled to offer Bruce his counsel, but realized Bruce's night had just begun. He had to get ready to save those kid's lives.

"Should I call anyone?" Clarke asked. Bruce said he was already taking care of it. He had been through a lot tonight, and Clarke really wanted to take a moment to make sure he was all right, but they both needed to get going.

"Thank you for calling, Bruce. I will head out there right now," he said, then added: "God bless you."

The line was silent for a moment.

"Thanks," Bruce said and the line clicked and went dead. Clarke turned to look at Sharon, who stared back, wide-eyed.

Gary pulled up to the volunteer fire building in Hebron. Dick was already there and had the truck running and the heater warmed up. Gary flipped the collar of his heavy and warm turn-out jacket up to circle around his neck and rubbed his gloved hands together. It was cold, and early. Too early for this, but these things were never convenient.

His job as a volunteer fire fighter kept life interesting, at least. It was a diversion from his regular job as a mail carrier in Hebron and nearby Belvedere, as well as the surrounding rural areas. Being a volunteer fireman broke up the monotony on occasion, even if the job was sometimes sad or tragic. Of course, he didn't create the tragedy; he just helped clean it up. Someone had to.

The call about the plane crash had come in from the Sheriff about a half hour ago. He didn't know much about it; just that a family had gone down and there was some hub-bub at the hospital with the survivors. He had never heard of a crash around here with survivors. But like most of them, there was death, too. His orders were to retrieve the body of a woman still out there in the field where the wreck happened.

Gary greeted Dick, and then slid in the passenger side of the big truck. They backed out of the driveway and headed out towards the old pond where the wreckage was reported to be. He had been out that way many times over the years, so knew right where it was. They turned north on Highway 81, past Monument Road, then turned right onto a dirt road that intersected the highway. He had no way of knowing that it was the same road Dad had lurched down a couple of hours prior.

Slowly they drove over the rough surface, occasionally slowing to shine their powerful spotlight over the darkened ground adjacent to the road. When they reached the pond, they moved slowly off the road, and across the dike that extended onto the field. Their headlights picked up the wreckage almost immediately.

"Jesus Christ!" Dick muttered.

He stopped the truck and they stared at the wreckage for a few moments, taking in the utter devastation that lay before them. Slowly, they got out of the truck, and armed with high power hand lights, walked across the field towards the corpse of the plane. Gary looked it over for a few minutes, and then turned to his right to move along the tree line, shining his light through the branches. Eventually he came to the spot where the plane had gone through the trees. There was a wide gap that the plane had carved as it slammed through. Trees lay broken and laid over and brush was strewn all around, mingling with scraps of metal and debris.

To the right he spotted what appeared to be the left wing of the plane, lying tangled in the thick brush in a crumpled heap. He shined his light up twenty feet into a large tree nearby and saw where the wing had impacted it, ripping the top ten or so feet off and flinging it several yards away. The tree was about five inches thick, and the force that sheared it off had to be incredible.

He turned and observed the rest of the newly established clearing. The other wing lay in a pile of brush and branches on the ground, mangled. All manner of other debris was strewn around the trees and had been carried out onto the field by the forward momentum of the impact. He considered the plum thicket that surrounded the thin forest. A section of it along the obvious path we had followed was smashed down. Apparently, the plane had slammed into the trees, and as it spun to the left, its inertia was taken and it dropped onto the bushy and thick plum trees. They must have acted like a cushion as the plane smashed through them, he thought. That's why, incredibly, the plane wasn't ripped apart when it hit the hard-packed ground of the field.

"Jesus," he muttered to himself. "If you were going to crash a plane, that's the way to do it."

His thoughts were cut short by Dick's shout over by the main hulk of the wreckage.

"Gary!" he called out. "I found her!"

Gary made his way toward the bright spot of Dick's light, where he stood over a white bulge on the ground. Both of them had seen their share of bodies before, but it was always a bit of a shock to see the seemingly infinite forms that death can leave a person in. This would be no different. They weren't machines in this job. They were painfully cognizant of the fact that those whom they recovered were once living breathing entities, usually just a short time ago.

Now they stood over the body of my mom, and had their own thoughts about her…someone's wife, someone's daughter, someone's mother. No doubt she never would have foreseen that her life would end here, literally frozen to the ground - dead in this field. Who could imagine that?

Dick stooped down and lifted the small blanket that covered her and tossed it aside, exposing the horror of her death to the glare of the bright lights that they carried. There was little doubt in either of their minds that she had died quickly. She probably died in the plane, before she was ejected, or maybe in the process of being ejected.

Either way, judging by the speed of impact indicated by the path of destruction Gary had seen, she never even knew what hit her. At least there was some comfort in that. Neither of them cared much for the idea of suffering, after all.

She certainly did not suffer.

Dick left Gary with her, and went back to the truck, starting it up and bringing it over to near where she lay. He extracted from the back a modified stretcher, known as a scoop that was used for the purpose of collecting the remains of bodies which were not fully intact.

They opened the scoop and placed each half on either side of her, then gently slid it closed under her, sliding it closed a few inches at a time, carefully breaking the icy bonds that held her fast to the frozen earth of the field.

Gary gingerly shifted her stiff body as necessary to aid Dick, and then the plates slid fully in place under her. Finally, she could be taken from that place. They covered her remains with a heavy wool blanket, which they gently tucked around and under her. Then they stooped and lifted the stretcher and carefully carried it to the back of the truck, sliding it into the interior and latching it down.

She would be taken care of now.

They drove in relative silence to the hospital, speaking only to express the disbelief at what they had seen in the field. It was hard to believe anyone had survived that. They had seen no shortage of gruesome and nasty accidents in the farms, fields, train tracks and roads around here, but that scene was truly amazing to both of them. Everyone in that plane should have been killed. Life is sometimes unbelievable, they both thought.

Eventually, they pulled up to the emergency entrance of the hospital without fanfare and quietly carried the basket containing Mom into the emergency area. The staff stood around, some of whom were preparing the little kids to be moved. Gary overheard they would be flown by helicopter to Lincoln.

Most of the staff just watched. A broken and bloody form of a man stood over one of the children watching intently as the staff stood by. It wasn't at all what Gary would have pictured this type of accident to be like.

A young sheriff stood by watching as well, standing near the man, talking gently to him. Marilyn saw them come in and moved over to Gary.

"Just put her there," she said, pointing to an out of the way spot near the admission desk. "We'll take care of her from here."

Gary and Dick obliged, gently placing the basket on the floor. Gary considered it for a moment. The form under the heavy blanket suddenly looked so small. He looked around at the man and the little kids, all of whom had been dragged through the worst that night, from what he'd seen at the crash site.

He suddenly felt sad for them. He had brought a family back together again for the last time, but he wished it could have been different. You just never get used to this.

Dick patted his shoulder as he passed.

"Let's go," he said. Gary followed him out of the hospital into the cold night. He took a deep breath of the cold, sharp air. They had done their job. Now they could go home.

He paused to look through the blood smeared glass of the entrance doors to the emergency room at the family beyond once more. His heart went out to them, and he hoped those kids would be alright. Then he turned and walked away, not looking back.

Bruce hung up the phone from his call to Clarke and got himself ready to go to the hospital to get everything ready. He knew that word was getting around about Dad and that lots of people would be showing up and would need to be managed. Everybody liked Dad. He was very popular with the staff and always treated all of them with respect and kindness. Now they would all want to help, he knew, and he wouldn't deny anyone that. It is important for people to help their friends. Not many people get to do that in the direct way that they would. It was a privilege of the medical profession, and he would get them all involved somehow. He was sure that the staff would be able to keep everyone busy tonight.

Another thought occurred to him as he was tying the laces on his shoes.

He sat up and stared into the dimly lit room. He steeled himself for the next call he had to make. Jim would be in no shape to do it so it had to be him.

They had to know.

He got up and went to his study to find his phone book in his desk. Dianne came in with a fresh cup of coffee for him. Her eyes were puffy and swollen from crying. She was really torn up over Mom. He produced the book from a drawer and found a number, and then he lifted up the receiver and held it to his cheek with his shoulder, listening to the dial tone, willing his fingers to dial. He took a deep breath and listened to the tones of the keys as he pushed them. Beside him Dianne had sat down and taken his other hand. She wept quietly.

In Fullerton, California, Uncle Ken woke up to the sound of the phone. Betty groaned a little beside him, but stayed asleep. Ken reached over and picked up the phone. He recognized the voice on the other end, but only vaguely.

"Uh, Ken, this is Bruce Miller, err, Jim Styner's partner." Bruce said.

Bruce? Of course, but why was he calling? He looked at the clock and saw it was a little after 2 a.m. west coast time. He was confused and still fuzzy with sleep.

"What can I do for you, Bruce," Ken asked groggily.

Bruce took a deep breath and told him what he knew about our plane and then about Mom. He told them that we had to spend the night in the field. He told him that we were all trying to get to the hospital right then, and still struggling to live.

Ken listened intently to Bruce's words and acknowledged them in stunned grunts, distracted by the increasing thud of his pulse in his head.

"I have to get to the hospital, now." Bruce said. "I'll be in touch later."

Ken thanked him in a muttered voice and hung up the phone.

He sat silent and motionless for what seemed a long time. Betty Lou awoke and sensed his tension. She rolled over to look at him sitting there staring into the space of the darkened room.

"Who was that," she asked. "What's wrong?"

Ken turned to face his wife. He had no idea how to say what he was about to say. He reached out and took her hand.

On the other side of the house my cousin Jeff was awakened from his deep sleep by the awful sound of his mother screaming her sister's name over and over again.

Chapter 11

Dr. Pumphrey walked through the ER and checked to make sure all was ready to go. It had been a long night and he was exhausted from the strain of the situation. His staff was emotionally chewed up from having to just watch, unable to do anything. It wasn't fair to them, but Dad had the final say. He could legally stop the care, and there was nothing the hospital could do. He refused to listen to their futile attempts to get through to him. If he was willing to risk his children's lives over what Dr. Pumphrey and Dr. Bunting agreed was a misunderstanding, and ignorance on Dad's part about how they managed their patients, then there was nothing he could do about it. That would be on Dad's shoulders. He knew Dad fairly well from the trips he had made to Hebron in the past and had always respected him as a very qualified surgeon, but now he was just interference. It was frustrating.

At the reception desk, Dr. Pumphrey glanced at the basket containing Mom's body. He got the attention of a nurse and pointed to it. No one had touched it since they had brought her in.

"Move her to an exam room, please," he said. "Dr. Bunting will care for her."

He shook his head, and then he walked over to Rick. They had removed his I.V. in preparation for the flight. He was well sedated now, so Dr. Pumphrey didn't see the need for it anymore. He reached down to feel Rick's pulse, which was strong, then stood back in silence.

Larry sensed Dr. Pumphrey's frustration as he walked through the ER. It was definitely a first for him. He stretched and yawned, twisting his head from side to side. It had been a long night. It would be good to fly home. He was satisfied at the job he had done. They had all done a good job. Just one more thing to do; get these people home.

He walked outside to wait for the big chopper that was heading their way, and scanned the northern horizon for a glimpse of it. A few minutes later, a distant speck of light appeared on the horizon and in a very short time emerged into the spectral thud of rotors beating methodically through the cold, still air.

Through the windshield of the Bell UH-1 Huey, National Guard Sergeant Ben Chesser of the 24th Air Ambulance Company peered over the pilot's shoulder toward the flashing white and green beacon of the Hebron Airport. It was a cold night, but was clear and calm. It was a beautiful night for a flight, actually. The beauty of it defied the purpose of their mission, which was to pick up a family of airplane crash survivors.

As the Crew Chief of this bird, he had been on emergency missions like this before, as the Guard was sometimes asked to do from time to time, but almost without exception they were neo-natal emergencies, where distressed expectant mothers would be ferried to nearby hospitals for critically needed care with regard to their unborn babies. Or sometimes there were burn victims. This was the first time they'd gone after plane crash survivors. He had never even heard of a civilian crash where there were survivors. He'd heard of lots of fatalities, though.

But there you go...and here they were. The hospital appeared and the pilot maneuvered the helicopter over it to get a view of the landing area that had been carved out of the parking lot before he committed to land. He caught a glimpse of Larry standing at one end and waving his arms slowly above his head. The pilot zeroed in on him and descended slowly with his nose pointed at Larry who guided him down until the skids gently thumped to the ground in a way that defied the 10,000 pounds of the big chopper.

The moment the skids touched and the strain of the engine was released, Ben grasped the handle of the door, turning it and sliding it back and open, pushing it toward the rear of the chopper till it locked securely into place. He could see people near the door of the hospital emergency room entrance who had prepared the victims for movement. The rotors of the big chopper slowly wound to a stop.

The Captain came on the intercom.

"Why don't you get in there and see what the situation is," he said. "Let me know when we're ready to go."

"Roger that," Ben replied and jumped out of the chopper. He walked over to Larry and they shook hands. Larry briefed him on the situation quickly and they turned to enter the hospital.

Inside, Ben saw Dad and went to him to make sure he was ready to go. He glanced over at Chris who stood near the door and was looking out at the big helicopter. Chris turned and watched them as they talked quietly.

He heard Dad ask Ben about Mom. Dad wasn't aware that they had already recovered her and she was there. Chris didn't know that either.

"Maybe I missed something," Dad said. "Maybe we can go out there and check one more time…"

Ben talked soothingly to Dad for a little while longer while the staff made the final preparations. When they were ready, he checked all of the gurneys to make sure we were good to go.

One of the doctors gave him a quick update on the situation. Dad and Chris could walk and sit once on board and there were the three stretchers with the children. Also, he and the nurse would come along. It would be tight, but Ben knew they'd make room. About that time the first of the gurneys rolled up to the door.

"Okay, Doc," Ben said. "Climb aboard with those two walking and get them strapped in. I'll get these gurneys aboard."

He looked toward the pilot's window and caught the eye of the captain watching the scene unfold through it, and held up four fingers, then turned his hand to make a walking symbol, and then he pointed at the gurneys and held up three fingers. The Captain nodded and gave a thumbs up.

Ben told the attendants standing near the stretchers to get them aboard. As they rolled past and were lifted into the big machine that would deliver us finally from the long nightmare, he could make out the little bodies of the children strapped to them once again.

Jesus, they were just little kids, he thought.

The nurse and the doctor then climbed aboard and began to strap themselves into the seats next to the other two. Ben made a quick check around the Huey and headed back to the hatch, climbed in and slammed the door shut. He went to each of the gurneys and passengers to make sure they were all secure and then snapped the yoyo chord of his helmet back into the intercom and keyed the microphone.

"We're all aboard, Sir!" he announced. "All clear!"

A few seconds later the helicopter whined to life and the intensity of the twin turbine engines quickly increased in a loud crescendo. Moments later, the Captain pulled up the throttle, forcing the blades to strain against the resistance of the dense cold air and gravity. Gradually, they lofted the helicopter upward and forward. The Captain moved the collective away from him and guided the chopper toward Lincoln.

As they slowly gained altitude, Ben looked at the nurse who had come on board. She stroked the side of one of the young boy's face, picking strands of blood matted hair out of his closed eyes, and then gently patted his leg. She never took her eyes off of him, as if she was willing him to stay.

Ben hoped it would be awhile before he did this kind of mission again.

Larry had caught a ride to the airport with another deputy sheriff and got his own helicopter ready to go. Bruce was waiting when he got there, and they did a quick preflight check of the bird and got it airworthy. When they got in, he quickly established radio contact with the pilot of the Huey and they agreed to fly to Lincoln together.

Larry and Bruce waited in the little bird until the Huey rose out of the trees near the hospital and began to move northeast. When he saw it, Larry lofted his helicopter into the sky and followed, taking a position off the left side and slightly behind the other chopper.

He looked at his watch. It was coming up on 4:30 a.m. The CAP team had secured after shutting down the ELT at the wreck, and he heard from Jon that they had all gotten back to Lincoln and gone home.

Jon mentioned the cadet who had found Mom was pretty shook up. And he probably wasn't even 18. He had his baptism into the dark part of the world of search and rescue, and Larry hoped he'd be alright. He could be proud of what he'd done, though. They all could be. They had done a good job.

Larry felt a particular satisfaction with how they all worked together that night, and the role he played. He felt that tonight he made a difference, which was why he had chosen this career. The life of a cop was tough and often thankless, but he knew he helped a family deal with a great tragedy tonight and he would remember this night for a long time.

Clarke approached the Lincoln airport from the other side of town. The helicopter carrying my family would be there soon. As he neared, he pulled up to a one-way street. The connector road to the airport was just down the street, but in the wrong direction. Clarke would waste precious time trying to go around and get on the right side of that street. He looked meekly in both directions. The street was dead empty. Perhaps the benevolence of his mission would get him a pass, he thought, and God would forgive him for breaking a traffic law.

He looked again and carefully turned his car and maneuvered up the wrong way of the street, quickly getting to the connector and carefully turning on to it. He was sure he was alone on that road, so no harm no foul.

He slyly congratulated himself for his courage and safely getting it done.

Just then, as if on cue, the reflection of blue and red blinking lights illuminated the scene around him. He looked in his rear-view mirror and saw the revolving lights atop the car that was quickly gaining on him.

Of course, he thought. A cop.

Clarke pulled over to the side of the street as the officer illuminated the car with his spotlight. After a seemingly very long time, the cop slowly exited his vehicle and approached where Clarke sat, shining a flashlight over the car as he approached.

Could he go any slower, Clarke thought? Clarke rolled down his window as the officer got there, and greeted him preparing to tell him his mission and ask his forgiveness. The officer cut him off and bluntly asked for his license and registration.

Clarke fumbled in the glove box and found the registration card, then pulled out his wallet to get his driver's license. He handed these to the cop along with his Hospital ID, and began to tell him what he was doing. At first the officer appeared to ignore him, but as he heard himself tell the story, he saw the young man's entire demeanor change.

The tough edge faded and he suddenly seemed much younger. Perhaps he had heard of the crash. He certainly had never heard that story as an excuse before. Anyway, it was too unbelievable to be a lie. The officer quickly handed Clarke the license and registration back.

"Well, you'd better get going, Pastor," he said. "You've got a big job to do."

Clarke thanked the young man and took back his registration and IDs. He watched the figure of the officer silhouetted by the bright spotlight in his mirror as he pulled away. He now had no doubt that God must be compelling him to go, and watched over him as he went.

In the helicopter, Helen gently touched my face again as I slept deeply. She carefully checked the bandage wrapped around my head that she helped Dad put on. It looked good. She patted my leg and thought I was so cold. She didn't know what had kept me alive that night, but was hoping that I could make it a little further. The lights on the ground below increased in quantity as the big helicopter approached Lincoln. Each passing second gave her new hope. Suddenly the crew chief stood up and held his hand over his microphone.

"Okay, were coming in for landing," Ben shouted, looking around to insure he had everyone's attention. "Everyone check your belts, and we'll be on the ground soon. Don't unlatch until I tell you to, okay?" Then he sat back down, and pulled a seat belt around him. The helicopter rattled its way to the Lincoln Airport.

Standing near the helicopter pad, Clarke watched the lights of the two helicopters approach against the blue-gold backdrop created by the coming dawn. Several ambulances were idling next to him, their medical staff handpicked by Bruce to be there. The thump of the rotors of the big military helicopter began to resonate with greater and greater intensity until they rattled the windows and other resonant objects nearby. Slowly it descended to the center of the pad, creating a gust of cold wind that blew into Clarke, causing him to grip the hat on his head in order to keep it from flying off. When its skids settled down, the high pitched whine of the engines sank and the immense power that lofted the huge machine was released by the pilot. The other small helicopter was descending to another pad 20 or so yards away.

Clark crouched and ran toward the door. The crew chief slid it open as he approached, and Clarke could see the stretchers and figures of the people inside. Dad, or some figure that looked like it may have been Dad, appeared and very slowly stepped out, aided by the others on board. Clarke grabbed his arm, and helped ease him to the solid ground. He was still shaky. To Clarke, Dad had always seemed a big man, both in size and stature. Suddenly he seemed so small and weak. Clarke looked at the mess of his face, catching his eyes through his swollen lids.

"Jim…" He whispered, horrified by his injuries. Behind them, the stretchers were quickly being unloaded, and people were shouting back and forth working out the transport details. Dad looked at him, and held onto his shoulders trying to stay balanced.

"Clarke, Char is dead." Dad croaked to him through chapped, bloody lips.

"I know, Jim," Clarke said. "I know, and it'll be okay…"

"She is still down there." Dad said. "I-I have to take care of the kids…please, take care of her and make whatever arrangement? I…have to go…"

Clarke gently pulled the broken man to him in an embrace. Jim hung in his arms, exhausted, on the verge of collapse.

"I'll take care of it Jim, don't worry." He said. Then he saw a little boy making his way out of the helicopter, his arm splinted to his chest.

My God, he thought, that's Chris!

He turned and stooped, holding his arms open to Chris. The little boy came to him, and Clarke grasped his arm gently. It was unmistakable to Clarke that behind that little bloody and dirty face, those eyes had seen what such young eyes should not see. Things that no one should see. Clarke pulled the boy into him. He looked at both of them.

"Listen to me, you made it, and you are going to be all right," he said. "You are alive, and everything will be all right. You have to believe that, okay?"

Chris nodded and looked at the ground. Dad had become distracted by the loading of the ambulance. Clarke patted Dad's back and motioned him to go to the ambulances. Dad nodded and stumbled toward them with the help of a nurse. Clarke turned to Chris again, and gently pulled up his chin. The boy looked at him with the eyes of an old man. Whatever he had seen was too much, Clarke could tell.

"It will be all right," Clarke said to him.

Chris nodded again and Clarke patted his shoulder gently. He stood and walked with him to the last waiting ambulance and Chris was rushed aboard. The doors slammed and in a chorus of whining sirens, the ambulances pulled away, rumbled toward the gate, and rushed out onto the street toward Lincoln General Hospital.

Clarke watched them go in silence, feeling drained and cold by the short experience. His attention was then drawn to the pilot of the other helicopter, who was walking toward him to get into the building that Clarke stood in front of. He was a policeman, by the look of him. Clarke caught his eye as he passed, and smiled at him with a nod. He always had liked policemen, but rarely more so than tonight.

"Rough night," Larry said as he passed. He spoke like a man who had just been through another day's work. Clarke murmured that he believed that it had been.

"Coffee inside," Larry said and opened the door to go in. That sounded good to Clarke. It was still cold and he could use some warmth. The sun was coming up though. To the east, dawn had begun to turn the dark grey of the twilight to a melding of silver, gold, and blue, slowly brightening, and washing over the barren winter landscape of the prairie. There were no more clouds in the sky. It was going to be a beautiful day.

The thought gave him pause, and he thought of Mom.

We all have one of these, he thought. The next morning that we don't get to see. He watched the brightening sky for a moment with mixed feelings. He didn't know if he was happy or sad that hers was so beautiful. He shivered slightly against the winter chill and followed the officer inside. He'd have that cup of coffee, but then he had work to do.

Betty Lou and Ken drove in silence toward Grandma's house in Cerritos. Betty Lou sniffed from the passenger seat and occasionally broke into full sobs, racked with grief. Ken found it hard to be stoic, but he had to. Jeff and Darren sat silently in the back seat.

Presently they pulled off the freeway and made their way into Grandma's neighborhood just off the 91 freeway, slowly working up the street and pulling up to the house. Ken shut off the car.

"Do you want me to do it?" he said.

Betty Lou clenched her jaw and shook her head, a fresh stream of tears welling from her eyes. She was about to do the hardest thing she had ever done, Ken knew, but she had to be the one to do it. She opened the door and got out. Ken guided Jeff and Darren and they followed her to the door. Betty produced a key, unlocked it quietly, and slipped in. Ken followed and directed my cousins to sit on a couch in the front living room, while he and Betty Lou made their way to the back of the house where Grandma's bedroom was.

They made their way across the kitchen where we had all sat yesterday morning for breakfast, a complete family. Betty Lou could still picture Mom, how she had been sitting there and sipping her coffee, laughing and…alive. The image brought a fresh wave of sobs which stopped her in her tracks for a full minute.

Grandma's room was off to the side of the kitchen. Betty Lou hugged Ken tightly for a few moments in the darkness of the kitchen, and then turned to walk into the room alone, closing the door behind her. Ken could see the light that filled the small hallway leading to the room through the crack under the door. He sat down at the table and listened to the murmur of Betty Lou's voice as she softly woke Grandma up. The murmuring became excited and suddenly the house resonated under Grandma's wail, followed by screams and hollering cries from both of them.

It was the worst sound Ken had ever heard.

He held his hands to his face and lowered his elbows to the table. His body began to tremble and he started to cry too.

The Lincoln General Hospital emergency room staff milled about near the entrance of the ER, in anticipation. Ron Craig had made all of the arrangements to receive us and Bruce had called some friends, too. Many of the hospital's staff came in as soon as they heard. Together, they had assembled there the most skilled group of medical staff any of them had ever seen. Dad was one of theirs, and now they would be taking care of him, and his family. No one else would die today, if they could do anything about it. And they all believed that they could.

The ambulances were on their way, and would be pulling in shortly. People chatted softly and got charged up with cups of coffee, but by and large the facility was quiet. It was a somber time, but a time to be as excellent as they all could be. That emergency room, like all, had seen its share of horror and mayhem, but this one had hit a little too close to home, and every one of them knew that by the grace of God they had a chance to make it right.

The wail of the sirens approached from the south. The morning sun was slowly beginning to brighten the landscape just beyond the glass doors of the ER. Suddenly the ambulances roared in and screeched to a halt right outside.

Bruce stood just inside waiting to receive us. After a few moments, the doors suddenly burst open flooding the foyer with bright sunlight in front of the first stretcher, which happened to be the one I was strapped to.

Someone directed it to an empty bed and Bruce followed it in. Rick and Kim were sent to two other rooms and Chris was immediately taken to get his arm X-rayed.

Bruce was now my savior and he quickly recognized me. He was a veteran ER doctor and trauma surgeon, but seeing me, his Godson and his son's best friend, like that--and still alive--shocked him. I was quickly transferred to the ER table and the stretcher was removed from the room. He made a quick assessment of my injuries. The deep gash in my leg was wide open and packed full of dirt and dried blood.

Bruce saw that the sharp piece of steel had incised the back of the knee and appeared to have sliced directly along the margin of my tibial nerve, which was now stretched and hanging out of the back of my leg, but seemed intact. It also sliced neatly right along the posterior artery of my leg, which had been packed deep into the wound but also appeared unscathed. A fraction of an inch to one side and I would not have ever walked on that leg again. A fraction of an inch to the other and I would have bled to death in minutes, long before Dad even dug me out.

The incision in my leg couldn't have been more precise if it had been done during surgery. Luck, Bruce decided, was on my side that night. But he shook off the thought and amazement. Now he had to fix it and that was what he did. He fixed these kinds of things, and he was damn good at it.

"Prepare an IV of lactate ringers and ready O.R. one," he told the ER nurse. "Prep him and get him up there stat! I am going to operate right now."

She departed the room and I was wheeled out to be prepped for surgery. Bruce could see the activity in the other parts of the ER. He could hear Dad's voice in one of the curtain draped-beds and poked his head into the room from which it came.

Dad was standing next to the bed of his little girl and was conducting himself more like a doctor than a patient. He was acting in charge of and still trying to direct the care, which he was capable of doing Bruce knew, but his friend needed to be a patient now. Bruce called to him and they connected eyes. Dad was a mess, but he was still a doctor, and having a hard time being a patient. Bruce motioned him to come over and they stepped into the brightly lit hallway between the curtained divided rooms of the ER.

"I've sent Randy to surgery," Bruce said. "I'm going to operate right away. He's going to make it. Why don't you sit down take it easy and I'll get scrubbed. Let them clean you up." Dad nodded and turned away. Bruce was satisfied with that and went to the doctor's lounge to get changed into scrubs for my surgery.

A few minutes later he reemerged. Before he went up to the operating room he went back to the ER to check on Dad. To his surprise, Dad was still up and again trying to direct the care of the rest of the kids. The staff was trying to calm him, but he was having a really hard time throttling down. Now he was more in the way than anything else. Bruce went to him and pulled him aside, speaking to him as gently but as firmly as he could.

"Jim, we've got them," he said. "You have to let us take care of them, and we are. But we need to take care of you, too."

Dad was physically exhausted, but there was determination in his eyes.

"We've got them…" Bruce said again and placed his hand on his friend's shoulder. Dad's eyes softened. Bruce wrapped Dad's arm around his neck and led him to an empty bed, bearing most of his weight, and caught eyes with a nurse who quickly hustled over and helped him lift Dad onto the bed. Dad lay back for the first time since he woke up a little over 24 hours ago. He finally closed his eyes. Bruce squeezed his hand.

"We've got them." He said.

Another nurse came into the room and they began to clean the wounds on Dad's face and head to prepare them for sutures. He'd need quite a few. Dad let out a long deep sigh and Bruce felt his body slump, completely exhausted. But finally he could just lie there. He had done more than he thought he would ever have to do that night, Bruce knew.

He was a hero, if that's what you want to call it. But the night was over. Now he had to rest and let the other heroes do their jobs.

Bruce looked over his friend once more, and sadly shook his head. A tear ran down Dad's cheek and he began to tremble. What did he go through tonight, Bruce thought?

Then he turned to go to the operating room and put me back together.

Dr. Bunting walked out of the emergency room at Hebron that morning, feeling drained. Helen and Dr. Pumphrey had just gotten back from the helicopter hop to Lincoln and had found him in the cafeteria sipping a cup of badly needed coffee. The family had made it, they had said. For what they had done, they had done it as well as could be expected. The family was safe, and that was what was important. They would put the fiasco of the night behind them.

Outside the sun was up. It was a clear and beautiful winter day, crisp and cold and not a cloud to be seen. The emergency room had been restored and cleaned up from the unfathomable crisis of the early morning, and there was little sign that anything out of the ordinary had even occurred. The on-call staff had all gone home and the place was quiet, except for a couple of staff coming in to start the day. No other emergencies had occurred last night, which he was very grateful for. Dr. Bunting could rest soon, but now he needed to take care of one more duty.

He opened the door to the small exam room and turned on the light. On the table, covered by a thin white sheet, Mom lay naked on her back. Beside the table, a plastic bag containing her clothes and effects had been placed. He picked it up and looked in. On top of the dirty and bloody blouse was a necklace that she had worn. It was a small white porcelain medallion depicting a windmill drawn in blue in the Dutch Delft style. He held it for a while, then closed his palm around it and looked at her. It gave him a glimpse into the person she had been, and he felt a pang of sympathy for her. He would make sure it made it back to the family with her.

They would all live, he was pretty sure. They survived the night with an almost total lack of care, except that given by the Dad. At least he was a doctor, and seemed to know for the most part what he was doing. Doctor Bunting just wished they could have helped more. It is very important to the staff to feel like they are doing something in cases like that. God forbid one of those kids died there. Some of the staff would have not been able to handle that, he knew.

He turned to the table and gently pulled the sheet back. Mom lay before him, exposed and vulnerable, just as she was when she came into the world only thirty-two years before. He carefully examined her body, noting to himself all of the broken bones and bruises she had suffered. It was very obvious that she had died immediately, and didn't have to sustain the pain from all of her wounds.

Most of her major bones were fractured, and cuts and contusions were present across her entire body. She had been subject to an incredible force when she had been ejected from that plane. The ghastly wound on her head was indicative of an impact by a flying object. Probably some piece of the plane, he thought. It had caused massive damage to her head.

Mom was dead before she was flung through the windshield and out onto the field a split second later, when the plane impacted into the ground. No one can say whether if she had been wearing her seatbelt she'd have survived. For me, I try not to wonder about it. I guess it doesn't matter now.

Doctor Bunting concluded his examination then signed the death certificate. He wrote the cause of death as a compound fracture of her skull. It didn't seem to do justice to the rest of what she had gone through. Rather, it seemed like such a simple thing, like a bump on the head. Someone else would have to fill in the blanks. That wasn't his job, as much as he'd have liked it to be.

The family minister in Lincoln had told Helen that a funeral home up there would be sending someone down to recover her later that day. Nothing more he could do. He hung the clipboard on the end of the bed by the paper tag that was tied to one of her toes and pulled the sheet back over my mother. He stretched and sighed deeply, rubbing his eyes. It had been a long night. He couldn't really recall a longer one. Hopefully he could get a little sleep before the next emergency.

He walked from the room, flipping the light off as he went and closing the door behind him. The dead body of the young woman who gave me life now was left all alone in the cool darkness.

A tan hearse pulled out of the garage at the Lincoln Memorial Funeral Home. It made its way to the interstate and headed west toward York where the driver could pick up Highway 81. Once there, it turned south, traveling several miles, past the road where my Dad had stood, past the wreckage of our plane three-quarter miles away, past a solitary monument to the pioneers, and into Hebron. It was the same exact route that Kim and I would follow thirty years later.

A black vinyl body bag lying on a rolling stretcher was awaiting the driver when the hearse pulled up to the hospital. They had said it was a woman killed in some kind of airplane crash. Without much ceremony, the driver signed the release, placed the bag in the back of the hearse, and pulled away, bringing my Mom the rest of the way home.

Chapter 12

They put us in one room of the pediatric ICU ward at Lincoln General Hospital. Kim, Rick, and I lay perfectly still, still deeply asleep in the beds, IV tubes dripping ringers lactate into our arms. Chris went home the day after we got to the hospital after having his hand stitched up and a cast placed on his broken arm. He had fractured both bones in his forearm. He had also been given a bed of his own for a few hours to catch up on his rest. What he needed most of all was sleep.

He left with some of the multitude of relatives that had begun migrating to our house after learning of the tragedy. It must have been a strange scene for Chris. On one side my Dad's sister, Mary Lou and her family were staunchly entrenched to protect my Dad from the heated emotions coming from my Mom's side. There was a definite unspoken rift among them, and Chris found himself caught up between it.

He didn't care, and just stayed out of it. He constantly thought of Mom in that field. He wanted to forget, but every time he closed his eyes, he was back there and staring at her. In some of his dreams, the little blanket that had covered her was gone, and she stared back at him with wide, terrified eyes.

He wanted her back.

Dad took refuge in the hospital. He had practically taken up residence there. It served two purposes. He wanted to be near us, but he also couldn't deal with the family tensions. He didn't want to see their accusing stares, especially from Grandma. He found himself alive but people wanted answers as to why Mom wasn't. But he had none to give. So, for a while he just stayed away.

Bruce took time from his rounds at the hospital every day to check up and keep an eye on his friend. Dad was wrecked. Bruce could see that he was trying hard to be stoic about the whole thing, but in reality, the entire impact of the accident just hadn't hit him yet. Dad was trying hard to keep up his humor and be his old self, but Bruce had known him for too long. Behind Dad's eyes was a pain the likes of which he did not like to see. It was painful for Bruce just to watch.

Bruce passed by our room and looked in. Aunt Sandy, Mom's youngest sister, was sitting with us. Bruce shook his head a little. He had done the best job he could putting us back together, as did the other docs. Larry Ruth, one of the best plastic surgeons around, had worked on our head wounds, and with any luck we wouldn't look like monster children with the scars that would form later on. We'd all have to have plastic surgery to tone them down at some point, but that was a long way off. The wounds he saw were awful and he thought again for the umpteenth time about how lucky all of us were to be alive at all.

Still, he had seen head injuries like that before, and had also known the consequences. The fact that we were children was a major advantage for us. The neurosurgeon, Lou Gollela, had told Dad that our relative youth would probably mean we would recover, as the injuries didn't kill us outright. Lou was a stand up guy and wouldn't lie to Dad, but Bruce still understood that even with the regenerative power of youth, there was a chance that we all could be severely disabled mentally and require lifelong care just to get by. He knew Dad was strong, but he had real concerns whether he was strong enough to handle that. Bruce didn't know if ever he was put in the same situation if he could, either.

Life can really be a bear, he thought. He turned away and went back to his rounds.

Uncle Ken was trying to stay out of the fray at our home as well. He and Betty Lou, Jeff and Darren, and Grandma had come to Lincoln first thing the morning after the crash, and had moved into our house to help make the arrangements for the funeral and care for Chris. Aunt Sandy and her husband, Jim, had come out from San Diego, too. Betty Lou and Sandy were rotating between meetings with Clarke to plan the funeral, and sitting shifts in the hospital with Rick, Kim and me. Dad's sister Mary Lou and her family had come too as had my Dad's parents, who were keeping things up at our house.

Uncle Jim also seemed quite aware of the tension floating in the air between Dad's and Mom's families. Everybody was just overcome by the whole thing. Tragedy will do that, Ken thought.

It was a morbidly strange reprieve when a few days later Uncle Jim suggested they go down to Hebron and see the crash site for themselves. Ken jumped at the opportunity, if only to get out of the tense scene for a few hours.

Jeff and Darren took the car and drove out of Lincoln east down I-80 to Highway 81. Just outside of Hebron, they turned up the dirt road where, unbeknownst to them, my Dad had walked to the highway. Soon they came to the pond we had flown over and the trees we had crashed through and guided the car over the dike and onto the field.

The corpse of our wrecked airplane still lay there, like the scene of a crime. People climbed around it, cutting out instruments and making measurements. Ken found out by talking to one of them that they were from the NTSB and were conducting their standard investigation. Ken and Jim walked off in different directions, surveying the scene. It was beyond description and like nothing either had ever seen. Dad had told him roughly where Mom had been, and Ken walked in that direction.

A small piece of wadded up cloth near the nose of the plane caught his eye and he went over to it. It was the small blanket that Dad had covered her with. Ken squatted down next to it and picked it up to examine it, realizing only then that it was stained with her blood. He gently put it down.

He stood and walked toward the wreckage, taking it all in. Suddenly his eye was drawn to a small object, laying in between clods of tilled up soil. It didn't appear to be a piece of the plane. He bent down and picked it up. It was small, about the size of a silver dollar, with crimson and light-colored strands, like corn silk. He considered it for a moment and turned it over to look at it some more, when with sudden horror he realized what it was he held in his hands. It was a piece of Mom's skull.

The realization made the blood drain from his face. He felt light headed and dizzy, like he should sit down, but his eyes would not move from the chunk of bone sitting there in his trembling hand. He looked around and was suddenly horribly conflicted at what he should do. Before he could think about it too much, he gently set the piece back on the ground where he had found it and for a moment just stared at it.

Under his breath, he said a prayer for my Mom, and then he turned around and walked away. He didn't tell me about that for thirty years, but when I heard I was glad that that he left it there. That part of her was still there in the place where she died. It just seemed fitting.

Aunt Sandy sat next to me still sleeping in the hospital bed. It was her watch. The blinds on the windows were all drawn and the room was dark and quiet. Every so often a nurse or two would come in to check on us or give medications. We were all on antibiotics, and Rick was being given other medications for his head injury. She wasn't sure what they all were for, but didn't really care, so long as they helped.

She would have stroked my hair, but a large helmet-like bandage was wrapped tightly around my head, securing the stitches that Bruce used to piece it back together. On my leg he had put a large cast that extended from my inner thigh to my ankle. Behind the protection of the dressings there were over one hundred sutures, all across my head and down inside and the outside of the back of my leg.

Sandy gazed woefully down at me. She was heartbroken. She had lost her big sister, and we had lost our precious mother, and were so badly hurt. It was such a large burden. She was almost glad that we didn't have to know. Not yet.

She touched her belly. Her own first baby was growing there, only a few months along. She had told Mom about the baby what seemed like such a short time ago and Mom had cried with joy. Sandy had been so excited that she would be able to introduce them some day. That was all gone now.

Kim and Rick both had head dressings just like mine. Sandy had gone back and forth to each of us that morning and spent time singing softly and telling stories to our unhearing ears. She had heard that that was a good idea. Now she sat next to me stroking my shoulder so that I could at least feel the warm touch of another, and softly sang a lullaby. She did not want to leave us.

A wave of motion from deep inside me gently rocked my body, ever so slightly. Sandy stopped and looked at me intensely, staring at my closed lids. Behind them, my eyes darted back and forth. Somewhere beyond, I swam in a dark liquid-like world of darkness swirling around me. It was now slowly beginning to drain, like if you were lying on your back in a full bathtub under the water after pulling the plug. The water slowly lowers toward you until the interface between it and air beyond reaches your nose.

Without a ripple or sound my body slowly broke the surface, and I opened my eyes, emerging from the fabric of my dreams.

Sandy looked back at me for an excited second and gripped my hand, joy pouring into her heart. I weakly smiled back at her, but did not speak. I had no idea where I was or what I was doing there.

"You wait here!" she said, barely able to contain herself, and shot to her feet. A tear ran down her cheek. She squeezed my hand and lifted it to her warm lips and pressed them against it, trembling, and then laid it gently across my chest.

"Welcome back," she whispered and hurried out of the room.

I stared up at the lifeless television bolted to the opposite wall and wished someone would turn it on.

Dad and Chris came to see me later on. Chris had a new cast on his arm. He said hey to me and then took off with some relatives. He tried not to act sad, for my benefit. Lots of other people came and went in the hours or days or weeks or whatever it was that passed. I had no reference for time, but it seemed like it went on forever. It was only shortly after I woke up that I asked the obvious question. I was hurt and wanted my Mommy. When I cried for her to come at some point, Sandy gently took my hand and told me that she couldn't come. Confused, I asked why.

She said Mommy had gone to heaven. Then dad came in and I asked him, not wanting to believe it.

"Mommy died, son," he said, his voice breaking as he did.

"Who killed her??" I asked breaking into tears of my own, not even really comprehending what that meant.

"She died in the airplane," Dad said, almost with a whisper and looked away from my wide-eyed stare.

My Dad, throughout my life has never told me a lie. So he couldn't tell me then that everything would be all right. His body hurt too, and he was still trying to make sense of it all. He wasn't so sure at that moment that it would be all right.

When they left and I was alone, I just lay there in stunned disbelief unable to comprehend the enormity of what Dad had told me. I don't think that feeling has ever really left me.

Kim and Rick still lay fast asleep and would be out for the next three days. Kim seemed to come around quickly once she awoke and got over her shock. I was sitting in my bed next to her watching TV and when I looked over, she had sat up and was quietly blinking at me. I swung my cast leg off the bed and carefully made my way to her. She smiled at me, and I held up a small stuffed dog someone had left near her so she could see.

A nurse came in and quietly moved me aside and looked Kim over, stroking her head.

"Randy's teasing me." Kim said with a smile. I smiled back, and the nurse laughed and quickly turned to get a doctor. My little sister had made it, and knowing that filled me with joy.

Rick wasn't doing so well. He had emerged from his coma a few days after Kim while I was out of the room, and when I saw him he seemed to be very slow and weak. He couldn't speak at all at first, and uttered strange words that only seemed to have meaning to him. They said he'd be okay in a little while and I believed them, but I was impatient. I wanted to play with my big brother again.

* * * * * * * * * * * * * *

It had started to rain again as Kim and I drove through the outskirts of Lincoln coming back from our trip to Hebron, rolling over endless rises and drops as the road snaked through the countryside. We had stopped at our childhood home along the way and looked around a bit before heading on. Doing so brought back many different kinds of memories, some good; some not so good.

Eventually we pulled up to a small church called Trinity Chapel situated up on a hill off of a small country road, and surrounded by farmland. It was the church that my family had dutifully attended for so many years so long ago. Clarke had been our pastor, and the memories of his sermons came flooding back as we slowed to a stop.

Clarke had a very '70's new age kind of approach to sermons. Oftentimes he would play that acoustic guitar to the hymns the congregation sang. He never spoke of God's wrath, but only God's love. He was a humble man, and a servant of the Lord, and it showed in how he was as a person day to day.

I was an acolyte there at the church in those days, along with my friend Kevin Anderson. Our jobs were to walk up the aisle on cue from our handler, usually Clarke's wife Sharon, solemnly holding the lit acolyte candles. These were long brass rods with long wicks that ran through them that could be slowly extended as they burnt down to keep the small flame lit, and a bell-shaped cup on the underside to extinguish candle flames. Our job was to light all of the candles in the candelabras at the front of the church as the introduction organ music played and put them out when the sermon was over.

I liked being an acolyte. It was a fun part of the service. We both took it very seriously. We got to wear long purple robes and sat in the front pew during the sermon. At the end, the organ music would play again, and we would watch Clarke until he nodded slightly to us, signaling us to go. We would go back up, light the wick again, and then extinguish all of the candles like we were supposed to. Then we would turn and walk to the back of the church and Clarke would follow us.

I don't recall when my family stopped going to the little church, or why. It was a few years after the crash, and the memories of it all are a blur to me and I don't know what they were, only that I left any formal relationship with God there the last time I left.

Kim and I got out of the rental car and walked across the wet gravel that crunched under our feet as we made our way toward the entrance of the church for the first time in almost thirty years. It had stopped raining long enough for us to not get wet as we walked up to the door. A man who had been diligently pulling weeds from a small patch of soil on the side of the church observed us as we approached and stood when we got near. We greeted him and told him who we were and that we had come to see the old church again. He said his name was Ken McQueen and it turned out he was now the pastor of the church.

We went inside and I was again transported back to my youth. Above the pulpit I saw the large wooden cross that had been placed on the wall so many years ago. It was the memorial to my Mom that my Dad had commissioned to be made. It was probably fifteen feet high and pointed at the tips. In its center carved symbols of the trinity were placed in circular wooden carvings. It was truly beautiful. I told Ken about it.

"That was put there for my Mom," I said. "She was killed in a plane crash back in '76. She was very active in this church." The pastor looked at me for a second, and then replied knowingly. Apparently he had heard of me.

"Yes..." he said. "Yes it is."

Kim and I stared at the old cross for a minute or two in silence, both contemplating the meaning of it as well as the meaning of us being there at that moment. The hall was musty with age and the rain. I remembered the smell of it from some distant corner of my brain.

We chatted with Ken for a short time and he showed us around the old church. We really didn't have a specific reason for coming, but we both wanted to, and I was glad we did. It was good to see the place again.

After a while, we said goodbye to Ken, left the church and walked back to our car. It began to rain again as we pulled out onto the road and drove away.

I felt as we drove away like there was a part of us still there. Maybe even part of my Mom, left over from her funeral. And I felt like maybe God was happy to see me again, even if only for a little while.

Dad handed over Mom's funeral arrangements completely to Clarke and Betty Lou in the days after the crash, and didn't really get involved. He asked me in the hospital if I wanted to go to the funeral, to say goodbye to Mom, as he put it. I must have said yes because a short time later I was fitted into a new suit jacket and shirt. The pants of my little outfit had to be cut up the seam so they would fit over my bulky cast. I thought that I looked pathetic and helpless.

Then I was placed in a wheelchair and trundled out of the hospital to a limousine and we drove through the dead and frozen countryside to the Trinity Chapel.

Two solemn young men in suits whom I didn't know lifted the wheelchair up the stairs at the front of the church. One of them maneuvered me up the aisle toward my family, gathered in the pews near the front. As I passed by, people stared at me with sad looks and stony faces. It made me feel quite self-conscious.

In one row, I saw my friend Greg Miller. He smiled meekly at me and waved slightly, but then looked away as if he knew that by doing so he was being bad for not exhibiting the proper sorrow. I smiled back at him anyway. It felt good to see him. And to smile again.

Nobody else smiled. Many were crying. Mournful organ music flowed through the chapel. I was wheeled to the front and stopped, sitting near the wall on the outside of the pew. I felt exposed and conspicuous. I felt ridiculous and stupid looking in the bandage that covered my head like some kind of grotesque helmet.

Just in front of the wide steps leading to the pulpit was a drape-covered cart. On it was a closed casket. It was made of light oak and very beautiful—not at all what I thought it would be. When my aunt told me what it would be like at the funeral, I pictured an elongated hexagonal coffin like those in old western movies or at Halloween parties. This one looked more like a nice piece of furniture, with elegant lines and understated accents—just like Mom.

Inside and well concealed, she lay in a blue dress that Betty Lou had picked for her. It was one that my Mom had told her once that she thought had made her look pretty. I wished then that I could have seen her once more, before they put her forever in the ground. I am glad now that I didn't.

Clarke surveyed the crowd that had amassed in the church. The pews were full and the space behind them was packed with people standing with no place to sit. The knot of people extended beyond the door and out into the parking lot where they stood straining to hear. People wept and dabbed at their eyes intermittently. In the tower, the bell tolled out slowly. The tragedy of my Mom had really brought out the community. It was good to see how many people she touched in life. I have heard others say that your funeral is the true mark of the life that you lived. If this was true, my Mom had a very rich life indeed.

The organ bellowed out hymns while everyone settled, then gradually merged into the signature ending chords of 'ahhhhhh-meeeeen!!" and fell silent.

For a few seconds, the only sounds were intermittent sniffles and the occasional cough. Clarke bowed for a moment to compose himself, and then lifted his head to the crowd that was bathed in the tinted sunlight that spilled through the stained glass windows of the little church. He began to speak.

Clarke spoke of our sorry mortal state and the need to accept God as a way to immortal life. Bruce and Ken both sang songs proclaiming

God's greatness. I don't know if I bought any of it or not. I don't think I did. I only stared at Mom's coffin. Its image would return again and again to haunt my dreams as the symbol of her for many years. It never has really left me.

When the sermon was over they wheeled her out and placed her in a white hearse. I was taken back to the limousine with my Dad and we followed the hearse out of the lot and towards town. They took her to a cemetery on the outskirts of Lincoln, and Clarke spoke a little more at the gravesite service. It was still cold, but the sun shined brightly. Clarke stood back as Mom's casket was prepared to be lowered into a grave, which had been excavated from the frozen soil. Her final resting place. The attendance was among the largest he had ever seen at a funeral. People had surrounded the grave ceremony in a large tight crowd, and he had to speak loudly for all to hear his words. He didn't mind.

Clarke stood dutifully by as the last few people sauntered slowly away, some approaching him first to shake his hand and congratulate his sermon. He felt good about it. He had done his duty and helped a family and friend in need. After a while he was all alone standing beside the grave.

Presently, workmen arrived and began to disassemble the grave service and fold up plastic chairs. Clarke looked at the coffin. He thought of Mom, and what she had been like. He thought about the pity of her death, and her kids, and Dad.

Then his thoughts turned toward his own kids and his own wife and his family. He was acutely aware in that moment that he loved them all very much.

Nearby, a large statue of Jesus stood. His head was bowed with an expression of solitude on his face. His crucified hands down and held with palms facing out to show the wounds to his mortal flesh caused by his Roman tormentors. He held them exposed - a gesture of comfort to those who would suffer their own wounds in this life. Clark walked over to him and read the inscription on the statue's base. It was a familiar passage from John 3:16.

It said, "For God so loved the world that he gave his only begotten Son, that whosoever believeth in him should not perish, but have everlasting life."

Clarke thought about that for a while and touched the icy cold stone robe of the statue. He didn't always understand God's plan, but he knew it was not his place to ask questions. He just knew that there was a plan. There had to be. He knew Mom believed in God and was a good Christian, and therefore had that guarantee of everlasting life, even through her tragic death. Even so, it had been a long and sad few days.

Suddenly he felt tired.

Emotion swelled up in him and with a sob, he bowed his head and began to cry at the base of the image of his Lord.

Nearby, my mother was lowered into the frozen ground.

Chapter 13

Dad looked around the large room in Ireland, and took in the stone still faces of all of the members before him. Then he looked back at his notes. They were blurry. His eyes were damp with tears, and the tears surprised him. But he had told the hard part of the story, and had gotten through it.

All eyes were on him. The room was dead silent; the audience rapt. Collecting himself once more, he began to speak again:

"Folks probably got tired of my criticism of the treatment we received prior to arriving in Lincoln." He said. "It was not so much that I was complaining about the care at any particular facility, but of the lack of a delivery system to treat the acute trauma patient in the rural setting. The statement in the ATLS manual 'When I can provide better care in the field with limited resources than what my children and I received at the primary facility, there is something wrong with the system and the system has to be changed,' emphasizes this observation."

"Simply put, you have to train them before you can blame them."

At the hospital and for the next year, Dad did complain. He felt very fortunate that all of us had come through, and were on a solid road to recovery. Eventually we all would recover fully, beyond everybody's expectations. Even Rick. At first and for a few months, it seemed that he had suffered a severe brain disability. He couldn't speak, or dress himself, and things did not look good. Then suddenly, just like that, he was fine. It was as immediate a transformation as Dad had ever seen. It was like he just snapped out of it and was a kid again.

For his part, Rick has no memory of his life leading up to that moment, but he'd be okay from then on. For that, and for all of us, Dad was profoundly grateful. But still, he couldn't shake the problems he had encountered in Hebron.

He wasn't even really sure exactly what he was complaining about, but the whole thing seemed so ridiculous. And it was causing him great consternation. He was trying not to be blameful of the hospital staff in Hebron, he was sure of that. He'd personally known those people and many others like them around the state. He had seen them work before and knew they were competent, caring people and professionals. They weren't bumpkins, and he felt bad that in the days after the crash he had given the impression to many people that they were.

Still, he felt angry and was having a very hard time getting over the closed ER doors he had encountered, but in reflecting on the events of that night he began to look more closely at the perceived errors he had seen and saw the whole fiasco that was created as secondary. It was only an indication, a symptom, of a much bigger problem.

It was really about the delivery system. It was so different from place to place. That was really what was bugging him, he realized abruptly one day.

"How could it be," he exclaimed to Ron Craig, "that such disparity in simple emergency treatment can exist in the modern world?" He demanded, to no one in particular, that someone needed to do something. Ron was intrigued by the problem as well and he and Dad began to talk, casually at first, about how to prevent the experience from happening to anyone again, and if it was even possible.

Ron and my Dad were friends and colleagues and Ron had nothing but respect for Dad, but he had gotten pretty sick of listening to Dad go on and on about it. He knew Dad was right about the delivery system, but if he was serious, then there was going to be work to do. A lot of work.

"Styner," he said one day after listening to another of Dad's tirades. "Quit you're bitching and put your money where your mouth is!"

I imagine that the jolt that hit him at that moment was very similar to the one that hit me when Shelley pointed out that the truth of the accident was still out there. These kinds of revelations happen in the simplest of moments, when everything lines up for a blip in time and a single word or phrase can change your entire outlook on life. Some call it epiphany, or divine intervention, or any myriad of things, but it is really only a matter of having the blinders torn off, and seeing the world in a new, unfiltered way.

Just like me, my Dad had been paralyzed. With Ron's words, he got up and began to walk again. And talk. His mind began to engage and soon the ideas were flowing from the two of them.

They had determined early in the conversation that what was really needed was fairly simple: There was a basic lack of consistency in trauma care and they needed a system to address this inconsistency. In other words, they needed a method to educate rural physicians in a systematic way to treat trauma that was applicable to all facilities all over the state. All of the doctors at these facilities were perfectly competent to treat their patients, but many were using out of date or obsolete methods because there was no consistent system, and even if there were, there was no way to deliver it.

The two of them soon managed to get together with a nurse who worked with the Lincoln Mobile Heart Team named Jodie Upright very early in their discussion. The Mobile Heart Team itself was a recent innovation that dealt with, as the name implied, cardiac trauma and the standardization of cardiac care.

The three of them hashed the issue out, comparing their own experiences, and quickly decided there was indeed a need for this new system. They were all aware that if this was possible, it would call for the creation of a training course for the small hospitals – ones like the hospital in Hebron. These kinds of facilities were literally all over the state, and Dad, Ron and Jodie all had the same conclusion through their individual dealings that very little consistency in trauma care existed among any of them.

And that's what had caused the problems Dad had encountered in Hebron—that lack of consistency. It wasn't the standard of care. Most of these facilities, including Hebron, could handle the emergencies, and most patients didn't suffer inadequate care. They probably could have handled us just fine if Dad hadn't lost it. But in trauma, there could be, and should be, a standard; a system to deal with all kinds of cases in a similar and by-the-numbers fashion.

They were all familiar with the work of another Lincoln physician named Steve Carvith, who had created a course with a similar objective called Advanced Cardiac Life Support, or ACLS, which addressed similar issues in cardiac care. Jodie had worked with Doctor Carvith on that project, so she was a good source of knowledge for how it came about and the format that was used. ACLS was a great idea and provided the level of consistency in cardiac care that Dad, Jodie, and Ron were looking for in trauma care.

Influenced by those concepts, and realizing that if something works you should go with it, they decided to use a similar format, and call the new course Advanced Trauma Life Support (ATLS). Not too original name, they knew, but it seemed to make sense to them, and it had a solid sounding ring to it.

The first thing they knew they had to do was to become experts on the conceptual framework that Steve had developed. Over the next several months they all took courses, and became certified ACLS instructors so that they could learn intimately how the course was organized. It was hard work and a huge commitment to their professional and personal lives, but they had all become entranced by the project, and to them it was well worth it.

As they went along, they began to see the enormity of what they had started. They could see that a lot of help would be needed, if this was going to work. Intensive training was the key to it, but it also needed a syllabus that arranged the concepts into a framework that presented a logical and consistent approach to all manner of trauma.

Somewhere along the way they had realized that the problem in many trauma cases was the wrong order of treatment. If a patient was bleeding profusely, it looks horrible and could certainly kill them, but the crushed chest that is ignored while treating the ghastly bleeding cut will kill them quicker than the bleeding itself. Simply put, a doctor had to understand the necessary order of treatment and treat people appropriately.

They got the idea that it would be more effective if a doctor could quickly evaluate a patient as soon as they came into the ER, know the severity of the various injuries based on known facts, then fix the worst ones first before attacking the next problem. As per their training, a doctor would look at every system involved and every problem, figure out which one to treat, and then begin treatment. That type of assessment was based on the individual doctor, who was, after all, human and limited by his or her level of training, knowledge, and experience. This created inconsistency.

They began to call their new concept of the correct order of treatment the ABC's of trauma.

As they expected, this idea created a bit of controversy and rumbling from the medical establishment as word of the ABC concept spread. As it is with many things, it is very difficult to get people, even highly educated and progressive people, to step out of their comfort zone, get away from what they know, and try something new. It is no different with doctors. Doctors see themselves, and rightly so, as the captains of their respective ships. The call may be right or wrong, but it was still their call. Some complained that the standardization of the process took away from them the ability to make good decisions.

In some cases, egos were getting in the way. But even the staunchest of critics couldn't argue away the simple logic of the concept, and it began to catch on. Soon that simplicity was implemented into the creation of the ATLS course as its central dogma. Everything else would be based on the ABC's.

Another doctor who quickly came on board early in the concept's development was a noted peripheral vascular surgeon in Lincoln named Paul "Skip" Collicott, who also happened to be a member of the distinguished American College of Surgeons. Dad and Ron both knew him personally and as a colleague, and also knew that he had the political connections and know how to get things going in moving the ATLS concept to a higher level. They all knew that the College's endorsement was critical to get ATLS accepted in any kind of broad way. Fortunately, Skip quickly became a true disciple of ATLS and gladly took the lead in presenting the course to the College.

By then, word of the innovation of ATLS had gotten around the Lincoln medical community and people liked what they heard. More and more doctors approached Dad, Jodie, and Ron about the course, joined in, and began to write chapters about their various specialties and the application of those specialties to the ATLS concept for the syllabus.

Among those that joined early in the development was a Lincoln Mobile Heart Team nurse named Irvene Hughes. She was so taken by the story of what had happened to Dad and what was transpiring before her with ATLS that they asked her if she would write the introduction to the course, where she told Dad's story and how it had led them all to that point. She became the Manager of the ATLS program for The American College of Surgeons Committee on Trauma and remained in that post for the rest of her professional career, spanning from 1982 to 2006.

The concept of the ABCs of trauma was further refined through numerous contributions and became the definitive way to prioritize the order of assessment and treatment. Nothing new was added, and there were no research-related discoveries or scientific revelations associated with ATLS. They all just took what was known and organized it in a different, more efficient way for treating the trauma patient. Simplicity was the key, and as ALTS worked, that key was being turned and would soon open a door bigger than any of them could have imagined.

Then it was done. The prototype course for ATLS was field tested in Auburn, Nebraska, in 1978 with the help of several groups and individuals who had by then become convinced of ATLS's relevance and importance to trauma medicine. It seemed to work. Armed with the early successes, Skip took the course and presented it to the University of Nebraska, which was also duly impressed and supportive. The University faculty threw their support behind ATLS by providing surgical training facilities to truly field test the concept. Next, Skip got the American College of Surgeons Committee on Trauma involved, and they too were impressed by what they saw.

Dad and his friends took the finished course to the thirteen regions of the College and presented their work. All of the doctors there were intrigued and inspired by what they had seen. Could it really be that easy? Could there really be a simple way to standardize trauma care and make it quickly available to all rural doctors?

It appeared so.

And, while they were at it, if it was good for them, why not the rest of the world? The College quickly distributed the course within each region, and ATLS was officially born. The United States military was one of the first major organizations to adopt it, and they still use it today as the basis of front line care for their wounded combat troops.

From its inception, the basic concepts have never changed for ATLS and it turned out to be more successful in its application than Dad, Ron and Jodie ever hoped for. Other states in the nation and Canada began to adopt the course through the American College of Surgeons and began to teach the concepts of ATLS to their respective trauma physicians. ATLS continued to prove incredibly effective and from the US and Canada it moved to other countries all over the world.

"Twenty eight years have gone by since that first course in Auburn and ATLS keeps on spreading and growing," Dad said to the audience, looking up from his notes. "Sort of like a real good malignancy."

The crowd chuckled, and Dad felt the mood of the room lighten. He loosened up a little and continued:

"What we thought would be a course for rural Nebraska, became a course for the world in all types of trauma settings, from the rural hospital to the Level One trauma center to the military.

"Ireland," he said giving acknowledgement to this crowd, "joined the ATLS family in 1991. Paramedics and the nurses all over the world now also have ATLS based courses tailored to them and their specific treatment scenarios. Everyone involved with the trauma victim speaks the same "ATLS" language. This ability to communicate and anticipate at all levels decreases morbidity and mortality in the 'golden hour.'"

That was what it was all about.

Dad left Lincoln and surgery and ATLS over a decade later in 1987, finally needing to slow down and take it easy. He moved to California and was content to work in obscurity as a physician there. But ATLS continued through all of those years, very similar to the first course that he, Ron, and Jodie wrote.

Several years later Dad started to go to Ayacucho, Peru, in coordination with medical missionaries there. The missions gave him a great deal of satisfaction, as well as a chance to do surgery again. The conditions made the work very challenging, and often included having restraint or traction devices or instruments made by a local blacksmith. He went down every year or so, and for many of the patients that he saw, he was their regular doctor. Peru had adopted ATLS in the years prior to him going there, but the hospital was still quite primitive by American standards.

During one of his trips, about 100 miles from the hospital in the mountains near Cusco, a fire fight occurred between the Peruvian Marines and the local insurgents known as the Shining Path. Two of the Marines were wounded during the battle and were subsequently brought to the hospital. One had AK-47 gunshot wounds to the abdomen and right arm. The other had stepped on a land mine during the melee, partially amputating the left leg, and sustaining a severe soft tissue injury to his other leg.

In the rather primitive ER, Dad helped stabilize the patients. The benefits of ATLS immediately were obvious to him. The Marine personnel and native doctors spoke Spanish, working along with Americans doctors that spoke English. There was only one doctor who was bilingual. It was the 'language' that was standardized in the ATLS course that became the common thread that was used by both groups to communicate outside the realms of their native languages, enabling efficient, effective assessment and stabilization of the Marines. They both lived.

"From the beginning of the course, over 500,000 students have trained in 46 countries within 25,000 ATLS courses." Dad concluded to the crowd before him.

"24,000 trained Physicians graduate each year from these courses," Dad said, wrapping up his speech with a smile. "It looks like we're on a roll. I think we might want to introduce it to the moon and Mars next."

"Compared to what happened in the recent tsunami in Asia," he concluded with seriousness, "9-11 in the US, the disaster on the Gulf of Mexico coast from hurricane Katrina, and the other natural and manmade disasters that have occurred in the past twenty years, my family's experience out in that field was just child's play. Hopefully what we have done, all of us who have become a part of the ATLS family, has played a part in saving some of these souls."

"Thank you."

The hall erupted in applause, echoing like thunder across the room. Everyone was on their feet, and beaming at him. He felt a little overwhelmed by it. But he was certainly grateful for the acknowledgement after all these years, even though he never did any of it for fame or money. He just threw it out and watched to see if it would stick. He was glad it did, but knew it was way bigger than just him. None of it could have happened without the help and interest he got from Ron and Jodie and all of the others.

The President of the college came up on stage and shook his hand vigorously. Dad smiled, and looked out at the crowd, still applauding. For a moment, he thought of Mom, and was both sad and grateful for her.

We all turned out okay in the end, I guess. "Okay" being a relative word. Life wasn't always easy, but is it ever? Through it all, we stayed together, and that is what's important. I think Mom would be content.

Chris is a successful real estate agent and businessman, and he and his wife Debbie are happy and have wealth beyond dollars.

Rick lost himself in the written word shortly after the crash and emerged after high school an academic. He began college at Nebraska Wesleyan University before ending up at Brown University where he got a Masters degree in Education.

Kim also went on to get a Masters degree in Human Resources. She is married and living happily with her husband Tim in Reno where she gave birth to her first son.

We all have people we love and who take care of us. And we remain close in spite of, or maybe because of, the tragedy we have all experienced.

The Hospital in Hebron, called the Thayer County Medical Center when I began this book, and now the Hebron Memorial Hospital, learned from the experience as we all did. The reader can easily look at the actions and decisions that were made over thirty years ago and judge them by today's standards, but one must realize that was just how things were done then.

That's the point. There was no ATLS. No standard of care.

But it was the same people who would later embrace these new concepts and the Hebron Hospital was one of the first in the country to embrace ATLS. The people there that night helped to implement it and my dad continued to travel to Hebron, along that same road or flying above the crash site, to assist them. Today it is an awesome facility.

What happened that night in 1976 will never happen again. But I met the people who were there and I love them and am grateful for them. I am sorry they weren't allowed to do more, but they did what they could.

Larry Russell thought about us a few times in the intervening years. Not long after he went looking for us, he was coming in for a landing at Lincoln in his helicopter. The locator beacon antennae that he had outfitted the helicopter with, the same one that had detected our signal, snapped off and flew into his tail rotor, shattering it and spinning the helicopter in what they call an auto-rotation. He managed to get it down, but it was a harrowing experience. He still has pieces of the rotor, as a memento of survival. He and the helicopter were flying together again in a few weeks.

A few years after that, he was flying a mission for the Lancaster County Sheriff department, and passed over a mountain ridge in Arizona in a Piper Cherokee when he hit what is known as a mountain wave. This happens when air cools rapidly as it crosses a ridge, and cascades down the other side, like a waterfall of air. Aircraft flying into one are helpless and at their mercy, as was Larry. One moment he was flying along and the next maps, cups, and McDonalds french-fries were levitating around him as he suddenly plummeted down the face of the mountain. He kept his wits and put the plane into a circular decent to slow it down, then at the last possible instant, managed to break free of the mountain wave and keep flying. It was only luck that the whole thing occurred over a deep valley; otherwise the results would have been much different.

His passenger, sleeping in the back, never knew anything had happened.

Jon Morris stayed on with the CAP and remained a cop with the Lincoln Police. He went on many more missions with the CAP, but the memory of our crash always stays with him. Another mission occurred a few years after our crash when he was on a recovery mission involving a commercial airline accident. After several hours on the scene, he was asked to take a look at the body of the copilot, who had just been recovered from the wreckage. It was only upon seeing him that he realized he was looking at his brother in law, who flew for the airline. He had to break the news to his wife. It was all part of the job with the CAP.

Jim Nitz stayed active in the Lincoln CAP, although he left Lincoln to move to North Platte to become a Disaster Planner for Lincoln County, Nebraska, where he lived till 2011 when he passed away, far too young.

Helen Boman, Gary, Dick, Marylyn, Blanche and Evelyn stayed in Hebron. Helen was still a nurse at the Thayer County Medical Center when I finally met her. Gary and Dick were still Hebron firemen. Evelyn and Marylyn both passed away in 2012.

Dr. Bunting retired and lived with his wife in a little nursing home directly across from the hospital. He died in 2013 at the age of 97.

Dr. Pumphrey moved away from Hebron to live in Omaha several years after our crash. His own son was killed in an airplane two years after Mom, and not far away. He was flying a crop duster near Hebron and had just finished a run when the wind shifted and blew the pesticide into him. He lost consciousness and crashed into the field he was spraying. Dr. Pumphrey himself died in 2012.

Clarke and Sharon Mundhenke stayed in Lincoln. Clarke left being a pastor at Trinity Chapel and turned towards working the local hospitals as a chaplain full time. He keeps busy.

Bruce Miller stayed in Lincoln and was the Chief of Staff at Lincoln General for many years. Bruce retired from medicine, but he continued to be a pilot. He and my father remained great and lifelong friends, as are his son, Greg, and I. Our lives were strangely parallel. But that's a different story...

Ron Craig also stayed in Lincoln to practice medicine. He became part of my family's club when he was flying his airplane out of Winslow, Arizona in 2006. The engine died at 300 feet as he was taking off. He managed to point the plane at a road, but it crashed into the desert just beyond and was destroyed. He and his wife walked away with only bruises. I would say miraculously, but I know there were no miracles - just a damn good pilot at work. He was flying again within a month. My kind of pilot.

I never saw Jill again. She died suddenly of an aneurism in 2010. She was young and healthy and no one can understand why she is gone either. I think of her sons a lot, and am saddened to know the pain they are now learning. I pray for them. I miss her.

Shelley is still my friend.

I don't know what became of Ricky Arnold or David McLaughlin. To me, they are two specters that appeared from nowhere to save us, and then disappeared back into the mist. I have heard that David lives in some tiny town somewhere in Nebraska but the letters I have sent have not reached him, I assume. I am still looking for both of them. I would like to shake their hands.

Dad remarried again and he lives in Los Angeles, near us and his first grandson. He will always be a doctor. He still wears his white coat, and I hope he always will. He flew a few times after the crash but will never land again. He says he made his last landing in that field. It took thirty years for us to go back in our minds to that night in the field and really work it out. But I know it has been good for both of us. We got to know each other like we never had. We are lucky.

As for me, I wrote about that part of my life. Learning about it gave me the opportunity to meet some amazing people and re-engage the others I did know who were there. It gave me the opportunity to share with all of them an experience that connected us to one another one cold February, long ago.

And in doing so I made some additional discoveries I had not anticipated—Discoveries having nothing to do with ATLS and that are not taught in any course.

I learned for certain that life isn't fair…like fairness has anything to do with anything. We come into this world as perfect little beings, and then are gradually contaminated and corrupted and pulled apart by life. If we are lucky we get to grow old, wear out, and die. We spend the time in between trying to figure it all out, but we probably never do. We try to avoid the thief of time and that's the best we can hope for.

But, through it all, there is goodness and beauty.

I have my family, who teach me about love every day. I have friends. I have mountains to climb and rivers and oceans to swim. I have clear blue sky to soar through and a wonderful world to explore. I have air to breathe and I breathe it. I have life. It'll never be perfect, but it doesn't have to be.

I took the things I learned and used them to unlock some old doors; let the bats out, clean the cobwebs. It has indeed been good for me, this journey to the truth. Better than I will ever know.

Each day that I find myself above the surface of the earth is indeed a good day, and a new blessing. I have no illusions about death. I don't fear it. I have dodged it once or twice, but I respect it. And I know someday it will find me, as it did her. As it does us all. But when it does, I intend that it will find me thoroughly used.

And maybe, somehow, its cold touch will finally bring me back to the arms of my mother.

And everything will be all right.

Epilogue

Gary guided the truck off of the highway just outside of Hebron and onto a dirt stretch called Monument Road. Kim, Helen, Dr. Bunting and I were squished into the king cab of his big pickup. Now Gary pointed it toward a nondescript clump of trees in the distance toward a place he had not been for thirty years. He knew right where it was, though, and had thought about it a great deal over that time.

"It's only a few miles from here," he said to Kim and me. I considered the clumps of trees in the distance toward where we were headed, and considered the last time I was there. I felt anxiety rise in me.

I had seen it in my mind so many times, an image created from the one dimensional colors of the handful of photographs I had perused in the intervening years. I had pictured a scraggly line of trees flanked by barren fields, and dark and gloomy skies. Something forbidding and not quite part of the world where decent and caring people live, like a graveyard in a Charles Dickens novel.

Gary took a left turn and continued up a dirt road that paralleled an empty field surrounded by barbed wire fences. That time of the year the corn hadn't been planted yet and the brown dirt surrounding us spread out towards the ends of the earth, as far as we could see. Then he made one more turn and slowed the vehicle down, stopping beside a small earthen dike leading toward a small tree-ringed pond.

"This is it," he said. We all got out.

Kim and I slowly walked a distance to where the trees met the field and stood in silence looking over it. It was like walking into some kind of time transporter, to another place. The empty field was level plowed dirt as far as we looked. It would have looked like this that day, roughly, empty and devoid of vegetation. I tried to grasp what I saw, but this was nothing like I had expected.

I had thirty years worth of dreams about this place, and the horror it would bring me to behold it. But now here I was, and I was transfixed. What I found defied my every expectation.

What I found was a lovely pond ringed by a beautiful and healthy strip of forest, mere yards from a section of the Oregon Trail. Pioneers heading to the California gold fields may have stopped at this spot at some point to refresh themselves in the shade of the trees or the clear water of the pond.

As we approached the woods, two large deer suddenly bounded from the trees on the opposite side of the pond and ran across the gently rolling ground to the shelter of another thicket nearby. The peace and tranquility that I felt at that moment so defied the picture of what I had known to be the truth for so long that it was hard to believe that this was really the place.

Kim and I walked along a faint cattle track that wound around the outer perimeter of the pond, just inside the ring of plum thicket that surrounded the woods. Kim continued to walk through the trees and I made my way through a gap in the thick plum bushes and then out onto the open field, taking it all in. I looked around, trying to identify the crash site, but from that spot, there was no trace. I again wondered seriously if this could really be the place. I figured there would be some sign, some indication of what we went through. Some monument that for a few dark hours we had laid there and fought for our lives. But it seemed like it was all gone.

I turned and went back into the woods to look for Kim. As I got to a corner of the pond, I suddenly noticed what appeared to be a gap in the tree line that surrounded it. I walked over to the spot and could see that much of the growth there appeared to be newer than the rest in the area. I worked into the gap and found myself in a tiny clearing a just few feet from the pond. Long dead branches and the remains of a couple of knocked down large trees lay around the area. I walked over to one dead and bare stump that was still standing. All that was left of it was a scrubbed clean trunk about twenty feet high. At the top of it, the wood was jagged and torn.

Suddenly I knew why.

I realized with a thump in my chest that thirty years before, it had ripped the wing off our airplane as we sheared through it. The path we had traveled began to resolve around me as I stood there and soon became clear. I could suddenly make out the entire thing. It was here, after all! It had happened right here!

My head spun. I had to find Kim and tell her! I turned and hurriedly walked back along the cow path through the trees looking for her. Then saw her. She stood a few meters away from the clearing I had found, in the shade of a few trees. She was looking intently at an object that she held in her hand. Dr. Bunting stood a few feet away. They glanced up at me as I approached a stunned look in her eyes.

"Look at this..." she said and handed me the object. "I found it on the ground right here."

I took it. It was a shiny metal chunk. It was obviously deformed as if it had been smashed by something. It was heavy chrome, so whatever twisted it, had done so with considerable force. The realization of it took me and I looked disbelievingly at Kim, and then looked over at Dr. Bunting.

"It's called a pitot tube," he said. "It's used to measure airspeed."

"From...the plane?" I asked in barely a whisper, still not quite getting the meaning of the artifact I now held in my very hands. He nodded.

I stared at it for a second, still in shock.

Never in my wildest imagination of this trip did I ever think I would actually hold a piece of our plane. I believed it all had simply vanished like a cloud into the passage of time and could not have possibly left any trace. I got hold of myself and directed Kim to follow me back to the tree. As I did I scoured the ground in case there were more artifacts. I stopped upon coming across a small jagged piece of clear, curved plastic.

I knew immediately it was from our windshield. I bent down and picked it up, studying it intensely. My head reeled. I felt like I was going to faint.

I am still trying to formulate the impact that that moment had on me and it is hard to put into words, but that moment was the instant that I really knew the truth. It was the moment I really became part of this whole thing and realized it had happened to me...all of this really happened to me. Up until that moment, I don't think I ever really understood that. To hold those pieces of that plane in my hands changed my whole perspective forever. They were the physical link to the puzzle that made it real - truly real - for the first time in my life.

It was as profound a moment as I have ever experienced. I have no other to compare it with.

I had come here to try and find for myself what it was my Dad had seen when he went into that field--foreboding, black, and thick with fog, like some horror movie. To try and relive what he must have felt when he had stumbled across what was left of his wife. To try and grasp the sensation he learned as our blood smeared his clothes while he tried to save and protect us. I had come here to get in touch with that horror and maybe get a taste of it so that I could know the truth of what had happened. So I could break through it and try to make sense of it all.

But what I realized instead was that it simply wasn't there. It was just a pond, and a forest, and a field, and the spring breeze, and the birds. It was just me and Kim walking through the trees. It was my new friends as they watched us. The horror was long gone. It had vanished long ago like the fog, maybe as my Dad left with us, maybe by the wash of Larry's rotors, maybe by the departure of the CAP team, or the wake of Gary and Dick's truck, or the wind from Looking Glass's engines. Maybe it only existed in the minds of those who witnessed that night from the same perspectives. At any rate, it was gone by the time I got there.

I felt as though I was too late when I realized that, and for a moment I was crushed because I thought that I wouldn't be able to tell the story without it. But then, as I stood in the shade of those trees, listening to the breeze and the birds, I suddenly realized that I didn't need it to tell the story. The horror wasn't the story. The words on this page are. The words from all those people. The impact of what came after. The life of my Mom. The healing that Jon spoke of. ATLS. That was the story. Not the pain. Not the dark. Not the death.

The life.

To my surprise, I was uplifted by the life I now saw all around me, like I was observing it for the first time. Suffice it to say that my own life took an entirely different meaning at that moment and it made me understand finally why I was standing there:

I was just supposed to tell this story – in the way that I could.

As I stood there, the truth was like being hit by an unexpected wave. I was stunned and amazed. Joyful and horrified. I simultaneously wanted to scream and laugh and dance and spin around and fall to my knees and pound the earth in rage on the very spot where my mother lay dead and bloody so long ago…but I couldn't make any decision of which one to do.

Instead I just stood there immobilized by the enormity of it, holding an old chunk of metal and a broken piece of plastic that had no meaning to anyone at that moment but me and Kim. All I could do was gaze around at it all and take it into my frazzled mind where it sloshed around like water in a bucket.

And yet in the midst of it all I was aware of a peace and calm slowly draping itself over me, the likes of which I had never before known.

Like a gift from my mother.

After awhile I forced myself to breathe, and then I found that I was able to move again. I looked over at Kim, then at Helen and Gary and Dr. Bunting with tears in my eyes. And I smiled. I affirmed for myself in that instant what it was that I had to do.

So I tell you the story…

And I am glad.

References:

1. **American College of Surgeons**. *Advanced Trauma Life Support (ATLS) student manual.* 7th ed. Chicago, IL: American College of Surgeons, 1997.
2. **American College of Surgeons**. *Pre-Hospital Trauma Life Support (PHTLS) student manual.* 7th ed. Chicago, IL: American College of Surgeons, 2004.
3. **Carmont, M.R.** *The Advanced Trauma Life Support course: A History of its Development and Review of Related literature.* Postgraduate Medical Journal 2005;81:87-91
4. **Federation of American Scientists**, *EC-135, Looking Glass*, Washington, D.C., viewed, 2 August 2005, http://www.fas.org/nuke/guide/usa/c3i/ec-135.htm
5. **Google, Inc.**, Google Search website, Mountain View, CA, viewed 28 February, 2005, http://www.google.com/
6. **National Transportation Safety Board,** *National Transportation Safety Board February 1976 Aviation Accidents, Washington, D.C.,* viewed 2 March 2005 http://www.ntsb.gov/ntsb/AccList.asp?month=2&year=1976
7. **The Pensy Web**, *USS Pennsylvania BB-38 website*, Murrieta, CA, viewed 3 January, 2006, < http://www.usspennsylvania.com/>
8. **United States Air Force Auxiliary,** *Civil Air Patrol website*, Maxwell AFB, Al, viewed 7 March 2005, http://www.cap.gov/index.cfm
9. **United States Department of Agriculture Forest Service**, *Aviation Incident/Accident Response Guide*, Washington, D.C., viewed 16 June, 2006. http://www.fs.fed.us/r2/fire/docs/Aircraft_Crash_SAR_Guide.PDF
10. **Yankee Publishing Inc.,** *Old Farmers Almanac Weather History*, Concordia Blosser MU, Kansas, for February 18, 1976, Dublin, NH, viewed 2 March, 2005 http://www.almanac.com/weatherhistory/oneday.php?number=725515&wban=99999&direction=next&day=18&month=02&year=1976&searchtype=zip